ACORN//

Vegetables Re-Imagined/
Seasonal Recipes from
Root to Stem

BY SHIRA BLUSTEIN
+ BRIAN LUPTAK

FOREWORD BY JULIA STILES
PHOTOGRAPHY BY GABRIEL CABRERA

appetite
by RANDOM HOUSE

Appetite by Random House® and colophon are registered trademarks of Penguin Random House LLC.

Library and Archives Canada Cataloguing in Publication is available upon request.

ISBN: 978-0-525-61026-7
eBook ISBN: 978-0-525-61027-4

Photography by Gabriel Cabrera
Photo on page xi by Sharon Radisch
Photo on page 135 by Michelle Sproule
Author photo on page 279 by Ryan Walter Wagner/
  Good Side Photo
Photo backgrounds and illustrations by Scott Lewis
Ceramics by Janaki Larsen
Book and cover design by Emma Dolan

Printed in China

Published in Canada by Appetite by Random House®, a division of Penguin Random House Canada Limited.

www.penguinrandomhouse.ca

10 9 8 7 6 5 4 3 2 1

appetite
by RANDOM HOUSE | Penguin
Random House
Canada

Shira | *For my daughters, Verona and Alita, to whom I pass the microphone. Sing loud and always from the heart. Don't be afraid to raise a little hell.*

Brian | *To Shira and Scott, for your trust, and just give'r mentality.*

The Acorn is located on the ancestral and unceded territory of the xʷməθkʷəy̓əm (Musqueam), Sḵwx̱wú7mesh (Squamish), and Səl̓ílwətaʔ/Selilwitulh (Tsleil-Waututh) First Nations. We recognize the many Nations of Indigenous People and their ancestors who have hunted, gathered, prepared, and shared meals on this land known as Turtle Island. As we celebrate food and share our stories in this book, we acknowledge our ongoing commitment to respect, honor and learn from the traditional knowledge keepers of this territory so that it can nurture future generations.

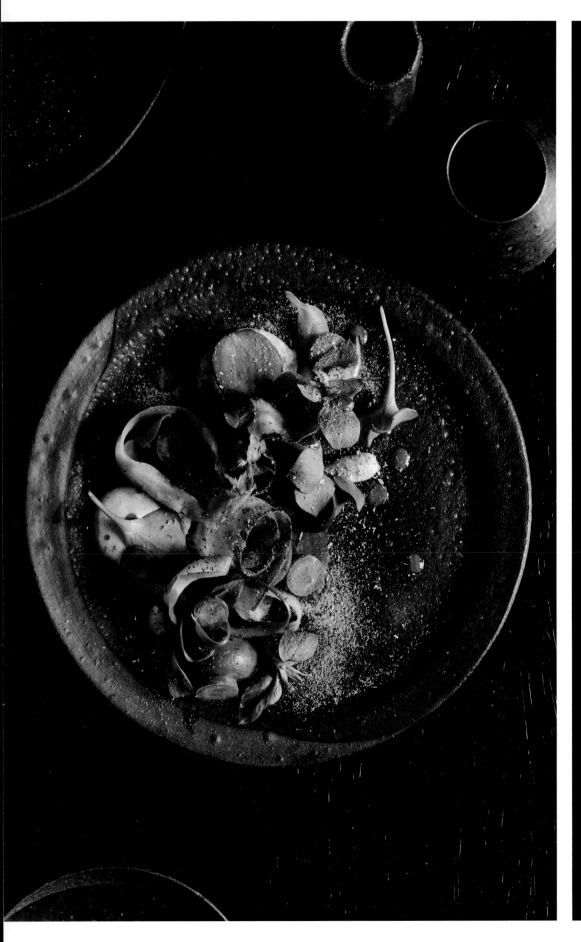

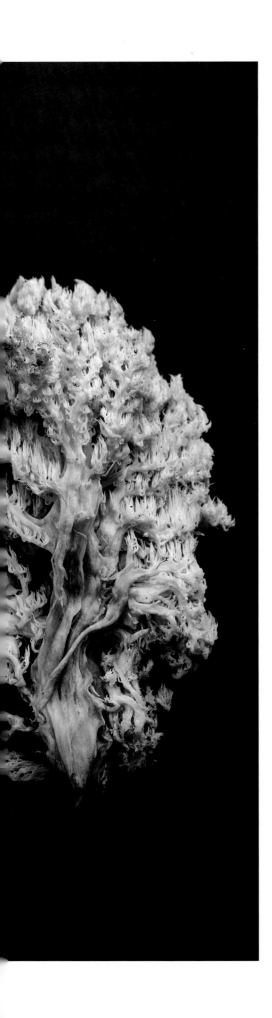

CONTENTS//

JULIA STILES // On any given night,

there's a line on the corner of Main and 24th connecting The Acorn to its more casual sister restaurant, The Arbor. I discovered the deliciousness that is The Acorn a few years ago, when I finally got the total carnivore I was dating to take me to a vegetarian restaurant. But you see, The Acorn isn't really a vegetarian restaurant—it's a restaurant for people who like good food. It just happens not to serve meat. So good is its reputation, that it was the total carnivore's pick.

I'm a home cook with vegetarian tendencies. The carnivore I was dating is now my husband, and he is an even better home cook, with fancier tendencies. People who enjoy cooking (like him) spend a lot of time figuring out how to procure and prepare the meat but disregard the figurative potato (or literal sunchoke, artichoke, radicchio, etc.). For omnivores, a meal without meat can feel incomplete. And if we home cooks are going out to eat, it better not be something we can make at home. Dining out is not just about skipping the dishes, but an experience to linger over. Dining at a vegetarian restaurant better be extra special then, because who wants to linger over tempeh and tofu? (Falafel, you say? You should know that after a summer spent touring music festivals, I vowed never to eat falafel again.) As a result, most vegetarian restaurants try too hard to make you feel you are getting your money's worth, forcing plants into shapes not found in nature, finding ways to replicate the meat they're scared their diners will miss. But like I said, The Acorn's not like other vegetarian restaurants. It's a place that all but reinvented the meatless menu and made plants the phenomenal focus of each plate.

At The Acorn, they celebrate the plant: enhancing it, pairing it, dressing it for a night of being the center of attention. Their produce is showcased in ways you can recognize, but these delicacies also require a little guidance to recreate—because it takes as much finesse to make a gourmet meal out of things that grow from the ground as it does from things that *eat* off the ground. Chefs Brian Luptak and Devon Latte hand-select their ingredients, all seasonal and all local, cooking them in a myriad of ways to bring the best out of them so we can enjoy these

flavors as they were intended. The first soup on their late-winter menu could describe the overall cuisine itself—simply put, an "Ever-evolving Assortment of the Freshest Ingredients Available."

Restaurants can often be defined by a central ingredient or specialty—steak, pasta, seafood, an ethnic influence from haute French cuisine to Jewish deli. Maybe because the founder, Shira Blustein, comes from a diverse background, The Acorn defies categories. Shira is a self-described "mongrel," a mother and a no-joke punk rocker. She and her partner, Scott, together with chefs Brian Luptak and Devon Latte, put so much care into keeping their menu as fresh as their ingredients. The Acorn's dishes are anything but predictable. This book allows us to be as adventurous with our veggies at home as The Acorn is on a nightly basis, and even mix and match some of the pairings. And if you don't have access to some of the ingredients mentioned? Don't worry, they offer this cookbook as a guide, not a rulebook, to inspire the farmer-chef in you. Enjoy!

SHIRA
BLUSTEIN // I always wanted to
open a restaurant, a dream I have come to realize
I shared with much of the world. My mom claims
it's in my genes. Her father was the head caterer of
a synagogue in Toronto, and they say the "crazy"
skips a generation.

I grew up in the largest city in the Canadian prairies, Calgary, Alberta, which, when I was a teen in the 90s, felt like a never-ending suburban sprawl designed solely to prevent my escape. My youth was spent finding creative ways to release the pressure of being an enraged and hormonal teenager. As luck would have it, my instinct to rebel against suburbia led me to a group of like-minded ratty teenagers looking to differentiate themselves from their conservative-leaning parents.

In my punk beginnings, I distinctly remember an old beaten-up VHS of *Faces of Death*, a pop-culture relic from the 70s whose controversial subject matter made it a must-see among the young, curious, and disillusioned. The film got passed around and was dubbed so many times that the video footage was full of static, often skipping and distorting, which was probably for the best. I found out only recently that most of the video was staged, save for the slaughterhouse footage. Still, it was enough to convince me that going vegetarian was a moral imperative, and I've never looked back.

I was 14 years old, loitering outside Megatunes, Calgary's independent record store, killing time with friends before a punk show was set to start. As memory serves, the bands were DBS, from Vancouver, and Anti-Flag, from Pittsburgh. Word carried that the show was canceled, that they had walked out of the venue after a fight with the promoter and had nowhere to play. Friends offered them their jam space as a makeshift alternative so their trip to Calgary wouldn't be a total bust. We piled into our friend's car and trekked out to the industrial suburbs. The circumstances and intimacy of their performance that evening encapsulated everything I was initially drawn to in punk rock—a community that supported one another creatively and stood up for what they believe in—and it cemented in me a set of values I carry to this day.

Between sets, everyone went outside for fresh air except for my girlfriend Mandy and me. Mandy, with a perfect Chelsea haircut and enough sense about her that we called her "Ma," pointed out that the PA system was still live and buzzing. Feeling inspired, we jumped on the mics and sang an a cappella version of "Walk Like an Egyptian," which quickly turned to death metal screams and growls. Unsurprisingly, someone heard our wails and interrupted

us to identify which scream belonged to whom. Mandy let out a deep, throaty, guttural growl and I unleashed a shrill, high-pitched, nails-on-a-chalkboard scream (later likened to that of a banshee in a show review). Unbeknownst to me, I had just participated in—and aced—my first band audition, discovering the secret door out of Calgary.

Touring North America as a DIY punk band in the 90s had a unique set of challenges. You had to cold-call and snail-mail cassette tapes of your music to promoters listed in *Book Your Own Fuckin' Life*—a resource guide published by the venerable *Maximum Rocknroll* fanzine—while plotting a tour route on a heavily creased road map. Often music venues were nearly condemned punk-house basements in yet-to-be-gentrified neighborhoods, where it fell within the realm of reason that the volume of our amps would bring an unwelcome start to the inevitable process of demolition. The drives were long and sleep was where you could find it, often under someone's kitchen table, packed like sardines in our sleeping bags. It was the furthest thing from glamorous, but glamor wasn't exactly on the menu.

Most of the meals we had on tour were fast and cheap. Sometimes, if we were lucky, a free meal would come by way of a co-op or collective like Food Not Bombs, or the promoter would make a huge vat of veggie chili. Admittedly, food was a low priority in those days, but on tour in the 90s, *vegetarian* was still treated as a four-letter word and *vegan* was another language altogether. We would occasionally come across a gem of a restaurant that would offer something beyond the side plates we relied on at mega-chain diners—and finding a hippie-run, vegetarian hole-in-the-wall in most of the United States and Canada was like finding an oasis in an arid desert. When a delicious morsel hit your tongue, the sensation rang deep, making the fact of our deprivation of basic nourishment even more evident.

After touring, coming home was another depressing reminder of how little people cared about vegetables. Calgary was, and still is, lauded as the beef capital of Canada. My mom, empathetic toward my vegetarian "condition," adapted her recipes and taught me how to cook. Our diverse multicultural background made for interesting dishes: Persian, Indian, Iranian, Polish, and Russian (all 100% Jewish) played their respective roles in the kitchen.

By 2002 the band had disbanded and I moved to Vancouver for film school. The intensive program only reminded me how much I missed playing music. I picked post-production sound to stay close to my auditory passions and eventually joined a band with several other Calgary expats. The music industry was still strong: record labels had money, CDs were selling, our band signed with an outfit from the United Kingdom, and I quit my film job to tour again. Funded with daily stipends and being slightly more mature made for food experiences that were more profound this time around. I was excited that views on vegetables seemed to be evolving beyond what amounted to a splash of color accenting the protein on the plate.

I would still return to Vancouver as a frustrated diner, though, knowing there was so much more potential and a niche to be filled for uncompromising plant-forward cuisine. Working the odd serving job in between tours, I knew the skills acquired from being in a restaurant, although incredibly valuable, were completely different from the skills required to open a restaurant. Intent on learning more, I studied business foundation courses at night. One of my bandmates, upon learning of my restaurant ambitions, introduced me to Andreas Seppelt, a Vancouver restaurateur driven by both passion and the mantra "work hard, show the love." Through his generous spirit, he offered endless resources and decades of experience. His vote of confidence gave me the push to open The Acorn.

The cards lined up on a well-loved corner at Main Street and 24th Avenue, blocks away from home, and I set out to realize my dream. Leaning on my community, I used all the goodwill I could muster calling upon friend after friend to come lend a hand in exchange for pizza and beer. The design was dark, angular, and edgy, inspired by the abundance of forest trees surrounding Vancouver and the dark artistic sensibilities I had been feeding for nearly three decades.

We opened in July 2012 to a flood of people who had that same hole in their heart for an elevated plant-based experience—or vegetable-forward, as we called it at the time. We were eager to fill that void. Our menu was simple, small, clean, and colorful. We were open until 2 a.m. and our friends DJ'd late in the night every Thursday. In 2013, we earned a spot on *enRoute* magazine's coveted "Canada's Best New Restaurants" list, the first time a plant-based restaurant had ever been acknowledged, cementing The Acorn as a restaurant of national regard—and a flag bearer for what would eventually become a larger cultural shift toward more conscious, vegetable-forward dining.

Year after year our global reach and recognition has grown. It has been incredible and humbling watching The Acorn evolve over the past 8 years. Our adventures have taken us from countless accolades and awards, to collaborative farm and wine dinners, to an edible art installation at the Vancouver Art Gallery, to opening a pop-up restaurant in the Lower East Side of New York City, to endless galas and fundraising events. We opened a sister restaurant called The Arbor in 2016, a less austere and more playful eatery on the same block. And my own family has grown, expanding from my husband, Scott, and me to include two young daughters.

The passion and focus of the team at The Acorn to source local, seasonal, foraged, and quality ingredients have deepened with every passing year, to what we can now proudly exclaim is a nearly 100% organic menu. The relationships we have with farmers, wineries, breweries, distilleries, foragers, and the neighborhood shopkeepers are the rewards for our hard work and dedication. I'm so proud of our front-of-house team who enthusiastically guide our guests through The Acorn experience, our dishwashers who are the backbone of service, and every cook who pushes our menu to be better through their collaborative spirit.

Since there are no rules with vegetables, we have limitless possibilities—as long as we continue to learn and grow together. It brings me back to that sweaty punk practice space 25 years ago, when I saw complete strangers working together, generously offering support to one another with a shared passion for community, creativity, and integrity. The Acorn's journey is just beginning.

BRIAN LUPTAK // Reflecting on the

influences that have made me the chef I am today, brings me back to my youth. I grew up surrounded by agriculture. Many of my friend's families were farmers, and much of my childhood was spent playing on those farms. Our small town sat right in the heart of apple country, and the first job I ever had was picking apples in the orchard right across the road from our house. Our town also butted up against Georgian Bay, which filled the nearby lakes and rivers with fresh fish. It is safe to say that my knowledge of where our food comes from was instilled in me at a young age. That knowledge is something I've kept with me, but never had an outlet for it until I became a cook.

Food was never a big focus in my life growing up. I am the youngest of three children, two of which were not the most adventurist eaters. As for my parents, they had their hands full trying to get us kids to all of our extracurricular activities. Time never seemed to be on their side, so convenience in the kitchen was key. Don't get me wrong, my mother is amazing in the kitchen, and went out of her way to make delicious dinners and elaborate holiday feasts. If it were left to my dad, we would have had toasted tomato sandwiches and canned soup seven days a week. I imagine my passion for cooking is a trait inherited from my great-grandmother. I was too young to ever know her, but the story of her journey from Slovakia to Canada and the tales of her cooking always amazed me. If there were one person I could cook with now, it would be her, hands down.

After countless random jobs as a teenager, I finally found one that opened my eyes to a world of endless possibilities, and to an industry that I would return to years later. That job was dishwashing. It was my gateway to the restaurant industry, and it led me to my first mentor, a Slovak chef with a strong demeanor and an even stronger handshake. People say that working as a dishwasher makes you a better chef, and it's true. This is where you learn to grind it out. Where you learn by observing how the cooks move and how the chef speaks. You're watching

how the front of house works in cohesion with the back of house—like hearing the serving staff come to the back to vent about the guests at table 12. It taught me a million invaluable little lessons that lay the groundwork for what would become my career.

From that first dishwasher job, I had some amazing opportunities to explore western Canada, going to places I never thought I would see, and all along the way working alongside some amazing cooks. Cooks from different backgrounds, of different nationalities, and with different skill sets. Cooks who showed me the discipline, speed, and creativity I'd need to grow in my own career. I'm forever indebted to those I have worked with over the years.

I found it trying over the years, to work my way up through the ranks at high-end hotels and never be able to truly, unapologetically express my artistic side. I reached a standstill in my career and knew that an independent restaurant was where I needed to be, so I reached out to The Acorn. I imagined that transitioning to a vegetarian restaurant would broaden my thought processes and inspire my creativity, and it did just that. However, I could never have foreseen just how much I would learn. Not only as a chef, but also as a consumer. A large shift in my approach to food and my perspective on the culinary arts started when forager Lance Staples came by the door for the first time with an assortment of wild edibles. Edibles that he had gathered from where he was living on Vancouver Island. Ingredients that I had never heard of. The farmers we work with, such as Klippers Organics, North Arm Farm, and Cropthorne Farm, have at times been mentors, as influential as the greatest chefs I have ever worked with. The respect, heart, and soul that they have for the land inspires and motivates me to pay homage to their product.

It has been an unbelievable voyage. One that has provided inspiration in the form of greens, mushrooms, blossoms and berries. My journey through the restaurant industry, and my years at The Acorn, have ultimately led to the creation of this cookbook, our giant art project. Writing the recipes in this book, and reflecting over my time as the chef of this oh-so-cozy 48-seat restaurant, has made me feel as though I am back in that small town where it all began.

WILDCRAFTED + UNIQUE INGREDIENTS // Central

to all we do at The Acorn is our ingredients. Our mission is to always to source locally and organic whenever possible, and utilize as much of a product as we can to minimize waste. We love the excitement of working with a new ingredient, trying to find the best way to showcase it while making sure it still complements the rest of our menu. Our dishes often have many components, and through these we weave elements from the ever-so-abundant seasons we have here on the west coast of British Columbia. Whether it's through preserving, pickling, or putting the ingredient front and center, we strive to make the most of each season and there is no challenge we don't welcome.

We use an abundance of wildcrafted items on our menu. Foraging connects us to our environment, giving us a deeper appreciation for the world we live in. We respectfully source foraged ingredients ourselves and through professionals, and they are then processed in our kitchen. Bear in mind, however, this book isn't a foraging guide! If you are unsure of the source or quality of your foraged ingredients, it's safest not to use them. In the descriptions below, we've done our best to offer alternatives to the foraged components of our recipes so you can make them with seasonal equivalents from your local farmers' market. We usually pick or source extra quantities of an item, and then preserve or freeze them so we can enjoy their unique flavor year-round. That is how you'll see us using summer produce in winter. Those hits of sunshine keep us mindful that the long, dark winter will give way to new growth, and brighter flavors will arrive to reawaken our spirits!

Here are some of The Acorn's favorite and unique wildcrafted ingredients; you'll come across them in the recipes of this book:

Big Leaf Maple Blossoms |
A spring delicacy, these green-yellow cluster buds can be collected from the Big Leaf Maple for a few weeks during the spring. They have a slight astringency, with a flavor that is a cross between a honeysuckle and an artichoke. At The Acorn, we take the fresh big-leaf maple blossoms and preserve them in vinegar for future bright, floral, and aromatic applications.

Blue Chanterelles | The unicorn of the mushroom kingdom. Blue chanterelles are a rare mushroom that cohabitate with a variety of coniferous trees. When found early in the season, they are luminescent with glowing white edges. The Acorn's main forager, Lance, had his greatest find at 4½ lbs. Since they're so rare, we like to pickle them to be able to enjoy them slowly over the span of the season. You can substitute blue chanterelles with the more common golden chanterelle, although they more closely resemble the pig's ear mushroom, also called the violet chanterelle, which actualy belongs to a different mushroom family, the Gormphaceae.

Cauliflower Mushrooms (or Sparassis) | These ivory cluster mushrooms are intensely aromatic and flavorful, and one of the most charming mushrooms to find. They grow naturally in British Columbia forests, usually parasitizing a live tree or feeding off a stump—often Douglas firs in our region. The name comes from their likeness in appearance to cauliflower, making them easy to identify in the wild. This mushroom is best foraged young when the flesh is whiter and firmer. If you don't have access to cauliflower mushrooms, you can substitute any lighter mushroom, such as oyster or chanterelle.

Chickweed | Packed with nutrients, chickweed is a great addition to any salad or dish. This cold-season annual is a tender, sprawling green, found in abundance in the colder months and spring in the Pacific Northwest, though it originates from Europe. Chickweed can also behave as a perennial green throughout much of the world. Farmers will use chickweed as a cover crop and it can also be found on vacant pastures, deciduous forests, and grasslands. You can use miner's lettuce in place of chickweed.

Hop Shoots | The young, tender shoots of hop vines, and a welcome indicator of spring in the Pacific Northwest. They have a brief harvest window when farmers need to trim the young shoots to strengthen the vines for maturation; hop shoots' edibility is a bonus for something that would otherwise go to waste. They are a unique and enjoyable delicacy, with a subtle flavor similar to asparagus. While hops are known for their bitterness, hop shoots have little to no bitterness at all. It's best to use the tender, young hop shoots from the beginning of the season. As the season progresses, hop shoots become tough and woody. When hop shoots are fresh, you can snap off the ends, such as you would with asparagus. If you can't find hop shoots, young asparagus will make an adequate substitute.

Japanese Knotweed | A wild edible with a bamboo-shaped stalk, best harvested in spring before the shoots become too woody. The shoots look like an oversized alien-like asparagus that tastes similar to rhubarb. Knotweed is one of the most invasive plants in the world and there are huge government efforts to prevent it from taking over. Great care must be taken if you find this plant, and choose to gather it. Cutting it without leaving any root stalks is the safest way to prevent further propagation. This plant is voracious and often unstoppable once it's been introduced. You can easily substitute this with rhubarb.

Juniper Berries | Available in the wild year-round. We like to pick, dry, and grind our own juniper berries, but you can also buy ground juniper berries from any specialty spice store.

Lamb's Quarters | Lamb's quarters is a lot like a "wild spinach", and it's no coincidence that they're related. Like many wild foods or greens, this species is nutrient dense, and also produces thousands of black seeds full of protein, vitamin A, phosphorus, calcium and potassium. Interestingly enough, it is closely related to Quinoa, which is cultivated specifically for its seed (they belong to the same genus, Chenopodium, which is in the Amaranth family). Lamb's quarters have mild flavored leaves that are a nice addition to a dish without imparting too much flavor. They do contain oxalic acid though, so it is important to not consume too much. You can substitute this with miner's lettuce or chickweed.

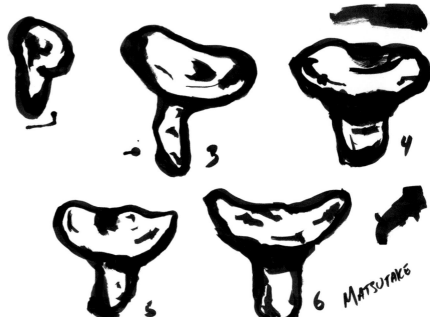

Larch | A member of the pine family, Larch trees are unique because they are the only coniferous tree that is not evergreen, meaning they shed their needles each year. In the spring and early summer, we clip small amounts of larch tree branches and freeze the branches with the needles for later use. We use Larch as a botanical, and we give the relish on page 131 an extra vibrant push with the help of the citrus and pine notes from a larch branch. If you don't have access to larch, you can use spruce tips or just omit this ingredient altogether.

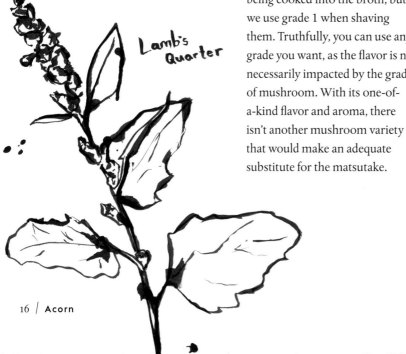

Lamb's Quarter

Matsutake (or Pine) Mushrooms | Among British Columbia's most-prized wild mushrooms. Rare and highly sought after for their firm texture and uniquely floral and pine aromas, their distinct flavors are best showcased in a clean broth and then delicately shaved on top. Matsutakes are rated based on the veil of their caps, with price points varying immensely based on grading. For the broth on page 85, we use grades 3 to 6 since they're being cooked into the broth, but we use grade 1 when shaving them. Truthfully, you can use any grade you want, as the flavor is not necessarily impacted by the grade of mushroom. With its one-of-a-kind flavor and aroma, there isn't another mushroom variety that would make an adequate substitute for the matsutake.

Morel Mushrooms | Wild mushrooms that thrive in post-fire-ravaged forestland, and also form relationships with deciduous trees where they grow in smaller numbers. These mushrooms are meaty, nutty, and highly sought after. Their honeycomb-like exterior makes them experts at holding sauce. We get our morels from a local forager, but you can find them, in the right season, at your local farmers' market. You can substitute with any wild mushroom, though morels should be easy enough to find dried.

Nootka Rose | A wildflower with a short-lived blossoming season in early summer. Its large vibrant pink petals have a sweet, delicate and uplifting floral aroma, and we jump at the chance to capture the flower's essence in vinegars and syrups. You could also use white beach or gallica roses.

Oxeye Daisy Bud

Oxeye Daisy Buds | One of the most prevalent weeds in the Pacific Northwest. These springtime buds must be harvested in a timely fashion, just before they are about to blossom. When pickled, the result is a larger, wilder, caper!

Pacific Crab Apples | A native apple to the Pacific Northwest, which can also, and, surprisingly, resemble a berry more than an apple. They are very crisp, tart, and acidic and stay fresh for quite some time for this reason. Pickling them softens the skins and flesh for a gentler texture. They may be hard to come by; feel free to thinly slice common crab apples in substitution.

Pineappleweed (or Wild Chamomile) | This introduced species is a member of the daisy family that grows in abundance all over the Pacific Northwest (even in sidewalk cracks) and can be quite common to find. It favors heavily compacted, poor soil, so finds a home in a variety of altered environments (choosing an uncontaminated site to pick it from is crucial). Its flavors are a balance between chamomile and pineapple. If you don't have access to pineappleweed you can use dried chamomile instead.

Red-Flowering Currants | Also known as pink winter currant or blood currant, this shrub is found to the west of the Cascades of Canada and the United States. The dark berries, which develop into the summer, are insipid and seedy, and are best left for the birds to eat and distribute their seed. The flowers on the other hand—which range from white to pink to dark red—release the most beautiful aroma. If red-flowering currants aren't available in your area, you could use any edible flower, including Nootka rose, lavender, or anything floral.

Reindeer Lichen | An edible moss-like plant that grows in British Columbia's forests. Its delicate, brittle branches form an airy puffball that's slightly bitter to the taste, with subtle flavors of the forest. Texturally, this might be one of the most interesting things you could ever try. When candied and dried, the tiny branches dissolve in your mouth, like a crispy cotton candy (as on page 191). Because Lichens are slow growing species that form complex relationships and take a long time to establish, great care is taken to ensure that it is gathered sustainability in small amounts. Lichen is so incredibly unique that there is no substitute for this plant.

Salmonberries | This member of the rose family grows abundantly along the west coast of North America, from Alaska to California. Salmonberries grow in brambles, much like blackberries, only they are much more tart and delicate in flavor. As one of the first summer fruits that we

Pineappleweed

get to use in the restaurant, it's a celebrated time of year for us! If salmonberries aren't available in your area you can use thimbleberries or wild raspberries.

Sea Asparagus (or Samphire) |
A naturally salty, crunchy, wild succulent, not unlike a thin green bean. It grows along British Columbia's shores and beaches and is often available at the farmers' market. You can substitute with other wild plants such as sea grass, sea plantain, or sea coriander.

Sea Coriander (or Sea Arrowgrass) |
A thin grass that grows wild along British Columbia's coastline and salt marshes. Its taste is similar to that of fresh coriander with a succulent texture. Young, fresh lighter green leaves are preferred, as this species has toxins (which are easily neutralized by heat), which occur in higher amounts in more mature plants. You can substitute with sea grass, samphire or sea plantain.

Sitka Spruce Buds |
These small male pollen-bearing "buds" are part of the flowering structure of Sitka Spruce Trees, appearing almost like little tree strawberries. They have a very short window of collection, barely 2 weeks. They pack an unbelievable aromatic flavor and are great for sweet or savory applications, as well as in cocktails. You can substitute with spruce tips (see right) for a similar flavor profile.

Spruce Cone

Sitka Spruce Cones |
Young, scaly cones that grow on Sitka spruce trees midway through spring. They should still be primarily green and anywhere from 1 to 3 inches in size. Since the young spruce cones are available for only a short period in spring, we pick extra and freeze them so we can enjoy their unique flavor year-round. You can substitute with spruce tips for a similar flavor.

Spruce Tips |
Spruce tips are the new growth on spruce trees that appears in the spring at the very tip of the branches. At The Acorn, we use spruce tips as a way to add citrus and brighten up a dish. You can freeze them by laying them out individually on a baking sheet until frozen, and then transferring to a freezer bag or container so you have them on hand to use all year long. If you don't have spruce tips, you can substitute 2 tbsp dried sumac for a similar (though less unique) flavor profile.

Wild Garlic |
Also known as crow garlic, wild garlic is a relative to the onion. It is a noxious weed that escaped cultivation and is now widespread in a variety of altered environments. Crow garlic can be confused with other potentially poisonous lookalike plants, but its strong garlic, onion-like aroma is a giveaway. If you prefer to source a more accessible ingredient, you can use thinly sliced leeks.

Wormwood |
A key herbal ingredient for making absinthe, wormwood is a plant native to Siberia, North America, and Europe. Historically used for a number of medicinal purposes, its herbaceous and bitter qualities are believed to help aid digestion along with other gastrointestinal ailments. In some cases, wormwood can be substituted with mugwort.

COOKING THE RECIPES //

At The Acorn, we strive to create dishes that are whole and unique. We name our dishes using just the key featured ingredient—often a single word—which gives an element of mystery and surprise, and creates dialogue about the stories behind the recipes. We continued that theme for many of the recipe titles in this book but expanded the descriptions so you have a better idea of what you're setting out to cook.

RECIPE COMPONENTS /

Our recipes are very much a sum of their parts, often comprising many different components. For the full Acorn experience, it makes sense to follow a recipe from top to bottom, but we also think food is about freedom of expression and we encourage you to choose your own adventure! Many of the recipes work well as stand-alone dishes or pair well with a recipe from another dish, so we have laid out the components for you to easily make them independently if you wish. The recipes are typically arranged in order of the components that you need to make first (or that take the longest to make, or need to be made ahead), but be sure to read a recipe through from start to finish before you begin, to avoid any surprises and to plan your time accordingly.

RECIPE NOTES /

As a general guide, recipes serve six unless otherwise noted. Most of the recipes will make a little extra, so we recommend experimenting with the leftovers. As in the restaurant, most of the recipes are vegan, but not all. Feel free to substitute vegan ingredients for dairy and eggs where you see them. We give some general plating guidelines at the end of most recipes, but we encourage creativity and individuality here. You've followed our way of doing things to get to this point—let your inner freak fly!!!

FOOD WASTE /

We work exceptionally hard to minimize food waste, and this is demonstrated in many of our recipes, where scraps are used in sauces, purees, or vinegars. Over the years, using scraps has led us to many new discoveries and new techniques and has given us good reason to think outside the box. This is easier to do in the restaurant kitchen setting than it is at home because we're using farm-fresh ingredients daily and always prepping ahead: the scraps from a melon being served that day in a salad can be used real-time for a vinegar that could take a month to set. If you find the recipe calls for scraps of a vegetable or fruit that you wouldn't otherwise keep on hand, have fun playing with new ideas for that ingredient first and then use the scraps. We encourage you to work your way through the seasons, making certain items such as vinegars and sauces first that you can store or refrigerate ahead of time until you are ready to serve them.

INGREDIENTS LEGEND / *Here is a guide for some of the basic ingredients we use in the restaurant and encourage you to use in the recipes of this book as well.*

Salt | kosher salt

Pepper | freshly cracked black pepper

Sugar | fair-trade organic cane sugar

Oil | olive oil is extra virgin olive oil; frying oil is organic Canadian canola (sustainable, local, and generally good for you!)

Eggs | always organic and free-range (we work with an SPCA-certified farm in Vancouver)

Agar-agar | thickening agent derived from red algae and a great plant-based substitute for gelatine

Barley koji powder and probiotic cultures | living microorganisms or bacteria that promote or kickstart the fermentation process (see page 22); we primarily use these in our nut cheeses and creams. You can buy probiotic capsules at most markets and health-food stores. The best ones are typically stored in the fridge as the cultures are hopefully still "alive." Some probiotics contain dairy, so double-check if you need a vegan brand.

Kelp | We get our kelp from either Dafne Romero at North Pacific Kelp in Haida Gwaii or from Canadian Kelp Resources, a family-run and sustainable harvesting company in Bamfield, British Columbia.

Nuts | While writing this book, we have been researching nuts and evaluating the impact that growing and harvesting them has on the environment. During our research, we discovered a local hazelnut farm and we couldn't have been more thrilled! Finding a local nut supplier has meant drastically reducing our carbon footprint for an ingredient we use extensively—and hazelnuts also require less water than almonds or cashews to grow, which is another environmental plus. While hazelnuts don't compare in creaminess and fat content to cashews, we still decided to phase out our use of cashews altogether, using hazelnuts instead, and we have limited our almond use too—all in the effort to keep things local and sustainable.

TECHNIQUES / *Here's an overview of a few techniques that appear throughout the book:*

Blanching | A key technique that we use in the kitchen on a daily basis. Essentially, blanching is par-cooking an ingredient in boiling water, then removing and submerging it directly into an ice bath (made up of two parts water to one part ice). This instantly halts the cooking process. The ingredient you are left with just needs a final, finishing cooking treatment before serving. It's a great way to ensure that you are always working with perfectly cooked and flavorful veg.

Blending | Our blender of choice is a Vitamix. Seriously, this is an absolute workhorse in our kitchen and the most-used piece of equipment at the restaurant. You'll see it being used in nearly every recipe. Our number-one blender tip: do not overload your blender. You will work faster and more efficiently if you don't. It may seem counterintuitive, but working in small batches will result in a more evenly pureed product. And always, *always* start your Vitamix on slow speed and work your way up to high. Warning: when blending hot items, you need to leave an air vent at the top of the jug so that the pressure and steam won't overflow. With the Vitamix, this means removing the plastic cap in the center of the lid and covering loosely with a kitchen towel. If you're using a different brand, leave the lid of the container slightly unsealed so that steam can be released.

Deep-Frying | We are not afraid of the deep fryer! We realize that most of you won't have access to a deep fryer at home, so the frying you do will be in a large pot. Make sure you have a pot thermometer on hand to maintain a precise oil temperature. When deep-frying with hot oil, it is important to control your environment. Use a heavy-bottomed, high-sided pot with ample room between the oil and the top of the pot. With ingredients that contain a large amount of water—like cauliflower, for example—the moisture will cause the oil to initially bubble up a few inches, so the extra room in the pot will make sure it doesn't bubble over.

Drying and Dehydrating | Many of our recipes involve dehydrating ingredients to transform them into dusts, powders, spices, and salts. Dehydration is a great way of preserving fresh produce to use at a later date, or just to take a dish to the next level. Here is a guide for some of the drying and dehydration times we use in the book. Moisture content varies between ingredients, so drying times should be adjusted accordingly:

INGREDIENT	DRYING TIME IN DEHYDRATOR @ 145°F	DRYING TIME IN OVEN @ 165°F
Beet slices	12 to 24 hours	6 to 8 hours
Pumpkin crumbs	12 to 24 hours (@ 120°F)	4 hours (@ 130°F)
Aleppo Pepper	18 hours	6 hours
Apple, diced	12 hours	4 hours
Cucumber slices	12 hours	4 hours
Carrot pulp	12 hours	4 hours
Espelette Pepper	12 hours	4 to 5 hours
Pineappleweed	11 hours	3 hours
Wild garlic scraps	6 hours	2 hours
Beet wedges (chewy)	6 to 8 hours	4 to 6 hours

Wash the ingredient and pat dry with a towel to remove any excess moisture. Lay the ingredient out in a single layer on a dehydrator tray (for the dehydrator method) or a baking sheet lined with parchment paper (for the oven method); do not overlap the ingredient (you may need more than one tray, depending on the amount that you're drying). For some lighter ingredients, place a dehydrator screen on top so the item does not fly around with the fans running.

Dry according to the drying guide above or until there is no moisture left in the ingredient when touched or compressed. If any moisture remains, extend the drying time. When using the oven method, it's important to leave the oven door slightly cracked open to allow for proper air circulation. This will also help cool your oven down if the lowest temperature setting available is 200°F.

Fermentation, Pickling and Preserving | Fermentation has become a process integral to our restaurant. It allows us to reach new, deeper flavors, and helps us to preserve the essence, texture, and aromatic qualities of ingredients so we can then use them out of season. We primarily rely on lacto-fermentation and use this method in many of our vinegars and pickles.

We find fermentation with salt is most successful when you work with the 2% rule: Calculate 2% of the weight of the ingredient you are fermenting, and that is the weight of the salt you'll need. This 2% rule provides the best pH (alkalinity) environment for healthy bacteria (lactobacillus) to thrive, while preventing bad bacteria from taking over—essentially, preserving your ingredients without letting them get overly salty!

Pickling and preserving allow us to enjoy farm-fresh or foraged seasonal ingredients during periods when less fresh produce is readily available—i.e., for us, the dreaded Pacific Northwest winter! They also augment the flavor profiles of some ingredients, allowing us to accentuate or draw out certain notes from an ingredient that would otherwise be thought of as inedible or unusable. And they are great ways to make use of vegetable or fruit scraps.

Successful pickling, preserving, and fermenting requires thoroughly cleaned ingredients and sterilized jars and utensils to prevent unwanted bacteria from interfering with the process, and to prolong the stable shelf life for your ingredients. Read more on page 40.

Smoking | The process of smoking an ingredient adds a depth of flavor to a dish that can be a real showstopper. As is usually the case in the kitchen, the trick is finding the right balance, so you don't want to overdo it. There are many ways to smoke food, but the methods used in this cookbook are simple, cold smoking techniques to add flavor to food that is already prepared or will be subsequently cooked by another method. We recommend using apple wood chips or shavings as they impart a mellower and less pungent smoke flavor—perfect for not overpowering the often-delicate fruits and veggies we're applying the smoke to. A word of caution: fire is hot and burns things, and this potentially includes parts of yourself and/or your house. Have a fire blanket or extinguisher at hand when smoking. And you probably don't want to smoke something directly under your smoke detector either!

Stove Top Method | Line the bottom of a large heavy-bottomed pot with aluminum foil and place approximately 4 tbsp of dry fine wood chips or shavings in a thin layer at the center of the foil (if you are using wood chips, soak them in water for 10 minutes first, then strain them out; soaking will help them smolder so they give off a more prolonged smoke). Place another piece of aluminum foil over top of the wood chips or shavings, and then place a 1- to 2-inch tall wire rack to the pot so there is space above the wood chips for air to circulate. Add your ingredients to the pot, either directly onto the wire rack for larger ingredients, or in a heat resistant dish for smaller ingredients. Cover with a heavy lid (if you do not have one, place aluminum foil around the edges of the lid and pot to keep it tightly closed). Heat the pot over medium or high heat for approximately 10 minutes, until there is smoke coming from the wood (you can peak inside to check). Reduce the heat to low and allow your ingredient to smoke for approximately 20 minutes more. Turn off the heat and allow the pot to cool (lid still on) so it retains as much smoke as possible.

Remove the lid and give the ingredient a stir (if it is the type of ingredient that can be stirred), then taste. Repeat the process if more smoke is required.

Smoking Gun Method | This method requires a cold smoking machine. At The Acorn, we use the Breville Smoking Gun, which is readily available at kitchen supply stores or online. Lay your ingredient of choice out onto a deep baking pan, spreading it out as much as possible so there's maximum surface area to be smoked. Cover the pan with plastic wrap, making sure that the edges are tightly sealed. Using a small knife, cut a ¾-inch slit into one end of the plastic wrap. Place the wood chips or shavings into the chamber of the smoking gun and insert its flexible tube into the slit in the plastic wrap. Turn the smoking gun on and light the wood chips in the chamber. You'll see the smoke coming out of the end of the tube. Let it run until the pan is filled with smoke. Remove the tube and cover the slit in the plastic with masking tape. Let everything sit until the smoke has dissipated.

Remove the plastic wrap, give the smoked ingredient a stir (if it is the type of ingredient that can be stirred), then taste. Repeat the process if more smoke is required.

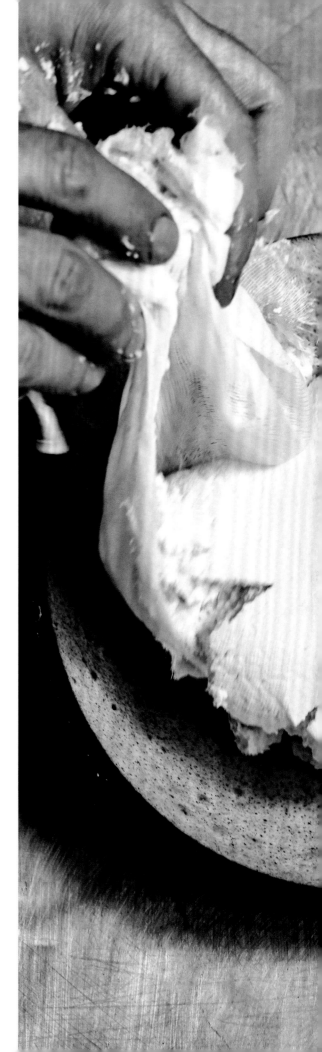

THE ACORN ESSENTIALS //

This section is all about the fundamentals. Recipes that transcend the seasons, or work to preserve them. We reference this chapter to cook many of the dishes throughout the book, but we hope you'll find a few standalone hits that you'll want to come back for.

PLANT-BASED ALTERNATIVES //

While most of this book is naturally plant-based, we wanted to put a few of our favorite plant-based alternatives in one place for you to reference. Most of these recipes can be used in multiple applications, be that as a dip, sauce, or spread.

AQUAFABA /

Aquafaba, or bean water, has revolutionized vegan cooking and baking in the last few years. As chickpeas (or other specific legumes) cook, they impart their proteins and carbohydrates into the water, leaving a viscous or syrupy liquid. This liquid acts similarly to egg white in cooking and baking, and can be used as a substitute (see Note). While it doesn't work as a straight replacement, it's a pretty remarkable ingredient in certain applications. You can use the cooked chickpeas afterward for any other favorite dish!

1 cup raw dried chickpeas

Makes ½ cup | Soak the chickpeas in 6 cups water overnight or for at least 8 hours. Strain the chickpeas and discard the soaking water.

Place the soaked chickpeas and 4 cups fresh water in a pot over medium to high heat, cover, and bring to a simmer. Reduce the heat to low and cook, stirring occasionally, for approximately 1 to 1½ hours, until the chickpeas are soft and tender. Remove from the heat and allow the cooked chickpeas to cool in the pot with the liquid. Once cool, transfer everything to airtight mason jars, seal and refridge overnight. This will help extract more proteins from the chickpeas, resulting in a more gelatinous aquafaba. Strain the chickpeas and use in salads, dressings, or your favorite dip (or just toss them in salt and cracked black pepper and enjoy as a snack). The liquid you are left with is the Aquafaba and should be just right to use in our meringue recipe (right); transfer it to an airtight container and store in the fridge for up to 5 days.

Note | **To use Aquafaba as an egg substitute in baking** | *Add the liquid to a small pot and bring to a simmer over medium-high heat until it reduces by a third; this will intensify the strength of the proteins even more. Depending on the viscosity of your Aquafaba, try 2 tbsp to replace 1 medium egg white or 3 tbsp for a whole egg.*

CHICKPEA MERINGUE /

We first experimented with using Aquafaba to make this Chickpea Meringue shortly after its universal discovery back in 2015—adding it to fresh and macerated berries with toasted macadamia nuts—and have been using it ever since!

3 tbsp Aquafaba (left)
¼ tsp cream of tartar
5 tbsp sugar
1 tsp vanilla extract

Makes 4 cups | In a stand mixer fitted with the whisk attachment, whisk the Aquafaba and cream of tartar until light and airy and soft peaks have formed. With the mixer on medium-high, gradually whisk in the sugar and vanilla until all the sugar is dissolved and stiff, glossy peaks have formed. Transfer to a piping bag as this meringue is best enjoyed directly after whipping; after an hour it will start to lose its stability and become airy and watery.

Note | *If you prefer a baked or crispier meringue, pipe the meringue onto a silicone dehydrator sheet and dry on medium (145 °F) for approximately 4 hours. Alternatively, you can pipe onto a baking sheet lined with a silicone sheet and bake in the oven at 275°F for 10 to 15 minutes.*

ALMOND CRÈME FRAÎCHE /

This vegan cultured almond cream is no match for crème fraîche, but it still delivers a tangy richness. Use this as your base recipe and play around with adding flavors, as we do for the cucumber variation to the right.

1 cup sliced raw almonds
1 tsp koji powder or 2 probiotic capsules
2 tbsp grapeseed oil
1 tsp agave syrup
Salt to taste

Makes 2 cups | Place the almonds in a bowl or container and cover with 2 cups water. Cover or seal the container and let soak in the fridge for 8 hours or overnight. Once ready, strain and rinse the almonds under cold water, then place them in a Vitamix. Add the koji powder, or open the probiotic capsules and pour the powder into the blender, discarding the shell. Add 1 cup water and blend on high until you've reached a silky-smooth consistency with no specks of almonds.

Transfer the mixture to a sterilized 32 oz mason jar. Cover with a towel or a piece of cheesecloth and secure with an elastic band or string. Store at room temperature (72°F) for 48 to 72 hours to ferment. Throughout the fermentation process, it will bubble and froth and increase in volume; this is normal!

Once fermentation is complete, place the mixture back into the Vitamix and blend on medium speed. With the blender running, slowly drizzle in the grapeseed oil until it is completely emulsified, then add the agave syrup and salt to taste. You want the finished consistency to be silky with the density of crème fraîche. Store in an airtight container in the fridge for up to 5 days.

CUCUMBER ALMOND CRÈME FRAÎCHE /

This flavored crème fraîche is the perfect cooling foil to lift any dense, spicy, or umami-rich dishes. It can also be used as a salad dressing, a vegetable dip, or a spread for your favorite sandwich. We've paired it alongside our Black Rice dish on page 65.

¾ cup sliced raw almonds
1 tsp barley koji powder or 2 probiotic capsules
1 large cucumber
1 tbsp maple syrup
Salt to taste

Makes 2 cups | Place the almonds in a bowl or container and cover with 2 cups water. Cover or seal the container and let soak in the fridge for 8 hours or overnight. Once ready, strain and rinse the almonds under cold water, then place them in a Vitamix.

Add the koji powder, or open the probiotic capsules and pour the powder into the blender, discarding the shells. Wash and roughly chop the cucumber, keeping the skin on, then add to the Vitamix along with the maple syrup. Blend on high until you've reached a silky-smooth consistency with no specks of almonds.

Transfer the mixture to a sterilized 32 oz mason jar. Cover with a towel or a piece of cheesecloth and secure with an elastic band or string. Store at room temperature (72°F) for 48 to 72 hours to ferment. Throughout the fermentation process, it will bubble and froth and increase in volume; this is normal!

Once fermentation is complete, place the mixture back into the Vitamix, season with salt, and blend on medium speed. You want the finished consistency to be silky with the density of crème fraîche. Store in an airtight container in the fridge for up to 5 days.

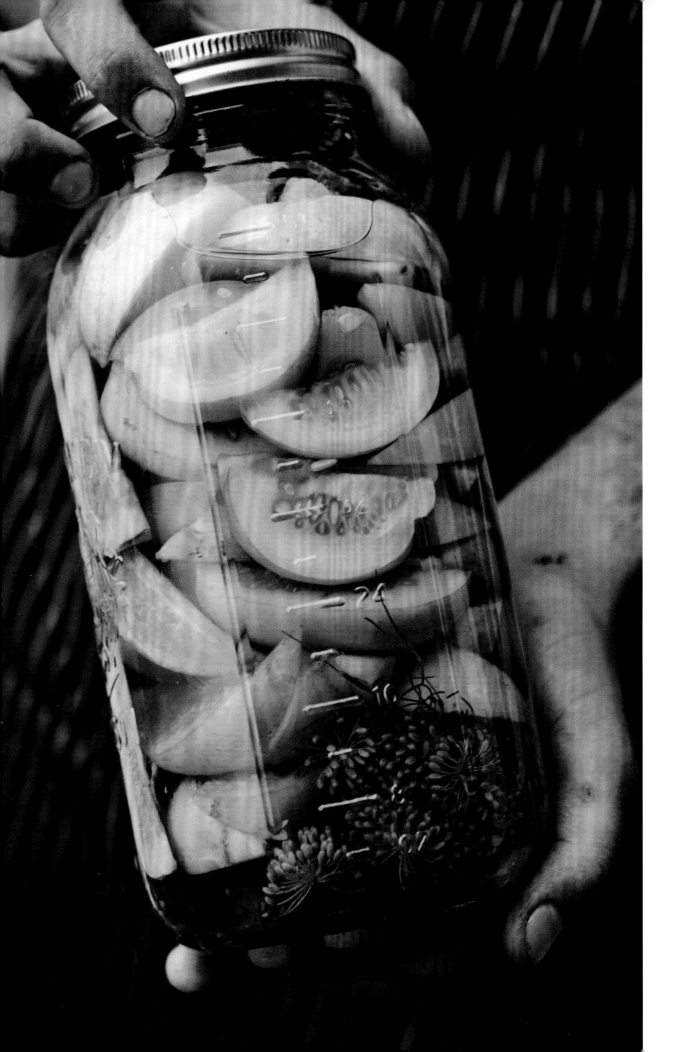

PICKLES //

We're big fans of preserving at The Acorn. Not only is it the best way to capture a micro season, but we rely on the flavor-balancing acid of pickles for many of our dishes. It's often the pickle bite that keeps you coming back for more. Our pickling program has increased so much over the years that we're always running out of space in the building to store our jars. We have a base Pickling Liquid that you can use for pretty much everything, but we change it up occasionally for the recipes that call for different flavors, juuust to keep you on your toes.

PICKLING LIQUID /

2 cups white balsamic vinegar
2 tbsp sugar
2 tbsp salt
3 bay leaves
1 tsp peppercorns
1 tsp yellow mustard seeds
1 tsp celery seeds
1 tsp coriander seeds

Makes 4 cups | In a medium pot, combine all the ingredients with 2 cups water and bring to a simmer. Turn off the heat and allow the liquid to steep for 5 minutes. Strain and reserve the liquid, discarding the solids. Allow the liquid to cool, then transfer to an airtight container. Store in the fridge for up to 6 months.

PICKLED OXEYE DAISY BUDS /

1 cup oxeye daisy buds
½ cup Pickling Liquid (above), cold

Makes 1 cup | Place the oxeye daisy buds in a sterilized 16 oz mason jar and pour in the Pickling Liquid. Seal and store in the fridge for a minimum of 24 hours before serving. Store in the fridge for up to 2 weeks.

PICKLED RAMPS /

20 ramp bulbs with stems attached,
    approximately 3 to 4 inches long
2 cups Pickling Liquid (left)

Note | *Both the Pickled Ramps and their vinegar in this recipe are used in the Radish dish (page 163), so be sure not to discard anything when you open the jar.*

Makes 4 cups | Clean the ramp bulbs thoroughly to remove any dirt, then trim off the leaves, reserving them for salads, pesto, or sauces. Add the bulbs to a sterilized 32 oz mason jar.

In a small saucepot, heat the Pickling Liquid until it reaches a simmer. Pour the hot liquid through a fine-mesh strainer over the bulbs. Allow the liquid to cool, then seal. Refrigerate for at least 1 hour before serving. Store in the fridge for up to 1 month.

PICKLED HOP SHOOT STEMS /

1 cup finely sliced hop shoot stems
    (from about 40 hop shoots, see Note)
1 cup Pickling Liquid (left), cold

Note | *This recipe makes use of the tougher, more fibrous part of the hop shoot stems. First, trim and discard the very ends of the hop shoot stems, approximately ½ inch.*

Finely slice the stems from the bottom into ⅛-inch pieces until you yield 1 cup, reserving the top 6 to 8 inches of the shoots for the Sautéed Hop Shoots (page 171).

Makes 1 cup | Place the sliced stems in a sterilized 16 oz mason jar, then pour the Pickling Liquid over top. Seal and refrigerate for 3 days before using.

PICKLED KNOTROOT /

1½ cups knotroots
¾ cup Pickling Liquid (page 31)

Note | *Knotroot (or crosnes) is a cultivated ingredient available worldwide that we think is pretty special. Knotroot, also known as Chinese or Japanese Artichoke is a little starchy tuber that has a similar appearance to a small grub. It has a subtle sweet and nutty flavor with lots of crunch, and it makes a strikingly unique pickle. You can substitute it with sliced water chestnuts or jicama.*

Makes 1½ cups | Soak the knotroots in cold water and rinse them well, being sure to remove any dirt inside the creases. Add the knotroots to a sterilized 16 oz mason jar. In a small saucepot, heat the Pickling Liquid until it reaches a simmer. Pour the hot liquid through a fine-mesh strainer and over the knotroots. Allow the liquid to cool, then seal. Let sit at room temperature for at least 2 hours before using. Store in the fridge for up to 1 month.

GARLIC PICKLED KNOTROOT /

1 cup knotroots
1 cup Pickling Liquid (page 31)
1 clove garlic, sliced
½ tsp red pepper flakes

Makes 1 cup | Soak the knotroots in cold water and rinse them well, being sure to remove any dirt inside the creases. Add the knotroots to a sterilized 16 oz mason jar. In a small saucepot, heat the Pickling Liquid until it reaches a simmer. Pour the hot liquid through

a fine-mesh strainer and over the knotroots. Add the sliced garlic and red pepper flakes to the jar. Allow the liquid to cool, then seal. Let sit at room temperature for at least 2 hours before using. Store in the fridge for up to 2 weeks.

PICKLED MOREL MUSHROOMS /

1 tbsp peppercorns
2 bay leaves
2 sprigs thyme
1 sprig tarragon
½ cup white wine vinegar
1 tbsp sugar
1 tbsp salt
1 cup sliced morel mushrooms (cut into ¼-inch rings, reserving the trim and scraps for future stocks and sauces)

Makes 1 cup | In a medium pot, combine all the ingredients, except the morel mushrooms, with ¼ cup water and bring to a simmer. Cook on medium heat for 5 minutes. Remove from the heat and strain, discarding the solids.

While the pickling liquid is cooking, pack the sliced morel mushrooms tightly into a sterilized 32 oz mason jar. Pour the hot pickling liquid over top and allow to cool for a minimum of 1 hour before serving. Seal and store in the fridge for up to 2 weeks.

PICKLED GARLIC SCAPE BULBS /

1 cup whole garlic scape bulbs, bulbs separated (see Note)
2 tbsp salt
1 cup Pickling Liquid (page 31)

Note | *Garlic scape bulbs, or bulbils, are the cloves that grow from the top seed head when the garlic scape stalk matures. Different varieties will produce different shapes and sizes of bulbils. The ones we use are typically the size of*

a small marble. These bulbils can be replanted, as they are genetic copies of the original plant. If you don't have garlic scape bulbils, you could use fresh whole garlic cloves instead. If this is the case, peel and cut each clove in half lengthwise and measure 1 cup.

Makes 1 cup | Wash the bulbs under cold water, removing any dirt. Add the salt to a large pot of water and bring to a boil. Blanch the bulbs for 30 seconds, remove from the water, and place directly into an ice bath. Once cool, remove from the ice and pull each bulb apart into the individual bulbils. Place the bulbils into a sterilized 16 oz mason jar.

In a small saucepot, heat the Pickling Liquid until it reaches a simmer. Pour the hot liquid through a fine-mesh strainer and over the bulbils. Allow everything to cool, then seal and refrigerate. Store in the fridge for up to 1 month.

PICKLED TOMATOES /

1 cup cherry tomatoes, halved
 (or quartered if especially large)
¼ cup basil, roughly chopped
1 tsp salt
½ tsp pepper
½ cup cold Pickling Liquid (page 31)

Makes 1 cup | In a medium bowl, gently mix together the cherry tomatoes, basil, salt, and pepper. Add the Pickling Liquid (making sure the liquid is cold, as you do not want to cook the tomatoes with any heat). Transfer to a sterilized 16 oz mason jar or airtight container and refrigerate for a minimum 1 hour before serving. Seal and store in the fridge for up to 1 week.

PICKLED SERRANO PEPPERS /

6 serrano peppers
½ cup Pickling Liquid (page 31), cold

Makes 1 cup | Wash the serrano peppers and thinly slice, leaving the seeds in. Transfer to a sterilized 16 oz mason jar and pour the Pickling Liquid over top. Seal and refrigerate for a minimum of 12 hours before serving. Store in the fridge for up to 1 month.

PICKLED SITKA SPRUCE BUDS /

½ cup sitka spruce buds
¼ cup Pickling Liquid (page 31)

Makes ½ cup | Place the buds in a sterilized 16 oz mason jar. In a small pot, warm up the Pickling Liquid to just under a simmer. Pour the hot liquid through a fine-mesh strainer and over the buds and allow to cool at room temperature. Seal and store in the fridge for up to 1 month.

PICKLED CARROTS /

2 yellow or orange carrots
1 cup Pickling Liquid (page 31)

Makes 2 cups | Clean the carrots, keeping the peels on, and trim off the ends. Slice into ⅛-inch-thick coins. Place the carrots in a sterilized 32 oz mason jar. In a small saucepot, heat the Pickling Liquid until it reaches a simmer. Pour the hot liquid through a fine-mesh strainer and over the carrots. Allow everything to cool, then seal and refrigerate for 1 hour before serving. Store in the fridge for up to 1 month.

PICKLED ONIONS /

2 Walla Walla onions
2 cups Pickling Liquid (page 31)

Makes 4 cups | Peel the onions and cut them into ½-inch wedges. Break the wedges apart and pack their petals as tight as you can into a sterilized 32 oz mason jar, trying to keep the integrity of the petal shapes without breaking them. In a small saucepot, heat the Pickling Liquid until it reaches a simmer. Pour the hot liquid through a fine-mesh strainer and over the onions and press down slightly as the onions soften. Allow everything to cool and sit for approximately 20 minutes before serving. Seal and store in the fridge for up to 1 month.

PICKLED MUSTARD SEEDS /

2 tbsp yellow mustard seeds
2 tbsp brown mustard seeds
½ cup Pickling Liquid (page 31)

Makes ½ cup | Place both types of mustard seeds in a small container and pour 2 cups water over top. Stir and cover, letting them sit in the fridge for 8 hours or overnight. Strain the mustard seeds from the water and place them into a sterilized 8 oz mason jar.

Pour the Pickling Liquid over the seeds, stir, and seal. Refrigerate for a minimum of 2 days before serving. Store in the fridge for up to 1 month.

PICKLED SHALLOTS /

4 shallots
½ cup Pickling Liquid (page 31)

Makes 1 cup | Peel the shallots and thinly slice them approximately ⅛ inch thick. Transfer to a sterilized 16 oz mason jar. Pour the Pickling Liquid over the shallots, seal, and refrigerate for 30 minutes before serving. Store in the fridge for up to 1 month, making sure the shallots are submerged under the Pickling Liquid.

PICKLED TURNIPS /

2 cups Pickling Liquid (page 31)
8 scarlet or Tokyo turnips (see Note)
2 shallots, thinly sliced
2 cloves garlic, thinly sliced

Note | *Scarlet and Tokyo turnips are similar in shape and size, but we prefer scarlets' gorgeous pink color for that* pop *on the plate.*

Makes 2 cups | In a pot, bring the Pickling Liquid to a boil, then turn off the heat. Wash and trim the turnips, removing the greens and the bottom stems (use the greens in a salad or in your favorite pesto), then cut the turnips into quarters. Transfer to a sterilized 32 oz mason jar and add the shallots and garlic. Pour the hot liquid through a fine-mesh strainer and over the turnips. Allow to cool at room temperature for at least 2 hours before serving. Seal and store in the fridge for up to 2 weeks.

PICKLED BLUE CHANTERELLE MUSHROOMS /

1 lb blue chanterelle mushrooms
2 tsp peppercorns
4 bay leaves
4 sprigs thyme
1 sprig tarragon
2 cups white wine vinegar
¼ cup sugar
1 tbsp salt

Makes 2 cups | The blue chanterelle mushrooms will be a dense cluster typically full of needles and debris. Using a brush, clean the chanterelles thoroughly and trim off the end of the stems, as they tend to be caked with dirt. It is best to tear off individual mushrooms from the cluster to clean these properly. Once fully clean, tear each mushroom into thin strips, approximately 2 inches long, until you have 2 cups.

Place the torn mushrooms into a sterilized 32 oz mason jar. Place the rest of the ingredients in a small saucepot, add 1 cup water, and bring the liquid to a simmer for no more than 5 minutes. Remove from the heat. Pour the hot liquid through a fine-mesh strainer ad over the mushroom. Allow everything to cool, then seal and refrigerate for 1 to 2 hours before serving. Store them in the fridge for up to 2 months.

PICKLED GINGER /

4- to 6-inch piece fresh ginger
2 tbsp mirin
2 tbsp rice wine vinegar
2 tbsp white wine vinegar
1 tsp salt

Makes ½ cup | Using a spoon, scrape the skin off the ginger, then slice the ginger into ⅛-inch-thick pieces and place into a small container or bowl. In a small saucepot, bring the mirin, rice wine vinegar, white wine vinegar, and salt to a simmer. Pour the hot liquid over the sliced ginger. Allow to cool, then transfer to a sterilized 8 oz mason jar, seal, and refrigerate for 1 to 2 hours. Store in the fridge for up to 1 month. The strength of the ginger will mellow over time; if you like a stronger, punchier ginger, use it sooner rather than later!

PICKLED FORMANOVA BEETS /

2 formanova beets
1 cup Licorice Fern Root Vinegar (page 46)
    or a neutral vinegar like white balsamic
    or apple cider vinegar
2 tbsp sugar
2 tsp salt
2 sprigs thyme, leaves picked

Makes 2½ cups | Remove the stems from the beets and thoroughly clean the beets to remove any dirt. Place the whole beets in a pot and cover with water. Bring to a boil, then reduce to a simmer and cook for approximately 30 to 40 minutes, until you can easily slide a knife through (be careful not to make too many holes when you're testing). Remove from the water and allow to cool slightly. Once cool enough to touch, but still warm, use a cloth to rub off the skin, then refrigerate for approximately 30 minutes. Use a mandoline to slice the beets lengthwise into ⅛-inch-thick strips and place them in a sterilized 32 oz mason jar.

In a small pot, bring the vinegar, sugar, and salt to a simmer for 2 minutes, then turn off the heat. Add the thyme leaves and stir, then let steep for 3 minutes. Pour the hot liquid through a fine-mesh strainer and over the sliced beets. Allow to marinate for at least 20 minutes at room temperature before serving. Store in the fridge for up to 2 weeks.

PICKLED PACIFIC CRAB APPLES /

1 cup Pacific crab apples
1 cup Peach Blossom Vinegar (page 49)
    or apple cider vinegar
2 whole star anise
2 cardamom pods, crushed
2 tsp salt

Makes 2 cups | Wash the crab apples and snip the stems off as close to the crab apple as possible. Place the vinegar, star anise, crushed cardamom pods, and salt in a small pot and heat until just warm enough to dissolve the salt. Place the crab apples in a sterilized 16 oz mason jar and cover with the pickling liquid. Seal tightly and allow to pickle in the fridge for 1 week before serving. Store in the fridge for up to 1 month.

PRESERVES //

If you're like us and never have enough freezer space, preserving your fruit is the next-best way to save them for future use! We make all our own jams and preserves at the restaurant. Here are a few recipes that we use within the book; you can also use this method as a guide to help you preserve your own favorite ingredients.

PRESERVED PLUMS /

3½ cups sugar
10 cardamom pods
5 lb Santa Rosa plums (the riper the better; see Note)

Note | *We especially love Santa Rosa plums for their juicy, low-acid, fruit-punch-like flavor, but you can use any ripe plum variety if Santa Rosas are not available.*

Makes 3 (32 oz) mason jars | Sterilize the Jars | To sterilize the jars, place a canning rack in the bottom of a large stockpot. Fill the pot two-thirds full with water and bring the water to a boil on high heat. Once boiling, turn the temperature down slightly. Remove the lids of three 32 oz mason jars and wash the lids with hot soapy water, then set aside on a clean kitchen towel. Using rubber-lined canning tongs, submerge the empty glass jars in the near-boiling water and position them in the canning rack. Allow to sit for 5 minutes in the boiling water. Carefully remove the jars using the rubber-lined canning tongs, and invert the jars on a clean kitchen towel until you're ready to use them. Use immediately to avoid any contamination.

Prepare the Preserves | In a medium saucepot, combine 8 cups water with the sugar and cardamom pods and bring to a simmer for 5 minutes to create a syrup. Remove from the heat and set aside, keeping warm.

Wash, halve, and pit the plums. Fill each of the sterilized jars with the plum halves, leaving 2 inches of space at the top of each jar. Gently tap the jars on a hard surface to settle them down; if this causes space

to free up, add more plums. Repeat until the jars are packed, always leaving 2 inches of space at the top of the jars. Carefully pour the still-warm syrup through a fine-mesh strainer over the plums, bringing the liquid up to 1 inch from the top of each jar.

Boil the Jars | Thoroughly wipe the top edges of the jars with a clean towel to remove any spilled syrup. Place the lids on the jars and twist until they are snug, then give a little twist back in the opposite direction; this will allow the lid to release air in the boiling process. Using a jar lifter, place the jars into the large pot of boiling water. When moving the jars, make sure the jar lifter is securely positioned just below the neck of the jar, and keep the jars upright—tilting could cause the contents to spill into the sterilized sealing area of the lid.

Once the jars are in the pot, you might need to add more hot water to make sure the jars are submerged at least 1 inch below the water (or at least 2 inches if boiling the jars for more than 30 minutes). Pour any added water around the jars and not directly onto them.

Turn the heat up to high and cover the pot with a lid until the water boils vigorously. Once boiling, set a timer for 20 minutes and keep the pot covered the whole time. You may lower the heat if needed, as long as a gentle but complete boil is maintained for the entire processing time. If the water stops boiling at any time during the process, you'll need to start over by turning the heat back to high, bringing the water back to a vigorous boil, and resetting the timer back at 20 minutes. When the timer goes, turn off the heat and remove the lid from the pot. Wait 5 minutes before removing the jars to allow the contents to settle.

Cool the Jars | Using a jar lifter, remove the jars one at a time, being careful not to tilt the jars. Carefully place them directly onto a towel or a cake cooling rack, leaving at least 1 inch of space between the jars during cooling. Avoid placing the jars on a cold surface or in a cold draft.

Let the jars sit undisturbed while they cool, from 12 to 24 hours. Do not tighten or push down on the lids until the jars are completely cooled. During this time, do not tighten the metal screw band, as air will continue to escape from the jar, helping it seal. Once cool, check to make sure the seal on the jar is tight. Look for a concave shape on the lid and press the center of the lid with your finger. The lid will not spring up to the touch if it is properly sealed. Tighten the metal screw bands. Store the sealed jars at room temperature for 1 to 2 years.

PRESERVED APRICOTS /

10 to 15 apricots
2 cups sugar

Makes 2 (32 oz) mason jars | Sterilize the Jars | See instructions on page 40, using two 32 oz mason jars.

Prepare the Preserves | Wash the apricots and cut them in half, removing the pits and reserving the pits for the syrup. Pack the apricots into the two sterilized mason jars as tightly as you can, leaving 2 inches of space at the top of each jar. Gently tap the jars on a hard surface to settle them down; if this causes space to free up, add more apricots. Repeat until the jars are packed, always leaving 2 inches of space at the top of the jars.

In a separate medium pot, combine 6 cups water, the apricot pits, and sugar and bring to a simmer for 30 minutes to extract the flavor from the pits. Remove from the heat and keep warm. Carefully pour the warm syrup through a fine-mesh strainer and over the apricots, bringing the liquid up to 1 inch from the top of each jar.

Boil and Cool the Jars | See instructions on page 40 for boiling and cooling the jars, but boil for only 10 minutes and allow to cool at room temperature for only 2 hours. Store the sealed jars at room temperature for 1 to 2 years.

PRESERVED MEYER LEMON /

8 Meyer lemons
2 cups salt
1 cup sugar

Note | *Meyer lemons are the overachieving little sister of conventional lemons. Smaller yet more fragrant, less acidic, and, dare we say, sweet?! Proof that size really doesn't matter. This recipe takes 2 weeks to make, so plan accordingly.*

Makes 2 (32 oz) mason jars | Sterilize the Jars | See instructions on page 40, using two 32 oz mason jars.

Destem and wash the Meyer lemons. Make two cuts lengthwise into each lemon, as though you were going to quarter it from the top of the stem down, stopping ½ inch from the bottom. Sterilize a 32 oz mason jar that will fit all the lemons.

Mix the salt and sugar together in a bowl (this will be your curing mixture). Pour a quarter of the curing mixture into the bottom of the mason jar. Dredge each lemon in the curing mix to evenly coat the inside and outside of the lemons; squeeze the bottom of each lemon to open it up like a flower, then pour some of the mixture inside each lemon to coat the wedges. Place the lemons one by one into the jar after coating them; sprinkle some more of the curing mixture over each layer and pack them down tight. Continue until all the lemons and curing mixture are packed in the jar. Cover with the lid and refrigerate for 2 weeks.

When ready, fully quarter the lemons and hollow them out (reserving the flesh to add to sauces or syrups). Small-dice the preserved lemon skins and piths. Store in a small airtight container in the fridge for up to 2 months.

VEGETABLE BOTTARGA //

Bottarga is the umami flavorbomb enhancer of the ancient world. Historically made from cured fish roe sac, this rich, funky, briny preserved condiment is typically shaved or grated on top of food to add that umami quality. We've created a plant-based version that provides a cleaner bottarga experience while still offering the same rich, robust, and salty flavor sensation.

In the restaurant, we use food scraps, "ugly" vegetables, and leftover waste from sauces to make our bottarga. Here, we give you a general outline for using raw product to achieve this tasty additive. Ultimately, it's up to you what you add to your vegetable mix—outcomes will vary, but all should be equally delicious and unique!

4 carrots

4 stalks celery

2 onions

8 cloves garlic

1 medium rutabaga

2 parsnips

1 medium celeriac

2 tbsp olive oil

1 tbsp salt

1 tbsp pepper

¾ cup tomato puree

2 tbsp sherry vinegar

Note | *You need to dehydrate the bottarga in your dehydrator for up to 2 weeks, so plan ahead for this.*

Makes 4 bricks | Preheat the oven to 400°F. Wash all the vegetables thoroughly and roughly chop them, keeping the skins and peels on (aside from the onions and garlic, which are peeled). In a large bowl, toss the vegetables with the olive oil, salt, and pepper until everything is evenly coated. Lay the vegetables out onto a baking sheet lined with parchment paper.

Roast the vegetables for approximately 45 minutes, stirring halfway through cooking. Once the vegetables have reached a dark caramelization, transfer them to a large saucepot on medium-high heat. Since the vegetables will have different cooking times, some of the veg might be slightly charred, and this is ok. Add the tomato puree to the pot and cook for 10 minutes, stirring often. The goal is to take the vegetables to an even darker caramelization.

Deglaze the pot with the sherry vinegar. Add 1 cup of water and cook on medium heat for another 5 minutes, then transfer the vegetables to a Vitamix or food processor. Blend the vegetables to a smooth consistency, then transfer the puree to a baking pan lined with parchment paper, spreading it out evenly to approximately 1 inch thick.

Turn the oven to 300°F and cook for 1 hour. This will release excess steam and moisture from the vegetables. Remove from the oven and allow to cool to room temperature. Once cool, shape it into four 1 × 3-inch rectangular bricks.

Transfer the bricks to a dehydrator and dehydrate on the medium setting (145°F) for approximately 2 weeks. The bottarga is ready when the bricks are completely dehydrated all the way through and rock-hard. If you're unsure whether they are ready, keep them in the dehydrator for the full 2 weeks. Store them in an airtight container in a cool and dry location for up to 6 months.

VINEGARS //

Each Vinegar Makes 4 cups | *The vinegars we make in-house are snapshots of the season, and often softer, less intense vinegars that are great for making light vinaigrettes and to finish dishes. We make the best use of our delicate wild-foraged ingredients that can't be ingested raw by extracting their flavors through vinegars. The vinegar recipes in this book typically yield more than what is needed for the recipes they're used in; we do so to make sure that we are taking full advantage of the long process (anywhere from 1 to 3 months) that it takes to make these vinegars.*

Note | *The best way to make a vinegar is with a vinegar mother—a clear jelly disk made up of acetic acid bacteria and cellulose—which can be used for multiple vinegars, so don't throw them away! You can buy vinegar mothers at your local homebrew/winemaking store, or you can make your own using a raw unfiltered vinegar (such as Bragg organic raw apple cider vinegar). Each recipe in this section includes the quantity of cider vinegar required to start a mother if you don't already have one, and they all follow the same method (on page 49). At the end of the process, you should have a tasty vinegar and a happy vinegar mother to use again. This way you have access to these amazing vinegar flavors to play around with all year round. Once you get the hang of our vinegar process, you can use it to make any vinegar with your own favorite ingredients.*

SPRUCE TIP VINEGAR /

½ cup fresh spruce tips, washed thoroughly
 (or ¼ cup dried spruce tips)
¼ cup sugar
1 vinegar mother or ¼ cup raw cider vinegar
4 cups dry white wine

BIG LEAF MAPLE BLOSSOM VINEGAR /

2 cups big leaf maple blossoms, submerged under
 cold water to remove any unwanted debris
2 tbsp sugar
1 vinegar mother or ¼ cup raw cider vinegar
4 cups dry white wine

QUINCE VINEGAR /

2 quinces, outside fuzz wiped off with a cloth
1 vinegar mother or ¼ cup raw cider vinegar
4 cups dry white wine

STINGING NETTLE SAKE VINEGAR /

2 cups stinging nettles, washed under cold water
 to remove any dirt and unwanted stems
2 tbsp sugar
1 vinegar mother or ¼ cup raw cider vinegar
4 cups dry sake

Note | *At The Acorn, we use the Junmai Nama sake from Artisan Sake Maker. There's no need to blanch the stinging nettles to remove the tiny needles that will cause your hands and arms to itch and burn. Just be sure to use tongs or gloves when handling.*

LICORICE FERN ROOT VINEGAR /

4 pieces licorice fern root, approximately
 4 inches long, thoroughly washed
¼ cup sugar
1 vinegar mother or ¼ cup raw cider vinegar
4 cups dry white wine

YARROW VINEGAR /

1 cup yarrow stems and leaves, rinsed under
  cold water to remove any dirt and debris
2 tbsp sugar
1 vinegar mother or ¼ cup raw cider vinegar
4 cups dry white wine

PEACH BLOSSOM VINEGAR /

3 cups peach blossoms, all stems
  and branches removed
¼ cup sugar
1 vinegar mother or ¼ cup raw cider vinegar
4 cups dry white wine

Note | *You can use this recipe as a guide for any other edible flowers or blossoms that you want to make vinegar with, such as Nootka rose.*

Peach Blossom

PEACH PIT VINEGAR /

1 cup peach pits
2 tbsp sugar
1 vinegar mother or ¼ cup raw cider vinegar
4 cups dry white wine

Note | *Instead of throwing out peach pits, use them to make vinegar!*

TOASTED CHICKPEA VINEGAR /

2 cups raw dried chickpeas, roasted (see Note)
2 tbsp sugar
1 vinegar mother or ¼ cup raw cider vinegar
4 cups dry white wine

Note | *Preheat your oven to 350°F and lay the chickpeas out onto a baking sheet lined with parchment paper. Roast for 20 minutes, remove them from the oven, and set aside to cool.*

Make the Vinegar | Add the solid ingredient (spruce tips, stinging nettles, quinces, etc.) to a sterilized 64 oz mason jar along with the sugar and the vinegar mother or raw cider vinegar. Add the white wine (or sake) and cover the top of the jar with a piece of cheesecloth or clean kitchen towel, secured tightly around the lip of the jar with an elastic band. Store in a dark area (a cupboard or pantry is great) for 1 to 3 months.

Check the jar once a week to make sure a vinegar mother is forming. Also make sure that no mold is growing. If you see mold developing, gently scrape it away. If it grows back again, you will have to throw out the vinegar and start again.

You'll also want to taste and smell the vinegar once a week to monitor the flavor progression. Once the smell of wine is completely gone and the taste is high in acidity with a depth of flavor, your vinegar is ready! Don't get discouraged if it feels like it's taking a long time; this process can take anywhere from 1 to 3 months (or potentially even longer) for maturation, so patience is key.

When ready, strain out the vinegar from the jar, discarding the solids and saving the mother for your next batch of vinegar. The vinegar can be used right away, or you can further mature it in an airtight container in the fridge for up to 1 year.

OILS //

Often in vegetable-forward cooking, where ingredients don't naturally contain fat, the best way to finish a dish is with a little drizzle of infused oil. Oils can impart a unique richness and flavorful mouthfeel to complement a dish without interfering with the existing salt, acid, or sweetness on the plate, keeping everything in balance.

WILD GARLIC OIL /

10 stalks wild garlic
1 cup chopped parsley
1½ tsp salt
2 cups grapeseed oil

Makes 2 cups | Remove the trim and scraps of the wild garlic stalks and reserve these for the Wild Garlic Powder (page 180). Chop the remaining stalks into 1-inch pieces (you need about 1 cup). Place in a Vitamix along with the parsley, salt, and grapeseed oil. Run on the highest speed for 5 minutes—you're using the friction here to heat the oil and infuse the flavors. If you don't have a high-speed blender, combine the ingredients in an airtight container and refrigerate for 2 days to give the flavors the chance to infuse.

Gently strain the oil through a fine-mesh sieve to remove any sediment. You can then further clarify the oil by straining it once more through a coffee filter or cheesecloth, making sure not to force the liquid through; let the oil drip slowly and naturally. Store in an airtight container in the fridge for up to 1 week.

LOVAGE OIL /

1 cup finely chopped lovage leaves and stems
½ cup finely chopped parsley
2 tsp salt
1 cup grapeseed oil

Makes 1½ cups | Place all the ingredients in a Vitamix and blend on high for 4 minutes. The heat from the blender will help infuse the flavor of the herbs with the oil. Gently strain through a coffee filter, making sure not to force the liquid through; let the oil drip slowly and naturally. Store in an airtight container in the fridge for up to 6 months.

Black Currant Leaf

BLACK CURRANT LEAF OIL /

2 cups packed black currant leaves
1 cup grapeseed oil

Note | *Black currant is a summer berry, famously used as the base for the liqueur crème de cassis. If you're picking them in summer, also pick some of their herbaceous leaves to create this deep-green infused oil—they're known for their medicinal qualities.*

Makes 1 cup | Place the black currant leaves and grapeseed oil in a Vitamix and blend on high for 3 minutes. The heat from the blender will help infuse the flavor of the herbs with the oil. Gently strain through a coffee filter, making sure not to force the liquid through; let the oil drip slowly and naturally. Store in an airtight container in the fridge for up to 6 months.

SMOKED SUNFLOWER OIL /

1 cup sunflower oil

Makes 1 cup | Place the sunflower oil in a shallow dish or bowl. Use one of our smoking methods (page 22) to smoke the oil. Smoke it twice to really infuse the flavor. Transfer to an airtight container and store in the fridge for up to 6 months.

BLACK SHALLOT OIL /

¼ cup peeled and sliced black shallots (see Note)
1 cup grapeseed oil
2 tsp salt
2 tsp sugar

Note | *Similar to highly adored black garlic, black shallots are produced using a similar method: left in their skins and allowed to slowly age at a controlled temperature for 3 weeks. This caramelizes the natural sugars in the shallots, leaving you with a uniquely dense, earthy, and sweet allium flavor.*

Makes 1½ cups | Place all the ingredients in a Vitamix and blend on medium-high speed for 1 minute, until the liquid has warmed and the sugar and salt are dissolved and well infused. Store in an airtight container in the fridge for up to 6 months.

AUTUMN//

// That feeling when the cool autumn air hits your lungs and you can sense the end of summer… It's a bittersweet moment for some, but for us it means one thing: mushrooms. Wild mushrooms thrive in the Pacific Northwest rainforests once the weather cools and the rains start. Their arrival is enough to keep us uplifted while others bear down for the cooler season ahead. Members of our team take to the forest for a pick on their days off, or we all go together on foraging education field trips. The importance of staying connected to our food is never more apparent than when respectfully picking a wild chanterelle or a cauliflower mushroom straight from the earth.

CAULIFLOWER RISOTTO //

Cauliflower Mushroom Risotto, Fermented Celery Leaf,
Potato Cauliflower Nests + Crispy Fried Cauliflower,
Sautéed Cauliflower Mushrooms

Serves 6 | Risotto. Often the only option for vegetarians in restaurants. What's that? Another risotto? Eye roll. Here's the thing: this book wouldn't be complete without it. We don't often have risotto on the menu, but when we do, it's always a hit. And the kicker is that it's *vegan*. We love this recipe's play on cauliflower, using both the vegetable and mushroom varietals.

The Potato Cauliflower Nests in this recipe made an appearance on the tasting menu we brought to New York when we did a five-night pop-up in the Lower East Side. They're delightfully crispy and add a touch of chaos to the plate.

Note | *The elements of this recipe are interlaced. For example, you need the trim from the Sautéed Cauliflower Mushrooms to make the Cauliflower Mushroom Stock, and the trim from the cauliflower used in the Potato Cauliflower Nests for the Crispy Fried Cauliflower. To best time this dish, we recommend frying the Cauliflower Potato Nests, Crispy Fried Cauliflower, and Sautéed Cauliflower Mushrooms while the risotto is cooking.*

FERMENTED CELERY LEAF + FERMENTED CELERY LEAF WATER /

4 cups roughly chopped celery leaves and stems
2 tbsp salt
2 tbsp sliced garlic

Note | *This recipe takes 4 days to ferment, so you'll need to make this in advance!*

Makes 4 cups leaves + 4 cups water | Wash the chopped celery leaves and stems well. Then, using your hands, massage the salt into the leaves and stems, making sure it gets into all the folds; don't be afraid of bruising them. Transfer the celery leaves and stems to a sterilized 64 oz mason jar or glass container. Pour in 4 cups water and the garlic and stir.

Fill a resealable plastic bag half-full of 2% salted water and seal it tight. Float the bag on top of the liquid, using it to keep the celery leaves and stems submerged under the water. Secure a towel or piece of cheesecloth over the container (rather than using a lid) so that the liquid can breathe—this is an important part of the fermentation process to let gases escape. Allow the leaves and stems to ferment at room temperature for 4 days, checking every day to make sure the leaves and stems are submerged.

After 4 days, strain the liquid into a separate jar or container, using a spatula or spoon to press the celery leaves and stems into the strainer to get as much liquid out as possible. Reserve the leaves and stems in a separate airtight container. Store both the leaves and stems and the container of celery water in the fridge for up to 2 weeks.

CONTINUES

CAULIFLOWER
MUSHROOM STOCK /

1 cup cauliflower mushroom stalks reserved
   from Sautéed Cauliflower Mushrooms (page 63)
1 cup sliced white button mushrooms
1 large onion, roughly chopped
3 cloves garlic
3 tbsp olive oil
1 tbsp salt
½ cup sliced celery
2 bay leaves
1 tbsp peppercorns
4 cups Fermented Celery Leaf Water (page 59)

Makes 12 cups | Preheat the oven to 400°F. In a large
bowl, mix together the cauliflower mushroom stalks,
sliced white mushrooms, onions, garlic cloves, 2 tbsp
of the olive oil, and the salt. Spread the mushroom
mixture on a baking sheet lined with parchment paper
and roast on the lower rack of the oven for 15 minutes
or until nicely caramelized (this gives more body to
the stock).

Remove from the oven and transfer to a large saucepot.
Add the remaining olive oil along with the celery,
bay leaves, peppercorns, celery water, and 12 cups
water. Bring to a simmer and allow to simmer for
30 minutes, stirring occasionally to prevent anything
from sticking to the bottom of the pot. Strain the
stock through a large-holed sieve or strainer. Store
in an airtight container in the fridge for up to 5 days.

POTATO CAULIFLOWER NESTS
+ CRISPY FRIED CAULIFLOWER /

1 tbsp salt + more for seasoning
1 tbsp cream of tartar
4 Yukon Gold potatoes
1 head cauliflower
3 tbsp olive oil
Pepper, to taste
8 cups canola oil

Note | *This recipe requires a spiralizer, which is a tool
used to turn vegetables into long noodles. It is best to choose
potatoes that are an even oval shape, as this will produce
longer, more uniformly sized noodles.*

Makes 6 servings | **Prepare the Potatoes** | In
a large bowl, stir the salt and the cream of tartar into
12 cups water. Wash the potatoes thoroughly, keeping
the skins on. Using a spiralizer, process the potatoes
into long noodles, creating the longest pieces possible.
Add the potato noodles to the water and soak for at
least 5 minutes, but no more than 10. This will help
soften the potatoes, making them less brittle when
you wrap them around the cauliflower.

Prepare the Cauliflower | Trim the cauliflower's
outer leaves and set aside six florets, approximately
2 inches each. Take the trim, stalk, and other scraps of
cauliflower and roughly chop into smaller pieces, then
add these to a food processor. Pulse until they're the
size of rice grains. Measure out 2 cups.

In a large bowl, season the reserved cauliflower florets
with the olive oil and some salt and pepper, and toss
to evenly coat. Using five or six potato noodles per
cauliflower floret, tightly wrap the noodles around
each floret, making sure to overlap two or three times.
You can make these 1 day in advance and store in an
airtight container in the fridge until ready to cook.

CONTINUES

Fry the Potato Cauliflower Nests | Line two plates with a kitchen towel or paper towel. Place the canola oil in a heavy-bottomed, high-sided pot. Using a pot thermometer, bring the oil up to 350°F. Working in small batches, fry the Potato Cauliflower Nests in the oil, rotating and flipping them until they are uniformly crispy and there are few to no bubbles of moisture escaping from the potato. Using tongs, carefully remove the nests from the oil and transfer to one of the prepared plates. Season with salt. After the nests are complete, working in batches, carefully sprinkle ¼ cup cauliflower scraps into the hot oil; be careful, as the moisture from the cauliflower will initially bubble up. Fry until they are an even golden-brown color and there are no more bubbles of moisture coming up. With a slotted spoon or spider, carefully remove the cauliflower and transfer to the other prepared plates. Season with salt. Repeat until all the cauliflower has been fried.

CAULIFLOWER MUSHROOM RISOTTO /

1 recipe Cauliflower Mushroom Stock (page 60)
¼ cup finely diced onions
2 tbsp olive oil
3 cups carnaroli rice
1 cup white wine
Salt, to taste
1 tsp white pepper

Note | *We like the higher starch quality of carnaroli rice for our risottos, as it absorbs the flavors of the stock a little better than arborio rice. Don't rinse the rice first; we want to keep those starches on the grain.*

Makes 6 servings | Place the Cauliflower Mushroom Stock in a medium pot and bring it up to just under a simmer. Maintain the temperature of the stock so that it's at the same heat as the rice.

In a large sauté pan on medium-high heat, sweat the onions in the olive oil until they are soft and translucent. Add the rice and toast for 3 minutes, stirring often. Add the white wine and cook for 1 minute, stirring often. Season with salt and white

pepper. Ladle in 1 cup hot Cauliflower Mushroom Stock. Let the stock cook, stirring constantly, until the rice is a little dry and screaming for more liquid. Add another cup of stock and stir until dry again, then add another cup of stock. Continue this process until the rice is cooked to a creamy texture, making sure it's still a little al dente; you may not need to use all the stock. Check for seasoning and serve immediately.

SAUTÉED CAULIFLOWER MUSHROOMS /

4 cups cauliflower mushrooms, stalks trimmed and reserved for Cauliflower Mushroom Stock (page 60)
2 tbsp olive oil
Salt, to taste
½ tsp pepper

Note | *This is a very fast sauté; you want to cook these mushrooms so they still retain their texture and structure.*

Makes 6 servings | Wash and dry the cauliflower mushrooms and cut into 2-inch pieces. Heat a frying pan on high heat and add the olive oil and mushrooms. Cook for 30 seconds, stirring often. Season with salt and pepper and serve immediately.

PLATING /

1 recipe Cauliflower Mushroom Risotto (left)
1 recipe Sautéed Cauliflower Mushrooms (above)
1 recipe Potato Cauliflower Nests (page 60)
½ cup Pickled Oxeye Daisy Buds (page 31)
1 recipe Crispy Fried Cauliflower (page 60)

Note | *If you don't have oxeye daisy buds to pickle, you can substitute the Pickled Oxeye Daisy Buds with capers for a similar, though less unique effect.*

Lay out six bowls. Evenly distribute the risotto between the bowls and add the Sautéed Cauliflower Mushrooms. Place one Potato Cauliflower Nest at the center of each bowl, and top with 1 tbsp Pickled Oxeye Daisy Buds. Finish with 2 tbsp Crispy Fried Cauliflower sprinkled over each plate.

BLACK RICE //

Black Rice, Pickled Blue Chanterelle Mushrooms,
Cucumber Almond Crème Fraîche, Puffed Black Rice

Serves 6 | This dish brings the drama. Shira's favorite color/not color is black, so she is naturally drawn to this dish. We treat the black rice in two different ways, with the Puffed Black Rice bringing a nutty texture that works wonders with the acid of the Pickled Blue Chanterelle Mushrooms. It's antioxidant-rich, tasty, and balanced with a depth of flavors that sing along with the creamy cooling qualities of the Cucumber Almond Crème Fraîche. What more do you need?

PUFFED BLACK RICE /

2 cups canola oil
2 tbsp forbidden black rice
Salt, to taste

Makes ½ cup | Pour the oil into a medium high-sided saucepot (you want it to be approximately 1 inch deep) and heat to 400°F. Line a baking sheet with a kitchen towel and have a fine-slotted spoon ready.

Add half of the rice to the hot oil; be careful, as in the first few seconds, the level of oil will rise and then settle. Stir with a spoon and cook for another 5 to 10 seconds until the bubbles dissipate. At this point most of the moisture will have been removed from the rice and you should be able see the whites from the inside of the rice as it puffs. Using the slotted spoon, quickly and carefully remove the puffed rice and lay out on the prepared baking sheet to soak up any excess oil. Season with salt. Repeat this process with the second half of the rice, making sure to maintain the temperature of the oil at 400°F. Set aside to cool to room temperature until you're ready to serve. If making this ahead of time, store it in a paper towel–lined airtight container at room temperature for up to 2 weeks.

BLACK RICE /

1 shallot, minced
3 cloves garlic, minced
3 tbsp olive oil
2 cups forbidden black rice
2 tsp salt
2 tsp pepper

Note | *We want to use the natural starches found in the rice to achieve a stickier finished product, so you don't need to wash the rice ahead of time.*

Makes 6 servings | In a medium pot on medium heat, sweat the shallots and garlic in the olive oil for approximately 1 minute, or until soft and translucent. Add the rice and toast for 1 to 2 minutes to give a nutty note to the rice. Add 6 cups water and the salt and pepper. (You'll notice that this is more water than you'd normally use, as we will strain the rice once cooked and save the rice stock for later use.) Bring the water up to a simmer and cook the rice, covered, until tender, approximately 40 minutes. Strain the rice and reserve the cooking stock. Spread the rice onto a baking sheet to cool it down quickly.

CONTINUES

Add the rice stock back to the saucepot and cook at a low simmer for approximately 20 minutes, or until it has reduced by two-thirds and has a thicker consistency. Add the cooled rice back to the pot and warm everything back up for serving, stirring so that the rice is evenly glazed in the reduced stock. Check for seasoning and adjust as needed.

PLATING /

1 recipe Puffed Black Rice (page 65)
1 recipe Black Rice (page 65)
1 cup Cucumber Almond Crème Fraîche (page 28)
36 pieces Pickled Blue Chanterelle Mushrooms
   (page 36)

Lay out six plates. Fold ¼ cup Puffed Black Rice into the pot of Black Rice. Spread evenly between the plates. (We use a 4-inch ring mold to press the rice into a cake shape, but you can plate it however you like!) Add a large 2 tbsp dollop of Cucumber Almond Crème Fraîche to each plate. Top the rice with Pickled Blue Chanterelle Mushrooms and garnish with the remaining Puffed Black Rice.

Blue Chanterelle

BRUSSELS SPROUTS //

Pan-Roasted Brussels Sprouts, Shiitake XO Sauce,
Black Garlic Mayo, Pickled Ginger, Crispy Shallots, Mizuna

Serves 6 | Brussels sprouts need no introduction, but for the love of God, stop boiling them! As a member of the cruciferous family, they have naturally occurring sugar that helps them caramelize, eliminating that astringent and bitter quality you remember from your childhood. Trust us, you love Brussels sprouts—you just have to cook them the right way. But what makes this dish really special is the accoutrements. We pack in the flavor with a vegan XO sauce, creamy mayo, and pickled ginger. There's no shortage of bold on the plate with this one.

SHIITAKE XO SAUCE /

2½ cups sliced shiitake mushrooms

3 (4 × 5-inch) sheets dried kelp

1 bird's eye chili pepper

2 tbsp minced ginger

2 tbsp minced garlic

3 tbsp tamari

2 tbsp mirin

⅛ cup rice wine vinegar

Note | *XO sauce is a flavor-enhancing umami bomb that originated in Hong Kong. Used as a condiment to impart savory and spicy flavors to a dish, it is traditionally made from fish, shrimp, ham, chilies, garlic, and ginger. Our version combines shiitake mushrooms with kelp to bring out those deep umami notes while remaining totally vegan.*

Makes 2 cups | Preheat the oven to 350°F. Using a brush, clean the shiitake mushrooms, removing any dirt or residue. Keep the stems on. Spread them out on a baking sheet lined with parchment paper. Roast for 25 minutes, until they have shrunken in half and have a deep roasted aroma. Remove from the oven and lay the sheets of kelp on top of the mushrooms. Roast for another 4 minutes to toast the kelp. Remove from the oven and let sit until cool enough to handle. Crush the kelp by hand and measure out 2 tbsp. Place the mushrooms and the 2 tbsp crushed kelp in a food processer and pulse until it is a fine crumble.

Remove the stem from the chili and finely mince, keeping the seeds in (if you're spice averse remove the seeds with the stem before mincing). Wash your hands and utensils thoroughly after handling the chopped chilies! In a medium saucepot on medium-low heat, slowly caramelize the minced ginger and garlic in the sesame oil. This will take some time, approximately 10 minutes, as you want to develop a slow caramelization. Frequently scrape the bottom of the pot with a spoon or metal spatula. Once a nice dark caramelization is reached, add the minced chilies, tamari, mirin, rice wine vinegar, and 1 cup water. Add the blitzed mushrooms and kelp and simmer on low for approximately 10 to 15 minutes, or until the liquid has reduced by half. Remove from the heat and store in an airtight container in the fridge for up to 1 week, or freeze; just re-blitz it in the Vitamix once thawed.

BLACK GARLIC MAYO /

1 (12 oz) package organic medium-firm tofu

2 tbsp blond or white miso paste

3 tbsp maple syrup

8 cloves black garlic

1 clove garlic

2 tbsp white balsamic vinegar

1½-inch piece fresh ginger, washed
    with the skin on, thinly sliced

1 tsp salt

1 tsp pepper

¼ cup grapeseed oil

CONTINUES

Makes 2½ cups | Remove the tofu from the package and rinse thoroughly. Set aside on a towel to draw out more moisture. Place ¼ cup water and the miso, maple syrup, both garlics, vinegar, ginger, salt, and pepper in a Vitamix and blend until smooth. Add the drained tofu and blend for another 30 seconds on high until fully incorporated. Reduce the speed to medium and slowly drizzle in the grapeseed oil until it is emulsified. Store in an airtight container in the fridge for up to 5 days.

CRISPY SHALLOTS /

6 shallots
2 tsp salt
½ cup cornstarch
8 cups canola oil

Makes 1 cup | Peel the shallots and keep them whole for slicing. If you have a mandoline, set it to ⅛ inch thick and slice the shallots into rings. You can also use a knife for this; just be sure to slice the rings to a consistent size. In a medium bowl, mix the shallot rings with the salt and set aside for 5 minutes; the salt will help extract moisture from the shallots. Using your hands or a kitchen towel, wring out any excess liquid from the shallots, then transfer them to a clean, dry bowl. Add the cornstarch and toss lightly by hand, making sure the shallots are fully coated. Transfer the shallots to a sieve and shake out any excess cornstarch.

Heat the oil into a high-sided, heavy-bottomed pot to 275°F. Working in batches of ¼ cup at a time, add the shallots to the oil and fry slowly until there are no more bubbles coming from the shallots. This will ensure you have removed any water during the frying. Line a baking sheet or plate with a kitchen towel. Using a slotted spoon, carefully remove the shallots from the hot oil and place on the prepared plate to soak up any excess oil. Repeat this process with the remaining shallots, making sure the oil stays at 275°F. Allow the shallots to dry completely at room temperature. Store in an airtight container lined with paper towel for up to 5 days at room temperature.

PAN-ROASTED BRUSSELS SPROUTS /

3 cups Brussels sprouts
3 tbsp olive oil
Salt, to taste
1 tsp pepper
½ cup Shiitake XO Sauce (page 69)

Makes 6 servings | Wash the Brussels sprouts and remove any bad outer leaves, then trim the very tip of the ends off and cut each Brussels sprout in half. Heat a large flat-bottomed saucepot on medium heat, add the oil, and lay the Brussels sprouts in the pan cut side down. Turn the heat to medium-high, season with salt and pepper, and cook the sprouts cut side down for approximately 6 to 8 minutes until you have achieved a nice deep caramelization. Add the Shiitake XO Sauce and cook for 1 minute, stirring often to coat the Brussels sprouts, then remove from the heat. Serve immediately.

PLATING /

1½ cups Black Garlic Mayo (page 69)
1 recipe Pan-Roasted Brussels Sprouts (page 69)
¼ cup Pickled Ginger (page 37)
1 recipe Crispy Shallots (left)
½ cup mizuna, washed and picked, or any
    mustard green or arugula, for garnish

Lay out six plates. Place ¼ cup Black Garlic Mayo on the bottom of each. Evenly distribute the Brussels Sprouts between the plates, making sure to scrape all the XO Sauce out of the pan. Top with the Pickled Ginger and Crispy Shallots, and garnish with mizuna.

SALSIFY
CAVATELLI PASTA //

Cavatelli Pasta, Salsify Sauce, Caramelized Black Salsify, Black Shallot Oil,
Preserved Meyer Lemon, Crispy Black Salsify, Goat Gouda, Celery Leaves

Serves 6 | As with everything else, we make all our pasta in-house at The Acorn. We love cavatelli for its ability to pick up and hold sauce. It's also an easy fresh pasta to store, as well as naturally vegan!

Note | *Salsify is a wonderfully interesting root veg, similar to a parsnip but sweet and earthy like an artichoke heart. While white salsify is furrier and requires a little extra prep, the black variety tends to be creamier with a little more sugar content, making it a great choice for caramelization. We get our black salsify from North Arm Farm, leaders in tasty root vegetables that benefit from the early first frost that covers the Pemberton Valley.*

CAVATELLI PASTA /

4 cups semolina flour + extra for dusting
2 cups water
2 tsp salt
Olive oil, for tossing

Note | *At The Acorn, we roll out our cavatelli using a hand-crank pasta maker. It produces an evenly sized pasta with ridges to help pick up the sauce. If you have a pasta maker at home, use it! This recipe will guide you to roll and cut the pasta by hand, which is equally delicious, just more time-consuming!*

Makes 6 servings | If making the cavatelli in advance, you can leave it on the baking sheet, covered, in the fridge for up to 5 days. Alternatively, freeze it on the sheet and, once frozen, transfer to a freezer bag or container and store in the freezer until ready to cook.

Make the Pasta | Warm the 2 cups water to 90°F. In a stand mixer fitted with the dough hook attachment, place the flour, salt, and warmed water and knead on medium-low speed for 5 minutes. Check the dough by pressing it with your thumb—if it springs back, it's ready! Remove the dough from the mixer and tightly wrap it in plastic wrap. Let it rest in the fridge for a minimum of 1 hour.

Remove the dough from the fridge and place on a clean work surface. Using a bench scraper, divide the dough into 6 equally sized pieces and roll each piece into a long strip approximately ⅓ inch in diameter. Cut the dough strip into little pillows ⅓ inch long. Lightly dust your work surface with flour. Using your index and middle fingers, press down the center of each pillow, roll it flat toward you, then roll it back again to make the shape of a mini rolled hot dog bun. Be careful not to overdust your work surface, as this will make it hard to roll back your cavatelli. Lightly dust a baking sheet with flour and transfer the prepared cavatelli to it. Repeat the dough-rolling process until all the dough is used up.

Cook the Pasta | In a large pot, bring 16 cups salted water to a boil. Drop in the cavatelli and boil for 2 minutes until cooked through and still al dente. Strain the pasta from the water. Place the cavatelli on a baking sheet lined with parchment paper and toss in some olive oil to prevent them from sticking together.

CONTINUES

SALSIFY SAUCE /

1 lemon
8 stalks black salsify
2 tbsp olive oil
1 onion, cut in medium dice
4 cloves garlic, sliced
½ cup medium-diced celery
1 tsp salt
1 tsp ground white pepper
1 cup white wine
3 sprigs thyme, leaves picked

Makes 4 cups | Make acidulated water by placing 4 cups water in a large bowl. Wash and cut the lemon in half and squeeze its juice into the water. Add the juiced peels to the water too and let sit.

Wash and peel the salsify stalks, reserving the skins in an airtight container at room temperature to fry into Crispy Black Salsify (right). Salsify oxidizes quickly, so place each peeled stalk immediately into the lemon water.

Cut the salsify into 1-inch pieces and measure out 2 cups. In a medium saucepot on medium-high heat, slightly caramelize the salsify in the olive oil. Add the onions, garlic, and celery and sweat until translucent. Season with salt and pepper. Pour in the white wine and continue to cook until the liquid reduces by half. Add 4 cups water and the thyme and simmer until reduced by half again. Working in batches, transfer the mixture to a Vitamix and blend until you reach a creamy, smooth sauce. Adjust seasoning as needed. Transfer the sauce to a bowl set over ice and allow to chill. Once chilled, transfer to an airtight container and store in the fridge for up to 5 days.

CRISPY BLACK SALSIFY /

3 cups canola oil
Skins of 8 stalks black salsify reserved
    from Salsify Sauce (left)
Salt, to taste

Makes 6 servings | In a heavy-bottomed, high-sided pot, heat the oil to 300°F. Make sure the salsify peels are thoroughly dry before frying, then, working in small batches, gently place the salsify skins into the hot oil and stir frequently. Once all the moisture bubbles have released from the salsify skins, carefully remove them using a slotted spoon and place on a kitchen towel to soak up any excess oil. Season to taste with salt. Repeat this process until all the salsify skins have been fried, making sure to keep the oil at a steady 300°F throughout.

CARAMELIZED
BLACK SALSIFY /

6 stalks black salsify, approximately 8 inches long
2 tbsp olive oil
½ tsp salt
½ tsp pepper
2 tbsp sherry vinegar
2 tbsp maple syrup

Makes 6 servings | Thoroughly wash the salsify
and cut on a bias into 2-inch pieces. In a large pan
(large enough to lay the salsify flat) on medium-high
heat, sauté the salsify in the olive oil until you've
reached some caramelization. Season with the salt and
pepper, then deglaze the pan with the sherry vinegar,
maple syrup, and 2 tbsp water. Continue to sauté until
all the liquid has reduced down. At this point, the
salsify will be sticky and caramelized.

PLATING /

1 recipe Salsify Sauce (left)
1 recipe Cavatelli Pasta (page 73)
Salt and pepper, to taste
2 tbsp Preserved Meyer Lemon (page 41)
1 recipe Caramelized Black Salsify (left)
6 tbsp Black Shallot Oil (page 51)
1 recipe Crispy Black Salsify (left)
Celery leaves, for garnish
1 cup shaved goat Gouda

Note | *For the finishing cheese on this pasta, we use a
firm goat Gouda from Smits and Co. in Chilliwack.*

In a large pan on medium heat, bring the Salsify Sauce
to a simmer, then add the cooked Cavatelli Pasta.
Simmer for 1 or 2 minutes. Check for seasoning and
add salt and pepper as needed.

Lay out six shallow bowls. Divide the pasta and
sauce evenly between the bowls. Garnish each bowl
with 1 tsp Preserved Meyer Lemon, four pieces of
Caramelized Black Salsify, 1 tbsp Black Shallot Oil,
and some Crispy Salsify and celery leaves. Finish
with a sprinkling of shaved goat Gouda.

Salsify

SEAWEED SALAD //

Vegan Kimchi, Apple Togarashi, Kimchi Mayo, Black Salsify Strips,
Crispy Kelp + Salsify Skins, Jade Radishes

Serves 6 | A version of this dish made an appearance at one of our Vintage + Veg events—a special dinner series where we pair a unique tasting menu with one specific local winery, distillery, or brewery. This one was particularly special because all the courses featured mushrooms hand-foraged by Lance Staples, who spent weeks in the forest gathering ingredients. We paired the dinner with wines from Summerhill Pyramid Winery, the first certified organic winery in British Columbia.

VEGAN KIMCHI /

2 medium heads napa cabbage

¼ cup salt

2 tbsp sweet rice flour

1 large onion, chopped

8 cloves garlic

3 red radishes, washed and halved

¼ cup chopped fresh ginger
    (washed with skin left on)

2 tbsp brown sugar

2 tbsp Korean red chili pepper flakes

1 bunch green onions, cut in 1-inch slices on a bias

Note | *The act of making kimchi is all about time and patience. Since the fermentation process is long (a minimum of 2 weeks), and kimchi evolves over time and has a very long shelf life (up to 6 months), we're going all in with this giant batch so you can enjoy it for months to come (or gift it to your besties).*

Makes 16 cups | Cut each head of cabbage into quarters and rinse under cold water. Lay them out in a large, 4-inch-deep glass baking dish. Sprinkle the salt over top and, using your hands, thoroughly massage it into the cabbage. Let the cabbage sit at room temperature for 1 hour to draw out the moisture, flipping and mixing it every 20 minutes.

Meanwhile, in a small saucepot on medium heat, bring 1 cup water to a simmer, then whisk in the sweet rice flour. Simmer for 4 minutes and remove from the heat. Place the onions, garlic, radishes, ginger, brown sugar, and Korean chili flakes in a Vitamix and blend until

smooth. Add the rice flour and water mixture to the blender and blend again to create a nice thick paste. Transfer the paste to a large bowl and stir in the sliced green onions.

When ready, squeeze the cabbage to wring out any excess water. Thoroughly wash and dry the glass baking dish to be used again.

Using your fingertips (and wearing gloves, to prevent the chilies from burning your skin), spread the green onion paste between each layer of the cabbage's leaves. Stack the cabbage quarters back into the glass baking dish and press down.

Pour any remaining paste into the dish, spreading evenly over the cabbage. Cover the surface of the cabbage with plastic wrap (rather than sealing the edges of the container) to eliminate the potential for aerobic bacteria to grow. Cover the container with a lid and let sit at room temperature for 48 hours, pressing down the cabbage after every 12 hours. If you don't have a lid, you can use a second layer of plastic wrap to seal the edges of the container.

After 48 hours, do your first taste test; it should taste tangy and sour. If the kimchi has your desired flavor, transfer it to the fridge, as this will slow down the fermentation process. Otherwise, seal it back up and let it sit at room temperature again for another 48 hours, again pressing down on the kimchi every 12 hours. Repeat the taste test; it should be sourer, slightly funky, and stronger-tasting now.

CONTINUES

Remove the kimchi from the dish and chop into 1- to 2-inch pieces. Pack the kimchi into sterilized 32 oz mason jars and cover tightly with the lids. Store the sealed jars in the fridge for a minimum of 2 weeks before serving, and up to 6 months. The kimchi will develop a stronger, deeper flavor as it continues to ferment over time.

APPLE TOGARASHI /

1 Granny Smith apple
2 (4 × 5-inch) sheets dried kelp
1 tbsp black sesame seeds
1 tsp white sesame seeds
1 tbsp red pepper flakes
2 tsp ground ginger
1 tsp salt

Note | *Togarashi is a Japanese seasoning mix typically made up of seven spices. Used as a natural flavor enhancer, this spice mix can be sprinkled on literally anything to add a little zip.*

Makes ½ cup | Wash and core the apple, then cut it into small dice, keeping the skin on. Lay the diced apples out on a dehydrator sheet and dry on medium (145°F) for 12 hours. Alternatively, you can dry them on a baking sheet lined with parchment paper in your oven at 165°F (with the door cracked open) for approximately 4 hours.

Preheat the oven to 450°F. Place the kelp sheets on a baking sheet lined with parchment paper. If the kelp sheets are too large, break or cut them to a smaller size so they fit on a single baking sheet. Toast the kelp on the lower rack of the oven for 4 to 5 minutes. Remove from the heat and allow to cool, then crush with your hands.

Heat a small frying pan on medium heat and dry-toast the black and white sesame seeds until they start to pop and crackle and oils begin to release. Remove from heat and allow to cool.

Place the dried apples, red pepper flakes, and ground ginger in a spice grinder or Vitamix and blend to a fine powder. Add the crushed toasted kelp and blend again until the kelp is in small flakes. Transfer the mixture to a bowl and add the toasted sesame seeds and the salt. Mix until everything is well incorporated. Store in an airtight container at room temperature for up to 6 months.

KIMCHI MAYO /

1 (12 oz) package organic medium-firm tofu
½ cup Vegan Kimchi (page 79)
1 tbsp maple syrup
2 tsp salt
1 tsp pepper
¼ cup grapeseed oil

Makes 2½ cups | Remove the tofu from the package and rinse thoroughly. Set aside on a towel to draw out more moisture. Place the kimchi, maple syrup, salt, and pepper in a Vitamix and blend until smooth. Add the drained tofu and blend for another 30 seconds on high until fully incorporated. Reduce the speed to medium and slowly drizzle in the grapeseed oil until emulsified. Store in an airtight container in the fridge for up to 5 days.

BLACK SALSIFY STRIPS /

¼ cup fresh lemon juice
20 stalks black salsify
2 tbsp salt

Makes 6 servings | Make acidulated water by mixing together the lemon juice and 4 cups water in a large shallow dish. Using a thin vegetable peeler, peel the salsify and reserve the skins in an airtight container for use in Crispy Kelp + Salsify Skins (right). With the skins removed, continue to peel the salsify into long, thin strips similar in shape and size to fettuccine noodles. Place the strips directly into the acidulated water.

In a large pot, bring 6 quarts water to a low boil and add the salt. Once all the salsify is peeled into strips, add them to the boiling water and blanch for 10 seconds. Transfer directly to an ice bath. Once chilled, remove from the ice bath and pat dry with a kitchen towel to drain off any excess water. Set aside for the Seaweed Salad.

SEAWEED SALAD /

3 jade radishes, approximately 4 inches long
½ cup Vegan Kimchi (page 79)
1 recipe Black Salsify Strips (left)
⅓ cup Kimchi Mayo (left)

Makes 6 servings | Wash and dry the radishes and trim off the very ends. Slice the radishes lengthwise into long, thin strips, then julienne. Transfer to a large bowl and add the Vegan Kimchi, Black Salsify Strips, and Kimchi Mayo. Mix well.

CRISPY KELP + SALSIFY SKINS /

8 cups canola oil
Skins from 20 stalks black salsify reserved from Black Salsify Strips (left)
Salt, to taste
6 (4 × 5-inch) sheets dried kelp

Makes 6 servings | In a heavy-bottomed, high-sided pot, heat the oil to 300°F. Make sure the salsify skins are thoroughly dry before frying. Working in batches, gently place a small batch of the salsify skins into the hot oil and stir frequently. Once all the moisture bubbles have released from the salsify, use a slotted spoon to carefully remove them and place directly on a kitchen towel to soak up any excess oil. Season to taste with salt. Repeat this process until all the salsify skins have been fried, making sure to keep the oil at a steady 300°F throughout.

Using your hands, break each kelp sheet into approximately four 2-inch pieces; you don't have to be precise here. Working in small batches and using the same oil, repeat the frying method above until you have fried all the kelp. Serve immediately.

PLATING /

1 recipe Seaweed Salad (left)
2 tbsp Kimchi Mayo (left)
1 recipe Crispy Kelp + Salsify Skins (left)
2 tbsp Apple Togarashi (left)

Lay out six plates. Portion the Seaweed Salad onto the center of each plate, using a twisting motion to maintain height. Dollop 1 tsp Kimchi Mayo beside each portion of salad. Top the salad with the Crispy Kelp + Salsify Skins. (If you have leftover skins, enjoy them as a snack!) Dust each plate with 1 tsp Apple Togarashi.

LANCE STAPLES, FORAGER //

Lance Staples trained as a chef and became curious about edible and medicinal plants when he traveled to South America on a wild foods ecotour. Back home in Victoria, British Columbia, he set out to learn everything he could about plant identification, wild foods, and herbalism. Foraging started out as his part-time passion, but within a few years, it turned into a full-time career.

Lance now spends his time in the forests of Vancouver Island and Lower Mainland British Columbia, respectfully and sustainably foraging wild foods like mushrooms, wild garlic, nettles, salad greens, watercress, herbs, microgreens, botanicals like wild rose, edible flowers like elderflowers, and edible weeds like dandelion. He then sells his foraged foods directly to a small handful of restaurants. Since Lance's work is often solitary, he says he's inspired and motivated by his part in The Acorn community. He works closely with the team to provide the unique ingredients that are an integral part of each menu.

Foraging helps create an understanding of biodiversity and that we're all part of a bigger ecosystem. Lance says he is encouraged when customers learn and appreciate that the ingredients in their meals are foraged. Unfortunately, he is also witness to the loss of more forestland every year to resource-based industry and development, but he says when people appreciate the value of land, we can begin to work together to protect it.

INSPIRATIONS | Wild foods, medicinal foods, herbalism, plant identification, biodiversity, forests.
THE ACORN-AT-HOME | Get curious about wild foods and learn what grows in your area. Immerse yourself in nature to understand the value and importance of biodiversity.

MATSUTAKE //

Matsutake Broth, Parsley Root Dumplings, Parsley Root + Lovage Puree,
Pickled Pacific Crab Apples, Shaved Matsutake + Lovage, Black Currant Leaf Oil

Serves 6 | Who knew that apples and matsutake mushrooms have such an affinity for one another? This super-clean dumpling dish is a stunner. The simplicity of the flavors unites this dish in a truly symbiotic way.

MATSUTAKE BROTH /

4 matsutake mushrooms, grades 3 to 6,
  approximately 4 inches tall
1 medium onion, diced
4 cloves garlic, sliced
2 tbsp olive oil
2 tsp salt
1 tsp peppercorns
2 bay leaves
3 tbsp maple syrup

Makes 4 cups | To clean the mushrooms, take a dry towel and wipe each matsutake to remove any dirt. Trim off the sandy ends, then roughly slice each mushroom.

In a medium pot, sauté the onions and garlic in the olive oil for 2 to 3 minutes, then add the sliced mushrooms. Add the salt, peppercorns, and bay leaves and sauté for another 10 minutes, until you have reached a light caramelization. Add the maple syrup and 6 cups water. Bring to a simmer and cook until the liquid reduces by a quarter. Remove from the heat and strain through a large-holed sieve or strainer into a glass bowl or container. Then strain again through a fine-mesh strainer. The broth should be clear with very little residue. Check for seasoning and adjust as necessary. If making ahead of time, allow the broth to cool at room temperature, then store in the fridge for up to 5 days.

PARSLEY ROOT + LOVAGE PUREE /

1 medium onion, diced
2 cloves garlic
2 tbsp olive oil
1 cup peeled and diced parsley root
¼ cup chopped lovage stems, reserve the leaves,
  wrapped in damp paper towel in the fridge,
  for the garnish (page 86)
1 tsp salt
½ tsp ground white pepper
1 tbsp maple syrup

Note | *Parsley root is a member of the carrot family, similar in shape and size to a parsnip with the flavor combination of carrot, parsnip, and celeriac. Lovage is perennial flat-leaf herb that we grow in our own garden. It has a distinct aromatic presence and a flavor that could be best described as a cross between celery and parsley. If you can't find lovage, celery leaves would make an acceptable substitute.*

Makes 2 cups | In a medium saucepot on medium-high heat, sauté the onions and garlic in the olive oil for 5 minutes, then add the parsley root and lovage stems. Add the salt, pepper, and maple syrup, turn the heat to medium-low, and cook for another 4 minutes to slowly caramelize the maple syrup. Add 2 cups water and stir. Turn up the heat, bring to a simmer, and continue to cook until the liquid has completely reduced. Remove from the heat. Carefully transfer the mixture to a Vitamix and blend until silky-smooth. Store in an airtight container in the fridge for up to 5 days.

CONTINUES

PARSLEY ROOT DUMPLINGS /

2½ cups red spring flour + extra for dusting
½ tsp salt
¾ cup warm water
1 recipe Parsley Root + Lovage Puree,
    chilled (page 85)
Olive oil, for baking sheet

Makes 6 servings | Make the Dough | Sift the flour into a large bowl. Add the salt and slowly pour in the warm water, mixing by hand until the dough comes together and starts to pull away from the sides. Dust a clean work surface with flour, then transfer the dough to the surface and knead for 30 seconds by hand, folding it over on itself and working it into a ball. Wrap the dough ball in plastic wrap and let it chill in the fridge for 1 hour.

Remove the chilled dough from the fridge and place it on a work surface dusted with flour. Using a rolling pin, roll the dough into a large rectangle until it is approximately ⅛ inch thick.

Using a roller cutter or knife, cut the dough into 2-inch-wide strips vertically, then cut these into 2-inch strips horizontally, leaving you with 2-inch squares. Dust the top of the squares with flour.

Create the Dumplings | Place the chilled Parsley Root + Lovage Puree into a piping bag. Line a baking sheet with parchment paper and dust it with flour. Set yourself up with a bowl of warm water and a pastry brush. Re-dust your work surface with flour if needed, and again, as you go, so the dumplings don't stick.

Working in sets of five, lightly brush the squares of dough with a little water, then pipe about 1 tsp Parsley Root + Lovage Puree into the center of each. Lift two opposing corners and pinch them together where the dough meets just over the filling. Lift the remaining two corners, pinching them together just over the filling. After doing this, the filling should be completely covered and sealed in by the dough. Twist the dough where you've pinched the corners together, resulting in a money-bag-shaped dumpling.

Transfer each finished dumpling to the prepared baking sheet. Repeat until you have stuffed and sealed all the dumplings. Place the sheet of finished dumplings in the fridge for a minimum of 30 minutes before cooking. If making in advance, freeze the dumplings on the sheet and, once frozen, transfer to a bag and store in the freezer for up to 3 months.

Cook the Dumplings | In a medium pot, bring 8 cups salted water to a boil. Drizzle a small baking sheet with olive oil and place this beside your pot of boiling water. Working in small batches, add the dumplings to the boiling water and cook for 1½ minutes or until they float to the surface. If cooking from frozen, the cooking time will be a little longer. Using a slotted spoon, carefully remove the dumplings and transfer to the prepared sheet. Repeat until all the dumplings have been cooked.

PLATING /

2 matsutake mushrooms, grades 1 to 2,
    approximately 2 to 3 inches tall
1 cup lovage leaves reserved from
    Parsley Root + Lovage Puree (page 85)
1 recipe Matsutake Broth (page 85)
1 recipe Parsley Root Dumplings (left)
½ cup Pickled Pacific Crab Apples (page 37)
1 tbsp Black Currant Leaf Oil (page 51)
    or sunflower oil

Note | *At the restaurant, we pour the hot Matsutake Broth over the dumplings tableside so our guests can experience the incredible aromas that get released from the mushrooms and the lovage when they come in contact with the broth.*

Clean, trim, and thinly slice the matsutake mushrooms and chiffonade the lovage leaves. Heat the Matsutake Broth and keep warm on the stove.

Lay out six shallow bowls and place five or six dumplings in each. Add to each bowl 8 to 10 Pickled Pacific Crab Apples and five to six slices of matsutake mushrooms. Garnish with lovage leaves and a drizzle of Black Currant Leaf Oil. Pour hot Matsutake Broth over top just the moment you are ready to enjoy!

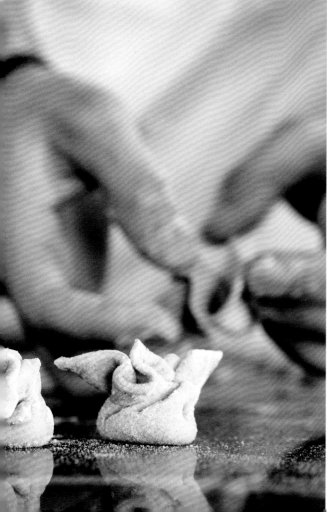

FERMENTED MATSUTAKE FOCACCIA //

Fermented Matsutake Mushrooms, Focaccia Bread

Serves 6 | This dish first appeared as an amuse-bouche for a collaboration dinner we did. Playing up the sour qualities achieved by fermenting the matsutake mushrooms, we wanted to create that sourdough-like quality, but in a simple focaccia bread. Once baked, the sweet and sour flavors of the mushrooms really come out, making this a unique bread to eat on its own, use as sandwich bread, or serve with a nice olive oil.

FERMENTED MATSUTAKE MUSHROOMS /

2.2 lb matsutake mushrooms (grades 4, 5, or 6)
20 g salt (2% of the weight of the mushrooms)

Makes 5 cups | Use a brush to clean the mushrooms, removing all dirt and debris, and trim off the very ends. Cut the mushrooms into 2-inch pieces and lay them out flat on a baking sheet lined with parchment paper. Freeze for 4 hours. (Freezing the mushrooms breaks down their cellular structure, allowing more of their liquid to be released for the fermentation process.) When ready, remove the mushrooms from the freezer and toss them with the salt, making sure to evenly coat.

Ferment the Mushrooms in a Vacuum Bag | Place the salted frozen mushrooms in a single layer in a vacuum bag, making sure to include all the salt. Vacuum on high suction and seal the very top of the bag in order to have room to puncture and reseal through the fermentation process.

Alternatively, Ferment the Mushrooms in a Jar | Place the salted mushrooms in a sterilized 32 oz mason jar, making sure to include all the salt. Fill a resealable plastic bag with 2% salted water and lay it on top of the mushrooms to stop any air interfering with the fermentation process. Cover the container with the lid, but leave a small gap to let gases out.

With either method, ferment the mushrooms at room temperature (72°F) for 4 to 5 days. Make sure to check the mushrooms daily. For the vacuum method, the bag may start to inflate with gas. You can make a small cut at the top of the bag to release the gas, and then reseal it. For the mason jar method, make sure that the mushrooms are completely submerged in their juices. You'll also want to taste the mushrooms; as the fermentation progresses, you will be able to taste the natural sweetness of the matsutakes as well as the developing acidity of the fermentation process. The flavor you're ultimately looking for should be a well-balanced sweet and sour matsutake.

Once you have the desired flavor, strain out the liquid from the mushrooms through a fine-mesh sieve. Reserve the liquid and the mushrooms separately in two airtight containers. Store these in the fridge for up to 3 months—keep in mind the fermentation will continue and the acidity will intensify.

CONTINUES

FERMENTED MATSUTAKE FOCACCIA /

2¼ tsp active dry yeast
2½ cups fermented matsutake liquid from
    Fermented Matsutake Mushrooms (page 89)
7¼ cups bread flour
1 tsp sugar
1 tsp salt
½ cup Fermented Matsutake Mushrooms (page 89),
    chopped in ½-inch pieces
5 tbsp olive oil
Sea salt, to finish

Note | *You can make this bread up to 24 hours in advance and still serve it fresh! Just wrap it tightly in plastic wrap once it's cooled to room temperature.*

Makes 1 (13 × 18-inch) loaf | Place ½ cup warm water in a mixing bowl. Sprinkle in the active dry yeast and gently stir with a fork. Allow the yeast to bloom in the water for 5 minutes, until it begins to bubble.

Either Make the Dough in a Stand Mixer | Transfer the bloomed yeast to the bowl of a stand mixer fitted with the dough hook attachment. Add the fermented matsutake liquid, bread flour, sugar, and salt. Mix on low speed to start; you may have to scrape down the sides of the bowl after 1 minute to make sure all the ingredients are being incorporated. Add the chopped mushrooms and increase to medium speed, kneading the dough for approximately 5 more minutes.

Or Make the Dough by Hand | Pour the bread flour into a mound on a clean work surface. Make a 4-inch well in the center with your fingers. Pour the bloomed yeast and fermented matsutake liquid into the well, along with the sugar and salt. Using your fingers, slowly work the flour into the liquid from the inside out until it all comes together. Once incorporated, press the dough down to flatten slightly and add the chopped mushrooms on top. Using a pastry scraper, fold and knead the dough onto itself for 3 minutes, evenly cutting in the chopped matsutakes throughout the dough.

Rise the Dough | At this point, the dough should be extremely elastic and very sticky. Place 2 tbsp of the olive oil in a large glass bowl and use your fingers to evenly coat the inside of the entire bowl with it. With a bench scraper or spatula, transfer the dough to the bowl and cover with a cloth. Set aside in a warm area for 2 to 3 hours, until the dough has doubled in size.

Add 2 tbsp of the olive oil to a 13 × 18-inch baking pan and spread the oil evenly to coat and grease the pan, making sure to cover all the inside edges of the pan. Using a bench scraper or spatula, scrape around the edges of the dough and fold it onto itself inside the bowl until it deflates, then turn it out into the greased baking pan. Lightly punch the dough down with your fingers to let out more air, then fold the dough over itself once. Turn the pan 90 degrees and fold the dough over on itself once more; the dough will be a lump in the center of the pan. Drizzle the remaining olive oil evenly onto the dough and cover its surface with plastic wrap. Let the dough rest for 10 to 15 minutes to relax the gluten.

Remove the plastic wrap from the dough (reserve the plastic wrap), then using your fingers, gently stretch and pull the dough out all the way to the edges and into the corners of the pan. If the dough starts to spring back, let it sit for 5 to 10 more minutes and start again. Once the dough is stretched to fill the entire pan, cover again with the same piece of oiled plastic and chill in the fridge for at least 8 hours and up to 24 hours.

Remove the pan from the fridge and set it in a warm spot until the dough is puffed and bubbly and nearly doubled in height, about 1 to 1½ hours.

Bake the Focaccia | Place a rack in the center of the oven and preheat the oven to 450°F. Remove the plastic wrap from the dough and oil your fingers with olive oil. Firmly press your fingers 1 inch apart into the dough, touching the bottom of the pan with your fingers. This will create dimples in the dough when baking. Sprinkle the top of the dough evenly with the sea salt. Bake on the middle rack of the oven for 25 to 35 minutes, until the bread is golden brown. Remove from the oven and let cool in the pan for 10 minutes. Gently remove the focaccia from the pan and place on a wire rack to cool completely.

MUSHROOM + WAFFLE //

Southern Fried Maitake Mushrooms, House Gluten-Free Waffles,
Mushroom Gravy, Bourbon Maple Syrup, Pickled Shallots

Serves 6 | This playful, vegan, and gluten-free take on chicken and waffles is the perfect sweet and savory dish for brunch. It's such a hit that it has remained on our menu ever since we launched our brunch back in 2014!

BOURBON MAPLE SYRUP /

½ cup bourbon
½ tsp salt
2 cups maple syrup

Makes 2¼ cups | In a small pot on medium heat, simmer the bourbon until it has reduced by half. Add the salt and whisk in the maple syrup until everything is evenly blended. Remove from the heat and cool to room temperature. Store in an airtight container in the fridge for up to 1 month.

MUSHROOM GRAVY /

20 cremini mushrooms, washed, dried,
    and quartered
1 medium onion, roughly chopped
1 carrot, peeled and cut in ½-inch slices
1 stalk celery, washed and cut in ½-inch slices
6 cloves garlic
1 tbsp salt
1 tsp pepper
¼ cup olive oil
½ cup tomato paste
1 cup red wine
10 sprigs thyme
1 bay leaf

Note | *This recipe will make more gravy than the dish calls for, but it's a pretty versatile gravy overall, and can be frozen for up to 2 months, so you'll be glad to have extra at hand.*

Makes 8 cups | Preheat the oven to 400°F. In a large bowl, mix together the mushrooms, onions, carrots, celery, garlic, salt, pepper, and olive oil until all the vegetables are evenly coated. Lay the vegetables out on a roasting pan lined with parchment paper and roast in the oven for 25 minutes. Check to make sure the vegetables are starting to caramelize, then mix in the tomato paste and continue to roast for another 10 minutes.

Once the tomato paste begins to turn a deep brownish-red, remove the pan from the oven and transfer the mixture to a large pot on medium heat. Sauté, stirring often, to prevent the tomato paste from burning. When the bottom of the pot begins to get sticky, add the red wine to deglaze the pan, scraping the bottom of the pan to pick up the caramelized bits. Simmer until the red wine has reduced by half, then add 8 cups water and the thyme and bay leaf. Bring the liquid to a boil, reduce to a simmer, and cook for 30 minutes or until the liquid has reduced by half. Remove from the heat and allow to cool down slightly.

Working in small batches, transfer the mixture to your Vitamix. Gradually working up to high speed, puree until fully blended. Pass the gravy through a fine-mesh strainer, using the back of a ladle to press all the liquid out. If making the gravy in advance, allow to cool completely, then store in an airtight container in the fridge for up to 5 days or in the freezer for up to 2 months. With either storing method, you should thaw and re-blitz the gravy in your Vitamix before reheating to serve.

CONTINUES

GLUTEN-FREE FLOUR BLEND /

1⅜ cups brown rice flour
¼ cup organic oat flour
2 tbsp psyllium husks
¼ cup tapioca starch flour
½ cup potato starch
¼ cup white rice flour

Note | *This blend is used for both the House Gluten-Free Waffles and the Southern Fried Maitake Mushrooms (below). You can use a store-bought gluten-free flour blend instead if you like, but this is our tried-and-true house blend.*

Makes 2¾ cups | Sift all the ingredients together into a bowl. Store in an airtight container at room temperature for up to 6 months.

SOUTHERN FRIED MAITAKE MUSHROOMS /

2 cups soy milk
2 tbsp fresh lemon juice
¾ cup Gluten-Free Flour Blend (above)
2 tbsp smoked paprika
1 tsp chili powder
1 tsp salt + extra to taste
½ tsp pepper
1 tsp sugar
3 maitake mushrooms, quartered (see Note)
8 cups canola oil

Note | *Maitakes are cultivated in a clean environment so typically don't need to be cleaned. Just check the mushrooms for any bad spots and trim them off.*

Makes 12 pieces | In a shallow bowl, mix together the soy milk and lemon juice and let rest for 5 minutes to curdle.

In a separate bowl, mix together the Gluten-Free Flour Blend, smoked paprika, chili powder, salt, pepper, and sugar. Add the maitake mushrooms to the bowl of soy milk and lemon juice, toss to make sure they are well coated, and let marinate in the liquid until after you've made the waffles (then return to this part of the recipe and follow the steps below to fry them).

Fry the Mushrooms | In a heavy-bottomed, high-sided pot, heat the oil to 350°F. Remove the mushrooms one by one from the marinating liquid and toss them in the bowl of seasoned flour, making sure to coat them well. Working in small batches, fry the mushrooms for 2 minutes, until crispy and golden brown. Using tongs, carefully remove them from the hot oil and place on paper towel to soak up any excess oil. Season with salt to taste, and serve immediately.

HOUSE GLUTEN-FREE WAFFLES /

1¼ cups unsweetened almond milk
1 tsp apple cider vinegar
¼ cup grapeseed oil
¼ cup maple syrup
¼ tsp vanilla extract
2 cups Gluten-Free Flour Blend (left)
1½ tsp baking powder
1 tsp salt
¼ cup soda water or carbonated water

Makes 6 waffles | In a large bowl, mix together the almond milk and apple cider vinegar and let sit for 5 minutes to curdle. Whisk in the grapeseed oil, maple syrup, and vanilla. In a separate bowl, mix together the Gluten-Free Flour Blend, baking powder, and salt. Add the curdled milk to the dry ingredients and mix until well combined. Evenly whisk in the soda water and set aside.

Heat a nonstick waffle iron on high heat. Spray with cooking oil, then ladle approximately ½ cup batter into the iron. Cook until crispy. Enjoy right away or keep warm in a 250°F oven until ready to serve.

PLATING /

6 House Gluten-Free Waffles (left)
1 recipe Southern Fried Maitake Mushrooms (left)
1½ cups Mushroom Gravy (page 93)
¾ cup Bourbon Maple Syrup (page 93)
6 tbsp Pickled Shallots (page 36)
Watercress, for garnish

Lay out six plates and place a waffle at the center
of each. Top each waffle with two fried mushroom
pieces. Ladle ¼ cup gravy off to one side of each
waffle, then ladle 2 tbsp Bourbon Maple Syrup over
the fried mushrooms and waffle. Top with 1 tbsp
Pickled Shallots and garnish with watercress.

CABBAGE //

Rosemary Roasted Cabbage, Red Chieftain Pomme Puree,
Burdock Red Wine Jus, Crispy Fried Cabbage

Serves 6 | We attack all our recipes with the same primary directive: flavor first. Without flavor, plant-based food falls prey to its stigma of "bland" or "boring." We've worked so incredibly hard over the years to push past those barriers and show the minds of the masses how different plant-forward food can be—winning over the hearts of some of the staunchest meat eaters! This dish is a prime example of our flavor-first mentality—and proof that you can enjoy your meat and potatoes, without the meat of course!

Note | *To time this dish right, you'll need to multitask, starting the Red Chieftain Pomme Puree while the cabbage is roasting and getting your pot of oil hot for the Crispy Fried Cabbage.*

BURDOCK RED WINE JUS /

2 medium onions
3 stalks burdock root, approximately 12 inches
   long, washed, skins on, and roughly chopped
   to fill 5 cups
2 carrots, washed with skins on, roughly chopped
2 stalks celery, washed and leaves removed,
   roughly chopped
6 cloves garlic
¼ cup olive oil
2 cups red wine
⅓ cup sherry vinegar
½ cup tomato paste
¼ cup brown sugar
1 tbsp salt
2 tbsp peppercorns
3 bay leaves
3 sprigs thyme
2 sprigs rosemary
1 sprig winter savory
2 tbsp potato starch

Note | *This jus is special because we apply the same technique and philosophy to it as though it were a classic meat jus. The earthiness from the burdock root gives it that meaty quality. It takes a while, but the most important rule for this sauce is, don't rush it.*

Makes 4 cups | Preheat the oven to 425°F. Peel and halve the onions. Using tongs, char them evenly over an open flame or barbecue. (If you don't have an open flame, you can skip this step, but the resulting jus will be lighter in color and flavor.) Remove from the heat and roughly chop.

In a large bowl, mix the chopped charred onions, burdock, carrots, celery, and garlic with the olive oil. Add the vegetables to an unlined baking sheet and roast on the center rack of the oven for 40 minutes, mixing the vegetables and scraping the pan halfway through. After 40 minutes, pull the pan from the oven and deglaze with 1 cup of the red wine, scraping the bottom of the pan to release all the charred bits.

Scrape all the ingredients from the pan into a large saucepot. Turn the heat to medium-high and continue to caramelize the vegetables, stirring occasionally. Once the vegetables darken and stick to the bottom of the pot, deglaze with the rest of the red wine. Reduce the red wine until the bottom of the pot becomes sticky once more, then add the sherry vinegar and reduce again, this time by half. Stir in the tomato paste and cook for 5 minutes. The tomato paste will darken and become less tannic. Add 6 quarts water, and the brown sugar, salt, peppercorns, bay leaves, thyme, rosemary, and winter savory. Bring the liquid to a slow simmer and let it cook for approximately 4 hours, reducing the liquid down to 4 cups.

CONTINUES

Strain the sauce through a fine-mesh strainer, using the back of a ladle to press out as much liquid from the vegetables as possible. Put the strained sauce into a clean pot, whisk in the potato starch, and bring the liquid back up to a simmer for 5 minutes, whisking periodically. Remove from the heat, check for seasoning, and serve the sauce right away or cool it down in a container set over ice, then store it in an airtight container in the fridge for up to 5 days. Alternatively, you can freeze this sauce, and when you're ready to serve it, thaw it to room temperature and add it to the Vitamix to bring back the smooth consistency.

ROSEMARY ROASTED CABBAGE /

1 head red cabbage
2½ cups olive oil
1 cup brown sugar
2 tbsp salt
2 tsp pepper
2 tbsp finely chopped rosemary

Makes 6 wedges | Preheat the oven to 400°F. Remove any bad or outer leaves from the cabbage and save them for the Crispy Fried Cabbage (right). Cut the cabbage into six pieces, first by cutting it in half vertically from the stem to the top, then cutting each half lengthwise into thirds.

In a large bowl, mix together the olive oil, brown sugar, salt, pepper, and rosemary. Taking one wedge of cabbage at a time, completely submerge it in the marinade and massage the marinade evenly around and into the folds of the cabbage. Repeat this step until each cabbage wedge is well coated. Lay the cabbage wedges on a baking sheet lined with parchment paper, leaving 2 inches of space between each piece. Roast for 45 to 60 minutes, until fork-tender. Halfway through cooking, rotate the pan and use a pair of tongs to flip the cabbage wedges. You should be able to slide a knife or fork right into the stem with ease when they're done. Serve immediately or keep warm in the oven until you're ready to serve.

RED CHIEFTAIN POMME PUREE

8 Red Chieftain potatoes
1 tbsp salt + more to taste
½ cup soft unsalted butter or 2 tbsp olive oil
2 tsp white pepper

Note | *Red Chieftain potatoes are sweet, velvety, and super flavorful. This is our potato of choice for mashed potatoes. We find using the ricer helps to keep these whipped potatoes light. If you don't have a ricer or a stand mixer, you can mash the potatoes by hand to remove as many lumps as possible and then whip them with a wire whisk in a bowl. Once they're broken down and silky, fold in the fat as directed below.*

Makes 6 cups | Peel the potatoes and cut them in half. Place them in a large stockpot with the salt and cover with water. Bring to a boil, then turn the heat down to a simmer. Cook for 25 minutes or until fork-tender. Strain the potatoes and allow them to rest in the strainer for 5 minutes, giving time for some steam to escape.

Process the potatoes through a ricer, then transfer to the bowl of a stand mixer fitted with the paddle attachment. Mix on medium speed for 10 seconds. Turn the speed to high for a few more seconds, then add the butter, a couple of pinches of salt, and the white pepper. Continue to mix on high speed for 10 more seconds until everything is well incorporated. You do not want to overmix these potatoes, as they contain extra starch and will lose their fluffy creaminess. Transfer the potatoes to a pot and keep them warm on the stove until you are ready to serve.

CRISPY FRIED CABBAGE /

1 cup cabbage trim from
    Rosemary Roasted Cabbage (left)
8 cups canola oil
Salt, to taste

Makes 1 cup | Place the cabbage trim in a food processor and pulse until it is chopped into small ½-inch pieces. In a medium high-sided saucepot, heat the oil to 275°F. Add ½ cup cabbage to the oil. Once the moisture bubbles and settles, add the other ½ cup. Continue frying until the cabbage is cooked and crispy. Using a slotted spoon, remove the cabbage and place directly onto a plate lined with a kitchen towel. Season with salt. You can make this ahead of time and store in a container lined with paper towel at room temperature for up to 5 days.

PLATING /

¾ cup Burdock Red Wine Jus (page 97)
1 recipe Red Chieftain Pomme Puree (left)
1 recipe Rosemary Roasted Cabbage (left)
1 recipe Crispy Fried Cabbage (left)
Sweet woodruff, for garnish (optional)

Reheat the Burdock Red Wine Jus in a small saucepot, stirring often to reincorporate. Lay out six plates and place 1 cup Red Chieftain Pomme Puree in the center of each plate. Using tongs, add one wedge of Rosemary Roasted Cabbage to the side of the potatoes. Ladle 2 tbsp hot jus over the potatoes. Sprinkle each plate evenly with the Crispy Fried Cabbage. Garnish with sweet woodruff leaves if you're looking for a little green on the plate!

Sweet Woodruff

APPLE CANNOLI //

Cannoli Shells, Apple Butter Cream, Apple Butter, Salted Diced Apple, Pickled Pacific Crab Apples

Serves 6 | We love this classic Italian dessert because you can truthfully fill the shells with whatever is in season! They're a flaky pastry vessel for anything sweet and delicious. We initially brought this on the menu and filled it with a vanilla aquafaba, then changed it to this Apple Butter for autumn. "Sometimes the menu changes so often that I can't even remember last week's dessert, but I do remember the cannoli being proper—tubby, addictive, and aesthetically quite pleasing!" says Chef Devon Latte.

Note | *You will need cannoli forms to make this recipe. You can buy them at your local kitchen supply store.*

SALTED DICED APPLE /

3 Gala apples, cut in small dice
3 Granny Smith apples, cut in small dice
2 tsp salt
¼ tsp freshly grated nutmeg
3 tbsp sugar
½ tsp ground cinnamon

Makes 1 cup | In a large bowl, mix all the ingredients together thoroughly, then spread the apples out evenly on a dehydrator sheet. Dry on medium (145°F) for 12 hours. Alternatively, you can dry them on a baking sheet lined with parchment paper in your oven at 165°F (with the door cracked open) for approximately 4 hours. Once fully dry and crispy, store in an airtight container in a cool, dry place for up to 2 weeks.

APPLE BUTTER /

6 allspice berries
5 cardamom pods
3 cloves
6 Gala apples, cored and sliced
½ cup pitted Medjool dates
1 cup brown sugar
1 tsp salt
1 tsp ground cinnamon
½ cup soy milk

Makes 1½ cups | In a medium saucepot on medium-high heat, toast the allspice berries, cardamom, and cloves for 30 seconds to 1 minute to release the oils and aromatics. Remove from the heat and place on a cheesecloth, then tie the cheesecloth into a sachet. Lower the heat to medium, add the apples and dates to the pot, and sweat until the apples start to caramelize. Add ¼ cup water and the sugar, salt, cinnamon, and spice sachet and cook, stirring often, until the liquid has completely reduced and the mixture is dark and caramelized. Stir in the soy milk and continue to cook for 5 more minutes then remove from the heat. Working in small batches, transfer the mixture to a Vitamix and puree to a smooth consistency. Store in an airtight container in the fridge for up to 5 days.

CONTINUES

CANNOLI SHELLS /

½ tbsp ground flaxseeds
1¾ cups all-purpose flour + ½ cup
   for dusting the dough
2 tbsp sugar
½ tsp ground cinnamon
2 tbsp vegetable shortening
⅓ cup soda water
8 cups canola oil

Makes 12 cannoli shells | To make a flax egg, place the ground flaxseeds and 1½ tbsp water in a small bowl and mix well.

Sift the flour into the bowl of a stand mixer fitted with the hook attachment, and add the flax egg, sugar, cinnamon, vegetable shortening, and soda water. Mix on low speed until everything is incorporated. Remove the dough from the bowl, form into a ball, cover with plastic wrap, and refrigerate for a minimum of 1 hour and up to 3 days. If tightly wrapped, this dough will also freeze well for up to 6 months.

Shape the Cannoli | Remove the dough from the fridge and split into 12 evenly sized balls (these will weigh about 0.4 oz and be approximately 1 tbsp of dough each). Using a rolling pin, roll out each ball to a 4-inch circle. Lightly dust each circle with flour. Set up a bowl of water with a pastry brush before you begin shaping. Using stainless-steel cannoli forms, wrap each circle of dough loosely around the forms, making sure there is a slight gap between the dough and the tube. Brush the edge of the dough with water to help the dough to stick to itself. Overlap the dough slightly by approximately ½ inch and press the dough down onto itself, pinching the edges lightly to secure.

Fry the Cannoli | In a heavy-bottomed, high-sided pot, heat the canola oil to 350°F. Working in small batches, carefully drop the cannoli tubes (still wrapped to the forms) into the oil and fry until golden, rotating halfway through cooking to make sure all sides are cooked, approximately 2 minutes. Using tongs, carefully remove the cannoli shells from the pot and transfer to a kitchen towel or paper towel to soak up any excess oil. Allow them to cool for 1 minute before handling. Carefully slide the cannoli off the forms and repeat this process until all the dough is used up. Allow the cannoli shells to fully cool, then store in a dry, airtight container until you are ready to serve. Store at room temperature for up to 5 days.

APPLE BUTTER CREAM /

1¼ cups heavy cream
½ cup + 1 tbsp icing sugar
1 tbsp milk powder
2 tsp vanilla extract
¼ cup Apple Butter (page 101)

Makes 6 cups | In the bowl of a stand mixer fitted with the whisk attachment, place the cream, icing sugar, milk powder, and vanilla extract. Whip on high speed until fluffy and thick. If you don't have a stand mixer, you can whisk the cream by hand—it just might take a little longer! Turn the speed down to medium and fold in the Apple Butter. Once folded, remove the bowl from the mixer and hand-mix with a spatula to make sure the Apple Butter is well incorporated. Transfer to a piping bag and chill in the fridge for at least 30 minutes before filling your cannoli shells.

PLATING /

1 cup semisweet chocolate chips
1 recipe Cannoli Shells (page 102)
1 recipe Apple Butter Cream (left)
½ cup Apple Butter (page 101)
1 recipe Salted Diced Apple (page 101)
¼ cup Pickled Pacific Crab Apples (page 37)
Icing sugar, for dusting

Line a baking sheet with parchment paper. Fill the
bottom of a medium pot with 2 inches of water and
bring to a simmer. Add the chocolate to a stainless-steel
or Pyrex bowl and carefully set the bowl in the hot
water to melt the chocolate. Stir occasionally to make
sure it's evenly melted. Once melted, dip each end of
each Cannoli Shell in the melted chocolate, then set on
the prepared baking sheet and allow to cool.

Cut the tip off the piping bag filled with Apple Butter
Cream and fill both ends of the cannoli with the cream,
making sure to add enough that it reaches the center
inside the pastry shell.

Lay out six plates and place two filled cannoli on each.
Garnish with dollops of Apple Butter, Salted Diced
Apple, and a few Pickled Pacific Crab Apples. Sprinkle
icing sugar over each plate.

WINTER//

// Winter in Vancouver can feel bleak. Our oceanic climate casts cold, wet, long winters. Sometimes the cloud cover is so low, you can touch it. At The Acorn, we greet the season with open arms and give it a long and deep embrace. Our intimate space fills with sweet warming smells from the kitchen as the hypnotic flickering candlelight dances around the room. Root vegetables carry us through the season with an abundance of varieties. We raid North Arm Farm's cellar and manage to keep things "fresh" by changing dishes often. Just when we think we've had enough, we add a sprinkling of the preserved fruits and veg we've set aside from summer to keep our spirits alive.

ROASTED CABBAGE //

Charred + Roasted Cabbage, Bavarian Mustard Cream,
Black Currant Leaf Oil, Sautéed Kalettes, Pickled Knotroot,
Pickled Turnips, Bavarian Mustard

Serves 6 | This dish is all about the friendship between cabbage and mustard. We char and roast sweet cabbage in mustard, then add a beautiful Mustard Cream Sauce and finish it off with a drizzle of super herbaceous oil and a little extra mustard to serve. It's a stunner.

BAVARIAN MUSTARD /

2 cups apple cider vinegar
1 medium onion, diced
½ cup brown sugar
1½ tbsp salt
1 cinnamon stick
6 allspice berries
6 cloves
2 tsp turmeric
½ cup yellow mustard seeds
¼ cup brown mustard seeds

Note | *Our version of this old-world mustard is a nice balance of sweet and sour, and it maintains a great texture. This is the kind of mustard you can put on anything, from your favorite (veggie) sausage to any sandwich. This recipe makes extra mustard—trust us, you'll want it around.*

Makes 4 cups | Place 1½ cups water plus all the ingredients, except the mustard seeds, in a pot and bring to a simmer. Turn the heat down to low—so that the liquid is not reducing in volume but the flavor is infusing—and cook for 10 minutes. Strain out the liquid, using a spatula to press the onions, getting them to release all their juices through the strainer. Place both mustard seeds in a sterilized 32 oz mason jar and pour the liquid over the mustard seeds. Give the seeds a stir, then seal the jar and store in the fridge for 24 hours.

After 24 hours, transfer the contents of the jar to a Vitamix and blend until you reach a creamy but still slightly coarse consistency, with some mustard seeds intact. In order to mature the mustard and remove

some of the sharp and bitter flavors, place the mustard back into the same jar and refrigerate for 1 to 2 weeks to taste; over time, the spice level of the mustard will lessen. Store it in an airtight container in the fridge for up to 3 months.

BAVARIAN MUSTARD CREAM /

1 medium onion, diced
2 cloves garlic, sliced
1 tbsp olive oil
¼ cup dry white wine
2 cups heavy cream or milk alternative
2 tsp salt
½ tsp pepper
1 tsp Bavarian Mustard (above)

Makes 2 cups | In a medium saucepot, sweat the onions and garlic in the olive oil until soft and translucent. Add the white wine and cook until the liquid reduces by half. Add the cream and season with the salt and pepper. Continue cooking until the liquid has reduced by one-third, then remove from the heat. Strain the liquid through a fine-mesh sieve into a bowl, using a spatula or wooden spoon to press out as much liquid as possible from the vegetables. Stir the Bavarian Mustard into the strained cream. Keep warm until you are ready to serve, or, if making ahead of time, place the bowl in a larger pan filled with ice water to cool the cream completely. Once cooled, transfer to an airtight container and store it in the fridge for up to 3 days.

CONTINUES

CHARRED + ROASTED CABBAGE /

3 heads caraflex cabbage, approximately
    5 inches long (see Note)
½ cup olive oil
2 tbsp Licorice Fern Root Vinegar (page 46)
    or white balsamic or floral vinegar
2 tsp salt
1 tsp pepper
2 tbsp Bavarian Mustard (page 109)

Note | *We love caraflex cabbage for its sweet, thin leaves and unique cone shape. You can use any white cabbage if caraflex isn't available.*

Makes 6 servings | Preheat the oven to 400°F. Remove the outer leaves of the cabbage and cut in half lengthwise. Brush the cut side of each cabbage half with a thin layer of olive oil. Heat a large skillet on high heat, then sear and char the cabbage, cut side down, for approximately 1 minute. Do not move or flip the cabbage, as you want only the one side to be charred. Place the cabbage, charred side up, on a baking sheet lined with parchment paper.

In a small bowl, mix together the remaining olive oil and the Licorice Fern Root Vinegar, salt, pepper, and Bavarian Mustard. Brush the charred side of the cabbage evenly with this mixture, making sure to use all of it. Roast the cabbage in the oven for 30 to 40 minutes, until you can easily slide a paring knife through the core of it. Keep warm in a 200°F oven until you are ready to serve.

SAUTÉED KALETTES /

24 kalettes
2 tbsp olive oil
1 tsp minced garlic
Salt and pepper, to taste
4 tbsp sherry vinegar
3 tbsp maple syrup

Note | *Kalettes are just cool. They're a hybrid cross between kale and Brussels sprouts; tiny little leafy bundles of everything you want to eat packed into a single bite. We should change the saying* cool as a cucumber *to* cool as a kalette.

Makes 6 servings | Remove any bad outer leaves from the kalettes and cut off the very bottoms of the stems. In a large frying pan on medium-high heat, heat the olive oil. Add the kalettes and sauté for 30 seconds. Add the minced garlic, season with salt and pepper, and sauté for another 30 seconds. Add the sherry vinegar and maple syrup and cook on high heat, stirring often, until the kalettes are nicely glazed. Serve immediately.

PLATING /

2 cups Bavarian Mustard Cream (page 109)
1 recipe Charred + Roasted Cabbage (left)
1 recipe Sautéed Kalettes (above)
24 pieces Pickled Turnips (page 36)
24 pieces Pickled Knotroot (page 32)
6 tsp Bavarian Mustard (page 109)
¼ cup Black Currant Leaf Oil (page 51)

Reheat the Bavarian Mustard Cream in a saucepot if needed, stirring often. Lay out six shallow bowls and place a wedge of Charred + Roasted Cabbage at the center of each, then evenly spoon the Bavarian Mustard Cream around the cabbage and place four Sautéed Kalettes on top of each cabbage. Add four quarters of Pickled Turnips to each dish, along with six to eight Pickled Knotroots. Garnish each dish with 1tsp Bavarian Mustard and a generous drizzle of the Black Currant Leaf Oil.

PUMPKIN //

Guatemalan Blue Pumpkin Tuilles, Cream Cheese,
Spruce-Cured Pumpkin Ribbons, Pumpkin Pearls, Pumpkin Dust

Serves 6 | This is a true representation of our zero-waste mentality. Here we take one squash—a Guatemalan blue pumpkin, to be exact—and use the flesh, scraps, and guts to make different components of this dish. From the cured ribbons to the crispy tuilles and the pop-in-your-mouth pearls, it's a real marvel. For a vegan option, sub out the Cream Cheese with our Almond Crème Fraîche (page 28).

Note | *Guatemalan blue pumpkins are a gorgeous blue-skinned varietal with an elongated shape and a firm, sweet yellow interior. We get ours from Klippers Organics, and you should be able to find one at your local farmers' market. This recipe takes at least 2 days and a night to complete, and the different components use the same pumpkin, so read through each section before beginning to cook.*

CREAM CHEESE /

4 cups whole milk
4 cups heavy cream
¼ tsp mesophilic culture
2 drops vegetable rennet

Makes 2 cups | In a nonreactive stainless-steel pot on low heat, slowly bring the milk and cream up to 82°F, then remove from the heat. Sprinkle the mesophilic culture evenly over the heated milk and allow to set for 5 minutes. Dilute the vegetable rennet in 2 tbsp water. Add the water and rennet mixture to the warm milk, and using a spatula, gently introduce the culture into the milk, stirring only four times in an up and down motion. Cover the pot with a lid and let sit at room temperature (72°F) undisturbed for 48 hours.

Fold a cheesecloth over itself so that you have four layers, and place it inside a strainer. Place or hang the strainer vertically over a larger container. Add the cheese to the strainer and cover. Allow the liquid to drip through the cheesecloth slowly, undisturbed, in the fridge overnight. (This will remove some of the excess liquid, resulting in a thicker, creamier cheese.) Remove the cheese from the fridge and turn out into an airtight container, discarding the cheesecloth. Store in the fridge for up to 5 days.

SPRUCE-CURED PUMPKIN RIBBONS /

1 Guatemalan blue pumpkin
3 tbsp salt
2 tbsp sugar
3 tbsp spruce tips
1 tsp barley koji powder or 2 probiotic capsules

Makes 6 servings | Wash and peel the pumpkin as you normally would, then, using the peeler, peel 36 long, wide strips of pumpkin, as long and wide as you can get them, rotating the squash as you go so it's evenly peeled. Set the ribbons aside.

Halve the remaining pumpkin, scoop out the guts, including the seeds, and set aside for the Pumpkin Pearls (page 114). Cut the flesh into 1-inch cubes and set aside in the fridge for the tuilles (page 114). Set aside the remaining trim and scraps for the Pumpkin Dust (page 114).

Place the salt, sugar, and spruce tips in a Vitamix and blend until it is a fine powder. Transfer to a bowl and mix in the barley koji powder to create a curing mix for the pumpkin ribbons. Lay out one layer of pumpkin ribbons on the bottom of a square cake pan, then dust some of the curing mix over top. Repeat until you have used all the pumpkin and curing mix.

CONTINUES

Cover the pan with a kitchen towel to allow the curing pumpkin to breathe. Leave the pan at room temperature for 8 hours to cure, then transfer to the fridge for another 8 hours. As the pumpkin cures, the curing mix will dissolve, and the salt will draw liquid out of the pumpkin ribbons. Rinse the liquid from the ribbons and transfer to an airtight container. Store in the fridge for up to 5 days.

PUMPKIN DUST /

1½ cups pumpkin scraps from Spruce-Cured
    Pumpkin Ribbons (page 113)
1 tsp salt
1 tbsp sugar
⅛ tsp citric acid

Makes ¼ cup | Place all of the ingredients in a food processor and pulse until you have reached small rice-sized pieces. Spread the minced pumpkin in a thin layer on a dehydrator sheet and dehydrate on low (120°F) for 12 to 24 hours, until no moisture remains. Alternatively, you can dry on a baking sheet lined with parchment paper in your oven at 130°F (with the door cracked open) for 4 hours. Once fully dehydrated, transfer to a Vitamix with the other ingredients and blend until it becomes a fine powder. Store in a clean, dry airtight container at room temperature for up to 1 month.

GUATEMALAN BLUE PUMPKIN TUILLES /

2 cups cubed Guatemalan blue pumpkin
    from Spruce-Cured Pumpkin Ribbons (page 113)
1 tbsp olive oil
2 tsp salt
1 cup all-purpose flour
⅓ cup grapeseed oil + extra for frying
1 tbsp maple syrup

Makes 6 tuilles | **Prepare the Pumpkin Puree** | Preheat the oven to 350°F. Toss the cubes of pumpkin with the olive oil and salt and lay out on a baking sheet

lined with parchment paper. Roast for 30 minutes or until tender. Remove from the oven and transfer to a food processor along with ½ cup cold water. Blend until it's a smooth puree.

Make the Tuilles | Preheat the oven to 140°F. In a large bowl, whisk together 1 cup pumpkin puree with ¾ cup water, and the flour, grapeseed oil, and maple syrup. Line a baking sheet with paper towel and set aside. In a medium nonstick pan, add ¼ inch of grapeseed oil and bring up to medium heat. Using a ladle, carefully pour some of the batter into the pan in a circular motion, pouring from the inside out to form a circle approximately 4 inches in diameter. Fry until golden, then carefully remove the tuille from the oil and lay it flat on the prepared baking sheet. Repeat with the rest of the batter to create six tuilles in total. Discard the paper towel and dehydrate your tuilles in the oven, with the door cracked open slightly, for approximately 4 hours. This will help to eliminate any remaining moisture in the tuilles.

PUMPKIN PEARLS /

1 cup pumpkin guts from Spruce-Cured
    Pumpkin Ribbons (page 113)
1 cup sugar
2 tsp agar-agar
4 cups grapeseed oil, chilled in the freezer
    until ready to use

Makes 1 cup | In a large pot on medium-high heat, combine the pumpkin guts and sugar with 2 cups water and simmer for 20 minutes to infuse the flavor and dissolve the sugar. Using a large strainer, slowly strain out the liquid from the guts, pressing lightly to get as much liquid out as possible while trying to keep the liquid clear and free of solids. Next, strain the liquid through a cheesecloth or coffee filter to further clarify it. Transfer to a medium pot and bring back up to a simmer. Whisk in the agar-agar for 30 seconds, then let the syrup simmer for another 5 minutes. Remove from the heat and allow to cool for 5 minutes.

CONTINUES

Pour 1 cup of the cooled pumpkin syrup into a squeeze bottle with a ¼-inch tip. Take the chilled grapeseed oil from the freezer and transfer to a deep bowl. Squeeze drops of the syrup in a zigzag motion across the chilled oil to create pearl shapes. Strain the pearls with a fine-mesh strainer and rinse under cold water. Store in an airtight container in the fridge for up to 5 days.

PLATING /

1 recipe Cream Cheese (page 113)
1 recipe Spruce-Cured Pumpkin Ribbons (page 113)
6 Guatemalan Blue Pumpkin Tuilles (page 114)
¾ cup Pumpkin Pearls (page 114)
6 tsp Pumpkin Dust (page 114)
Bittercress, for garnish

Note | *We plate this dish to add height to the tuille so it doesn't just sit directly on the plate, but feel free to get creative with your own ideas.*

Lay out six plates. Add three dollops of Cream Cheese (approximately ½ tsp each) to each plate. The goal is to create three points for the tuille to sit on, so space them out accordingly. Fill in the spaces with smaller dollops of cheese (we like to add the cheese to a piping bag so that we can pipe the cheese onto the plates, which creates a cleaner look overall).

Pat the pumpkin ribbons with a kitchen towel to remove any excess liquid. Curl three ribbons on each plate, in and around the cheese. Gently place a warm tuille on top of the cheese and pumpkin ribbons. Pipe or dollop more cheese on top of the tuille, being careful not to break it. Curl three more ribbons in and around the cheese on top of each tuille. Sprinkle the top of each tuille with Pumpkin Pearls and 1 tsp Pumpkin Dust. Garnish with bittercress.

PARSNIP + POTATO PÂTÉ //

Smoked Caramelized Parsnip + Potato Pâté, Red Russian Garlic Confit,
Fresh Horseradish, Pickled Mustard Seeds, Sweet Walla Walla Onions, Taro Root Crisps

Serves 6 | We always have a seasonally rotating pâté on the menu—it's the perfect start to a meal or snack to enjoy with a cocktail. We throw down a little party trick in how we serve this one, trapping a little smoke inside the jar of pâté that is then released when the guest opens it at the table. The smoke imparts flavor to the top layer of the dish, while adding alluring visual and aromatic elements. It's a sensory adventure.

TARO ROOT CRISPS /

- 1 medium taro root
- 1 tbsp salt
- 1 tbsp sugar
- 12 cups canola oil

Note | *These crisps are an addictive snack on their own or with any of your favorite dips or sauces, especially our Herbed Hazelnut Dip (page 197) or Ashed Spring Onion Almond Sauce (page 163). We're making enough for 10 crisps per person with this recipe, but feel free to make more if you have extra taro root left over.*

Makes 60 crisps | Peel the taro root. Using a mandoline set to approximately ⅛ inch thick, slice it into 60 slices.

In a small mixing bowl, mix the salt and sugar together and set aside. Line a baking sheet with paper towel and set aside.

In a medium heavy-bottomed, high-sided pot, heat the oil to 325°F. Working in small batches, carefully drop the taro slices into the oil, stirring often at the start with a slotted spoon. Once there are no more bubbles releasing from the taro, carefully remove them with a slotted spoon and place on the prepared baking sheet to soak up any excess oil. While the chips are still warm, season with the salt and sugar mix. Repeat this process for the rest of the crisps. When cool, store in an airtight container lined with paper towel at room temperature for up to 1 week.

SWEET WALLA WALLA ONIONS /

- 2 Walla Walla onions
- 1 tbsp olive oil
- 2 tsp sugar
- 1 tsp salt
- ½ tsp pepper
- 2 tbsp Spruce Tip Vinegar (page 46) or a neutral vinegar like white balsamic or apple cider vinegar

Makes ¾ cup | Peel and finely dice the onions. Heat a medium frying pan on medium-high heat, then add the olive oil and onions and cook for approximately 3 minutes. Stir in the sugar and cook for another 2 minutes, stirring often. Once there's a nice golden-brown caramelization, season with salt and pepper and deglaze the pan with the Spruce Tip Vinegar. Continue cooking until the vinegar has reduced down and the onions are semidry and glazed. Remove from the heat and cool over an ice bath. Store in an airtight container in the fridge for up to 5 days.

CONTINUES

RED RUSSIAN GARLIC CONFIT /

8 cloves Red Russian garlic
½ cup olive oil

Note | *We love Red Russian garlic for its sharp and intense garlic flavor, which doesn't get lost to the sweetness once cooked. If you don't have Red Russian, you can use any garlic variety available.*

Makes 8 cloves | In a small saucepot on low heat, cook the garlic cloves in the olive oil for 1 hour, or until they are soft and have a golden caramelization. Do not let the oil get too hot, as this will overcook the garlic and burn it. Remove from the heat and allow the cloves to cool in the oil for 10 minutes, then strain and set aside. Alternatively, leave the garlic in the oil and store as garlic confit in an airtight container in the fridge for up to 2 weeks.

SMOKED PARSNIP + POTATO PÂTÉ /

POTATO PUREE
2 large Yukon Gold potatoes
1 recipe Red Russian Garlic Confit (above)
1 tsp salt
½ tsp white pepper
¼ tsp freshly grated nutmeg

CARAMELIZED PARSNIP PUREE
2 tbsp olive oil
2 large parsnips, peeled and diced
½ cup diced onions
3 cloves garlic, sliced
1 tsp salt
1 tsp white pepper
2 tbsp sherry vinegar
1 tbsp maple syrup

Note | *If you're smoking the pâté, the exact size of the jar doesn't matter as long as you can fit all the ingredients in and seal it quickly to trap the smoke inside. At The Acorn, we use wide-mouthed, straight-edged, hinge-top clamping jars that we buy from our local general store, Welk's, down the street.*

Makes 3 (8 oz) swing-top jars, or 3 cups |
Make the Potato Puree | Peel the potatoes and cut into 2-inch cubes. Place in a medium pot and cover with lightly salted cold water. Bring to a simmer and cook until fork tender, approximately 25 minutes. Strain out the potatoes and transfer to the bowl of a stand mixer fitted with the whisk attachment. Add the garlic confit, salt, white pepper, and nutmeg. Whip on medium-high speed for 30 seconds, then stop the mixer and scrape down the sides of the bowl to make sure all the ingredients are incorporated. Whip on high for another 30 seconds, then again scrape down the sides of the bowl, making sure there are no lumps. Be careful not to overwhip the potatoes or they'll start to get gluey. Wrap the potatoes with plastic wrap and set aside.

Make the Parsnip Puree | In a medium frying pan on medium heat, add in the olive oil, parsnips, onions, and garlic. Cook until caramelized, stirring often to make sure they don't burn. Season with the salt and white pepper and continue stirring. Once you have reached a dark caramelization, deglaze the pan with the sherry vinegar and maple syrup. Continue cooking until the volume of the sherry vinegar is reduced by half, then add 2 cups water. Cook again until the water has reduced by half, then remove from the heat. Working in batches, puree the parsnip mixture in a Vitamix until silky-smooth.

In a large bowl, thoroughly mix the potato and parsnip purees together. Cool the mixture over an ice bath. Fill three 8 to 16 oz swing-top jars with approximately 1 cup puree each. Set by tapping the bottom of the jars with your hand to knock out any air bubbles. (You can also transfer the puree to a serving bowl instead of the jars if you don't plan to smoke the pâté.) If making in advance, seal the jars (or cover the bowl) and store in the fridge for up to 5 days.

PLATING /

1 recipe Smoked Parsnip + Potato Pâté (left)
¾ cup Sweet Walla Walla Onions (page 119)
3 tbsp Pickled Mustard Seeds (page 36)
3 tsp fresh-grated horseradish
1 recipe Taro Root Crisps (page 119)

If you're plating the Parsnip + Potato Pâté in jars, evenly distribute the Sweet Walla Walla Onions between the jars, spreading the mixture over the pâté. If you're serving in a bowl, evenly spread the Walla Walla onions over the surface of the pâté. Add 1 tbsp Pickled Mustard Seeds to one side of each jar on top of the onions, or distribute the 3 tbsp around the top of the bowl. Garnish with the fresh-grated horseradish. If you're smoking the pâté, use your smoking gun to fill the jar with smoke, keeping the lid as close to the tube as possible. Once you have achieved a thick, dense smoke, quickly seal the jar, trying not to let any smoke out. Serve immediately with the Taro Root Crisps.

CARROT //

Lacto Caramelized Thumbelina Carrots, Carrot Jus,
Pickled Carrots, Carrot Dust, Almond Crème Fraîche

Serves 6 | One of our obsessions is finding ways to use all parts of a vegetable and minimize waste. Here the carrot is extremely versatile in many forms: pan-roasted, pickled, shaved, reduced into a sauce, and dehydrated into a dust. We Love Carrot!!!

LACTO CARAMELIZED
THUMBELINA CARROTS /

20 thumbelina carrots
Salt (2% of the weight of your carrots)
2 cloves garlic
1 tbsp olive oil
2 tbsp brown sugar
3 sprigs thyme

Note | *Thumbelina carrots are a mini, sweet, and plump carrot variety. They are the perfect little snack—since you can eat them with the peels on—and they also roast evenly due to their consistent shape. An overall winner in our books. This recipe has a couple of extra carrots so you can taste them along the way.*

Makes 6 servings | In a large pot, bring 16 cups salted water to a boil. Blanch your carrots for approximately 1 minute, until they are tender but still have some crunch. Strain the carrots out and place directly into an ice bath to cool down. Transfer the cooled carrots to a sterilized 64 oz mason jar (or divide evenly between 2 smaller jars if needed), add the salt and garlic cloves, and cover with 8 cups water. Fill a large resealable plastic bag half-full with 2% salted water and place on top of the carrots to keep them submerged. Cover the jar with a towel or cheesecloth and allow the carrots to ferment at room temperature for 3 or 4 days, until they have developed a slight tangy and acidic flavor.

When ready to serve, add the olive oil to a medium pan on medium heat. Remove the carrots from the fermenting liquid and transfer them to a kitchen towel to quickly dry off. Add the carrots to the pan to the pan and sauté them for 2 to 3 minutes until nicely caramelized on all sides. Add the brown sugar and thyme, and cook until the brown sugar has reached a deep caramelization.

CARROT JUS /

10 large orange carrots
½ tsp salt

Makes ½ cup | Clean the carrots, making sure to remove all the dirt from the skin, then peel and trim the ends. Using a juicer, juice the carrots, reserving the carrot pulp for the Carrot Dust (page 124). In a medium pot on medium heat, combine the carrot juice and salt and reduce the liquid down by a quarter of its original amount; do not let the carrot juice boil or simmer too rapidly. The bubbles at this point will be like that of a simple syrup and will appear very sticky. With a rubber spatula, periodically scrape down the sides of the pot and mix the scrapings back into the juice—this is very important, as it will help with the final color and flavor of the jus.

Once reduced, remove from the heat and transfer to a Vitamix. Blend the liquid until it has all come together. Store in an airtight container in the fridge for up to 10 days.

CONTINUES

CARROT DUST /

Carrot juice pulp from Carrot Jus (page 123)
Salt, to taste
Sugar, to taste
Pinch citric acid

Note | *The yield for this recipe will depend on the amount of pulp you get from your juicer after juicing the carrots for the Carrot Jus (page 123). As such, seasoning will also vary.*

Makes varied (see Note) | Season the carrot pulp with salt and sugar to taste—you're trying to achieve a balance between sweet and salty, so if your carrots are very sweet, you'll need less sugar and more salt, or vice versa—and mix in. Spread the carrot pulp in a thin layer on a dehydrator sheet and dehydrate on medium (145°F) for 12 hours or until the pulp is dry. Alternatively, dry on a baking sheet lined with parchment paper in your oven at 165°F (with the door cracked open) for 4 hours.

Once dried, transfer the pulp to a Vitamix along with a pinch of citric acid (approximately ⅛ tsp for every ½ cup of dried carrot) and blend to a fine powder. Store in a dry airtight container at room temperature for up to 1 month.

PLATING /

2 rainbow carrots
1 recipe Lacto Caramelized Thumbelina Carrots
  (page 123)
1 cup Almond Crème Fraîche (page 28)
1 recipe Carrot Jus (page 123)
1 cup Pickled Carrots (page 35)
Chickweed, for garnish
1 recipe Carrot Dust (left)

Clean and peel the rainbow carrots and trim off the very ends, then use a thin peeler to peel them into long ribbons. Place the ribbons in ice-cold water until you're ready to plate them, to allow the carrots to firm up and curl.

Lay out six plates. Cut the Lacto Caramelized Thumbelina Carrots in half and distribute them among the plates. Add approximately 2½ tbsp Almond Crème Fraîche to each plate and drizzle approximately 1 tbsp Carrot Jus in and around the carrots and Almond Crème Fraîche on each plate.

Remove the carrot ribbons from the water and pat dry with a kitchen towel, then fold and distribute them around the plates. Add the Pickled Carrots to the plates. Garnish with chickweed leaves, and using a small fine-mesh strainer, top each plate with a sprinkling of Carrot Dust.

FRIED
POACHED EGG //

Fried Poached Eggs, Pasilla Pepper + Tomato Roasted Butter Beans

Serves 6 | Brunch at The Acorn isn't your typical breakfast fare. We like to keep things interesting with our menu and started by tasking ourselves to create something fun and unique with eggs. Crispy on the outside with oozy yolks on the inside, these eggs go well with any of your favorite brunch menu items, or follow our lead by serving them in a bowl of butter beans along with our house Focaccia Bread (page 226) for dipping.

PASILLA PEPPER + TOMATO ROASTED BUTTER BEANS /

½ cup small-diced onions

1 tbsp minced garlic

2 whole dried pasilla peppers, soaked for 1 minute in hot water and diced (soaking water reserved)

2 cups small-diced canned sweet red peppers

1 tsp ground annatto seeds

1 tsp epazote

2 cups tomato puree

1 tsp chili powder

½ tsp black pepper

¼ cup fresh lime juice

2 cups butter beans, soaked for 12 hours

2 tsp salt

Note | *These beans get a herbaceous kick from the epazote, which, when cooked with beans, eases digestion. Sweet with just a hint of spice, these beans are great on toast, over rice, or served immediately with our Fried Poached Eggs.*

Makes 6 servings | In a medium pot on medium-high heat, sweat the onions and garlic until soft and translucent. Add the pasilla peppers, sweet peppers, annatto seeds, and epazote and continue to cook for 5 minutes, stirring often. Add the tomato puree, chili powder, black pepper, lime juice, and the leftover liquid from soaking the pasilla peppers. Stir until the mixture is blended. Add the butter beans, cover with 16 cups water, and bring to a slow simmer. Once simmering, cover partially with a lid to let steam escape. Cook for

approximately 1 hour, stirring every 10 minutes. After 45 minutes, season with salt; seasoning with salt too early will firm up the shells of the bean, making the cooking time much longer and resulting in uneven cooking. Continue to cook the beans on low heat until they are tender and the liquid is thick and saucy. The length of cooking time may vary, so make sure you are patient and don't rush the process!

FRIED POACHED EGGS /

¼ cup white vinegar

1 tbsp salt

6 eggs

BREADING

½ cup all-purpose flour

2 eggs, beaten

1½ cups panko bread crumbs

8 cups canola oil

Salt, to taste

Makes 6 eggs | **Poach the Eggs** | In a high-sided pot, bring 6 quarts water and the vinegar and salt to just under a simmer; the water temperature should be approximately 180°F to 190°F. (You can omit the salt if you want; we use it in the restaurant to help firm up the egg whites and make them easier to handle.)

CONTINUES

Once at the right temperature, stir the water in a clock-wise motion and crack one of the eggs into the center of the pot; stirring the water first will help encapsulate the egg white around the yolk. You can add the rest of the eggs now, one after the other, or work in small batches for more control. Allow the eggs to poach for approximately 2 minutes for a soft poach (you can cook them longer if you prefer a firmer yolk).

Using a slotted spoon, carefully remove the eggs one at a time and place them directly into a bowl of ice water to sit for 4 minutes. Make sure the eggs are completely cooled and firm to the touch before removing. Remove the eggs from the ice water and transfer them to a baking sheet lined with a kitchen towel to dry.

Bread the Eggs | Set up your breading ingredients in small bowls side by side in the order of flour, eggs, and bread crumbs. Working with one poached egg at a time, carefully dust the first egg with flour. Then coat it in the beaten eggs, rolling it around to make sure it's evenly coated. Then place directly into the bread crumbs, again making sure it's thoroughly coated. Place the breaded poached eggs on a plate and refrigerate until you are ready to fry them.

Fry the Eggs | Line a baking sheet with a kitchen towel and set aside. In a medium high-sided pot, heat the canola oil to 350°F. Gently place the eggs in the hot oil one at a time. Fry them for only 1 minute; if you fry them any longer, the oil will further cook the eggs. Using a slotted spoon, carefully remove the eggs and place on the prepared sheet to absorb any excess oil. Season with salt and serve immediately.

PLATING /

1 recipe Pasilla Pepper + Tomato Roasted
   Butter Beans (page 127)
1 recipe Fried Poached Eggs (page 127)
Red frilly mustard greens, for garnish
Salt and pepper, to taste

Lay out six bowls and divide the butter beans between them. Place a Fried Poached Egg at the center of each bowl and garnish with red frilly mustard greens. Season with salt and pepper.

BEETS //

Seaweed + Beet Gastrique Glazed Chewy Beets, Pickled Formanova Beets, Beet, Redwing Onion + Larch Tip Relish, Hazelnut Cream, Beet Chips, Sorrel

Serves 6 | Beets, the mascot of plant-based cooking. A model vegetable with antioxidant-anti-inflammatory-detoxification bragging rights, and a versatile root in both color and texture. This book wouldn't be complete without our interpretation of this wondrous ingredient. North Arm Farm beets carry us through winter like a valiant horse galloping through a wheat field.

Chewy beets! In this recipe we cook, dehydrate, and then rehydrate these beets in an umami-rich caramelized glaze that takes beets to the next level. Time-consuming, but totally worth it. You haven't tried a beet quite like this before. Also, in this recipe you'll discover that beets and hazelnuts have a total flavor affinity! And we give you that classic "yogurt" and beet pairing in a dairy-free way that's still rich and creamy. We had to do our model vegetable justice.

Note | *To save time, cook the beets all at once, making sure to cook the golden beets in a separate pot to the red to maintain their color. Cooking times may vary depending on the different sizes of beets.*

BEET CHIPS /

1 large golden beet
¼ cup sugar
1 tsp salt

Makes 1 cup | Trim, wash, and peel the beet. Using a mandoline, slice the beet into ⅛-inch-thick medallions. In a small pot, bring 1 cup water and the sugar and salt to a simmer, then add the sliced beets and cook for approximately 5 minutes. Using a slotted spoon, remove the beets and lay out the slices in a single layer on dehydrator sheets; you can keep them tight together, as they will shrink dramatically as they dry.

Dry on medium (145°F) for 12 to 24 hours. Alternatively, dry them on a baking sheet lined with parchment paper in your oven at 165°F (with the door cracked open) for 6 to 8 hours. You want the dehydrated beet chips to be devoid of any moisture. To check if they're fully dry, remove the beets from the dehydrator and let them stand at room temperature for at least 1 minute; the heat from the dehydrator softens the sugars, so you can't tell if they are crispy until they have tempered. Once dry, store the beets in an airtight container lined with paper towel at room temperature for up to 5 days.

BEET, REDWING ONION + LARCH TIP RELISH /

2 large red beets
1 redwing onion, cut in small dice
2 cloves garlic, minced
2 tbsp olive oil
½ tsp salt
1 tsp pepper
¼ cup sugar
½ cup Spruce Tip Vinegar (page 46) or a neutral vinegar like white balsamic or apple cider vinegar
6-inch larch branch, washed thoroughly

Makes 2 cups | Trim the stems from the beets and thoroughly clean the beets to remove any dirt. Place them whole in a medium pot and cover them with water. Bring the water to a boil, then reduce to a simmer and cook the beets for approximately 40 minutes, depending on the size, until you can easily slide a knife through them. Strain out the beets and, while still warm, rub with a clean kitchen cloth to remove the skins. Allow the beets to cool fully before dicing, then dice into ¼-inch cubes.

CONTINUES

In a medium saucepot on medium heat, sweat the onions and garlic in the olive oil until they are soft and translucent. Add the diced beets, salt, pepper, sugar, vinegar, 1 cup water, and the larch branch. Continue to cook on low heat, stirring often, until the liquid has almost completely reduced. Remove the larch branch and transfer the relish to a sterilized 16 oz mason jar or airtight container. Cover and store in the fridge for up to 1 month.

HAZELNUT CREAM /

1 cup raw hazelnuts
1 tsp salt
1 tbsp maple syrup
⅓ cup grapeseed oil

Note | *Truth is, this Hazelnut Cream is highly versatile. Use it as a spread, dip, or sauce to balance out higher-acid fruits and veg.*

Makes 1½ cups | Preheat the oven to 350°F. Spread the hazelnuts on a baking sheet and toast for approximately 10 minutes or until they become aromatic and start browning. If there are skins on the hazelnuts, allow the hazelnuts to cool slightly, then rub them vigorously with a dry kitchen towel to remove as much of the skins as possible. Place the hazelnuts, ⅛ cup water, the salt, and the maple syrup in a Vitamix and blend until it starts to become smooth; use the tamper to help keep the ingredients moving evenly in the blender. Slowly pour in the grapeseed oil and blend until the texture is silky-smooth and creamy. Transfer to an airtight container and allow the cream to cool completely in the fridge before using it. Store in the fridge for up to 5 days.

SEAWEED + BEET GASTRIQUE GLAZED CHEWY BEETS /

4 medium red beets
2 tbsp crushed and toasted kelp or kombu (approximately one 4 × 5-inch sheet)
1 shallot, minced
4 cloves garlic, minced
1 tbsp minced fresh ginger
4 tbsp olive oil
1 tsp salt
1 tsp pepper
¼ cup sherry vinegar
1 cup brown sugar

Makes 6 servings | Trim the stems from the beets and thoroughly clean the beets to remove any dirt. Place them whole in a medium pot and cover them with water. Bring the water to a boil, then reduce to a simmer and cook the beets for approximately 40 minutes, depending on the size, until you can easily slide a knife through them. Be careful not to put too many holes in the beets, as you will be cutting them into wedges once they're cooked. Strain out the beets and, while still warm, rub with a clean kitchen cloth to remove the skins. Cut into 2-inch wedges and lay them out on dehydrator sheets. Dehydrate on medium (145°F) for 6 to 8 hours. Alternatively, dry on a baking sheet lined with parchment paper in your oven at 165°F (with the door cracked open) for approximately 4 to 6 hours. Dehydrate the beets until they have shrunken by one-third of their original size. Don't be alarmed by their appearance; it's not about the look of these beets, it's about the flavor and texture.

Larch

Preheat the oven to 350°F. Place the kelp on a baking sheet and toast for 10 minutes or until lightly browned. Transfer the kelp to a bowl and crush it with your hands until you've reached a fine-grained consistency.

Meanwhile, in a medium saucepot on medium heat, sauté the shallots, garlic, and ginger in the olive oil. Cook, stirring often, until you've developed a nice dark golden caramelization. Add the salt, pepper, ground toasted kelp, sherry vinegar, brown sugar, and 2 cups water. Simmer for approximately 5 minutes, then add the dehydrated beets. Cook the beets on low heat for 15 minutes, stirring often; during this time the beets will rehydrate as they soak up the glaze. Remove the beets and pour any remaining glaze into a heatproof container or bowl.

PLATING /

1 recipe Seaweed + Beet Gastrique Glazed
   Chewy Beets (left) + any leftover glaze
1½ cups Hazelnut Cream (left)
1 cup Pickled Formanova Beets (page 37)
¾ cup Beet + Redwing Onion + Larch Tip Relish
   (page 131)
1 recipe Beet Chips (page 131)
Red-veined or wood sorrel leaves, for garnish

Lay out six plates. Divide the chewy beets between the plates, and add 3 tbsp Hazelnut Cream to the bottom of each plate around the chewy beets. Place three ribbons of Pickled Formanova Beets artfully around the plate. Add 2 tbsp relish in and around the beets. Drizzle each plate with 1 tbsp glaze left over from the chewy beets. Top with a sprinkling of Beet Chips and garnish with fresh-picked sorrel leaves.

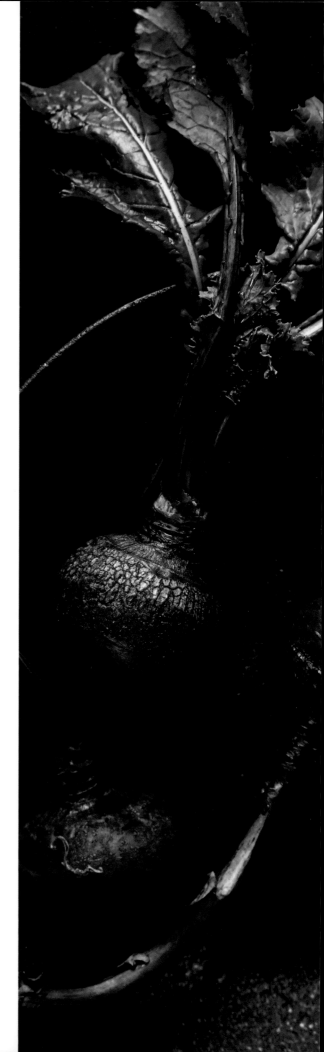

NORTH ARM FARM //

North Arm Farm's very first crop was an acre of sweet corn. Shortly after purchasing their picturesque property in the early 90s, Trish and Jordan Sturdy asked a neighbor for farming advice and started growing. They were both working full-time, so they'd pick corn in the morning before work and place it in a wheelbarrow by the side of the road with an empty peanut butter jar alongside it. When they returned at the end of the day, the corn would be gone and there would be money in the jar.

Today their family farm—which is nestled in a valley basin beneath Mount Currie near Pemberton—grows 50 to 60 crops a year with organic and sustainable practices and has expanded to 45 acres of land. The Sturdys supply select restaurants with their unique, prized produce and love to invite the local community to the farm to buy freshly harvested produce, pick their own, or just walk around and see how things grow.

The Acorn cooks with North Arm Farm produce all year round, including the winter, when the farm is renowned for its cellar and root vegetables—their purple Brussels sprouts are a particular favorite! Trish says the farm is thrilled to be part of The Acorn family because we share the same values of creating community, working locally and seasonally, and finding joy in a vast spectrum of colorful vegetable varieties.

INSPIRATIONS | Mountains, valleys, food and farm communities, colorful varieties, and a deep appreciation for vegetables.

THE ACORN-AT-HOME | Go visit a farm! See what it looks like, learn what goes into the food they're growing, and enjoy harvesting with you-pick berries and pumpkins.

GNOCCHI //

Squash + Chanterelle Gnocchi, Preserved Apricots,
Sautéed Wild Mushrooms, Squash Puree, Pickled Blue Chanterelle Mushrooms,
Lacto Fermented Chanterelle Butter

Serves 6 | Gnocchi is a fan favorite, both at home and in the restaurant, so these perfect pillowy doughballs often make an appearance on our menu. The soft texture of the gnocchi really complements the different textures of the mushrooms in this dish—and we're using many different mushroom varieties, all belonging to the chanterelle family, to showcase the diversity of British Columbia's mycelium. While the butter in this dish is specifically used to finish the gnocchi, you can use it anytime, anywhere, anyhow.

LACTO FERMENTED CHANTERELLE BUTTER /

1.5 lb golden chanterelle mushrooms
15 g salt (2% of the weight of the mushrooms)
1 lb unsalted butter

Note | *This recipe takes 5 days to ferment.*

Makes 1½ lb | Using a brush or kitchen towel, clean the mushrooms, removing all dirt and debris, then trim off the very ends. Break the mushrooms up into small pieces with your hands and lay out flat on a baking sheet lined with parchment paper. Freeze for 4 hours. (Freezing the mushrooms breaks down their cellular structure, allowing more of their liquid to be released for the fermentation process.) Remove from the freezer and toss with the salt and ¼ cup water.

Place the salted mushrooms and water in a sterilized mason jar with a lid. Fill a resealable plastic bag half-full with 2% salted water and lay it on top of the mushrooms to stop any air interfering with the fermentation process. Cover the container with the lid but leave a small gap to let gases out. Ferment the mushrooms at room temperature (72°F) for approximately 5 days. Check the mushrooms daily to make sure that they are completely submerged in their juices. You'll also want to taste the mushrooms after a few days to check the acidity of the liquid; it should be tart but not too overpowering, and you should skim off any kahm yeast growth (a white stringy yeast often mistaken for mold) that may start to form on the surface or around the edges. Use a clean spoon to skim off the kahm yeast, making sure to remove as much of it as possible so you don't have to start the fermentation process all over again. The final product you're ultimately looking for is a tangy umami flavor, balancing salty and sour with an aroma of mushroom.

After 5 days, or once you have achieved the desired taste, strain out the liquid from the mushrooms through a fine-mesh strainer. Reserve the liquid in an airtight container in the fridge for the Sautéed Wild Mushrooms (page 141). Place the fermented chanterelles in a Vitamix and blend until the mixture is a smooth puree.

Soften the butter at room temperature until it is easily spreadable. Once tempered, place the butter and 3 tbsp chanterelle puree in a bowl and evenly mix together. Transfer to an airtight container and store in the fridge for up to 5 days. Freeze any extra chanterelle puree and use in sauces, or with pasta.

CONTINUES

SQUASH PUREE /

3 cups small-diced blue hubbard squash (see Note)
½ cup diced onions
6 cloves garlic, sliced
3 tbsp olive oil
2 tsp salt
1 tsp white pepper
2 tbsp maple syrup

Note | *This squash puree is used for making the gnocchi and to finish the dish. You can use any type of squash available. Just make sure that with whatever squash you use, you have cooked out all the excess moisture, as some types of squash contain more than others.*

Makes 4 cups | Preheat the oven to 350°F. In a large bowl, toss together all the ingredients and spread them out on a baking sheet lined with parchment paper. Roast for approximately 30 minutes or until the squash is fork-tender. Remove from the oven and allow to cool at room temperature. Transfer to a bowl and stir in ½ cup water. Working in batches, blend this squash mixture in a Vitamix until smooth. Store in an airtight container in the fridge for up to 1 week.

SQUASH + CHANTERELLE GNOCCHI /

2 lb (4 medium) russet potatoes
2 tsp salt
1 tsp white pepper
2 cups red spring flour + extra for dusting
¼ tsp ground nutmeg
1 large egg
½ cup Squash Puree (above)
Olive oil, for cooked gnocchi

Note | *The secret to making perfect gnocchi is to remove any excess moisture in the potatoes. This is done by ricing the potatoes and spreading them out on a baking sheet to release steam as soon as the potatoes are cooked through and are still hot.*

Makes 6 servings | Preheat the oven to 425°F. Wash the potatoes and pierce with a paring knife three times on each side. Bake the potatoes for approximately

1½ hours, flipping halfway through. Once cooked soft all the way through, remove from the oven.

Working carefully so as not to burn yourself, slice the top of each potato lengthwise and pinch the potato to allow steam to escape immediately. You want your potatoes to be as dry as possible before adding the wet ingredients, so it is important to work quickly in the next step. Cut each potato in half lengthwise and scrape the potato flesh out of the skins. Pass the cooked potatoes through a ricer while they are still hot; this provides a smooth texture in the finished gnocchi and allows more steam to escape. Spread the riced potatoes out on a baking sheet to allow more steam to escape. Let the potatoes cool, then season with the salt and pepper.

Transfer the potatoes to a large bowl. Add the flour and nutmeg and mix everything together with your hands until you achieve a fine crumbly texture. Crack the egg into the mixture and add the Squash Puree, mixing again until the dough comes together and the egg and puree have evenly dispersed.

Dust a clean work surface with flour and turn the dough onto it. Work the dough lightly just to help smooth it out and bring everything together a little more. Press the dough out into a 6-inch square and then cut the square into 4 quarters. Roll each section evenly into a long tube, about 1 inch in diameter. Using a pastry scraper or sharp knife, cut each tube into 1-inch pieces.

Bring a large pot of salted water to a boil and work in batches to blanch the gnocchi, dropping only a dozen or so pieces in at a time and cooking each batch for 2 minutes. Using a slotted spoon, remove the gnocchi from the water and transfer to a baking sheet. Toss the cooked gnocchi in olive oil to help prevent them from sticking. Repeat the process for all the gnocchi and let them cool completely on the baking sheet. If you're preparing this ahead of time, lay the uncooked gnocchi on a baking sheet and freeze them right away. Once frozen, transfer to a sealed container or bag.

CONTINUES

SAUTÉED WILD MUSHROOMS /

6 golden chanterelle mushrooms
6 white chanterelle mushrooms
6 hedgehog mushrooms
6 pig's ear mushrooms
24 yellowfoot chanterelle mushrooms
¼ cup unsalted butter
Salt and pepper, to taste
4 sprigs thyme
3 tbsp fermented mushroom liquid from
   Lacto Fermented Chanterelle Butter (page 137)

Note | *Since each mushroom has a different density and moisture content, it's important to add them to the pan by order of firmest to softest, as they have varied cooking times.*

Makes 6 servings | Clean all the mushrooms with a pastry brush to remove all dirt and debris. Trim off the base of the chanterelles (these can be saved for stocks or soups). If the mushrooms are large, break them up into even bite-sized pieces with your hands.

In a frying pan on medium heat, melt the butter, then add the golden and white chanterelles. Cook for approximately 30 seconds, then add the hedgehog and pig's ear mushrooms. Season with salt and pepper, and add the sprigs of thyme. Cook for 1 minute, then add the fermented mushroom liquid. Cook until the liquid has reduced by half, then add the yellowfoot chanterelles to the pan and cook for 30 seconds more. Remove from the heat and serve immediately.

PLATING /

2 tbsp olive oil
1 recipe Squash + Chanterelle Gnocchi (page 138)
2 tbsp Lacto Fermented Chanterelle Butter (page 137)
Salt and pepper, to taste
1 recipe Sautéed Wild Mushrooms (left)
1½ cups Squash Puree (page 138)
24 halves Preserved Apricots (page 41)
30 pieces Pickled Blue Chanterelle Mushrooms
   (page 36)
Sweet alyssum flowers and watercress, for garnish

Note | *If using the gnocchi from frozen, follow the Squash + Chanterelle Gnocchi recipe method for blanching them first, adding an extra 30 seconds to 1 minute to the cooking time.*

Heat a large pan on medium-high heat and add the olive oil. Sear the gnocchi on each side until they are heated all the way through. Once cooked, add the Lacto Fermented Chanterelle Butter and season with salt and pepper. (If your pan is too small to fit all the gnocchi, use two pans and divide the olive oil and butter between the two.)

Lay out six large shallow bowls. Evenly distribute the seared gnocchi and Sautéed Wild Mushrooms between the bowls. Place dollops of the Squash Puree (about ¼ cup per plate) throughout the gnocchi, and add four pieces of Preserved Apricots to each bowl (halving large pieces as necessary). Top each dish with Pickled Blue Chanterelle Mushrooms and garnish with sweet alyssum flowers and watercress leaves.

POTATO
PINE NUT SOUP //

Caramelized Garlic, German Butter Potato + Pine Nut Soup,
Aleppo Pepper Powder Potato Chips, Smoked Sunflower Oil

Serves 6 | No more lies! Soup on a restaurant menu should be an indication that the kitchen is working to minimize food waste, using up any vegetable trim and scraps that would otherwise end up in the landfill. We always have a rotating soup, one that helps us to make the best use of our ingredients while remaining seasonal. With that, we couldn't help but include this recipe for one of our favorite winter soups. It's as comforting as it gets, like your favorite oversized wool sweater. Feel free to get creative and add any clean vegetable trim you have lying around.

ALEPPO PEPPER POWDER POTATO CHIPS /

ALEPPO PEPPER POWDER
15 dried Aleppo peppers (see Note)
1 tsp salt
2 tsp sugar
¼ tsp citric acid

POTATO CHIPS
4 German butter potatoes
12 cups canola oil

Note | *Aleppo peppers are a milder red pepper. If you're using fresh Aleppo peppers, there are many methods for drying them. We usually dry them in the dehydrator for around 18 hours at 145°F, or in the oven at 165°F for 6 hours. Before drying them, wash thoroughly, cut off the stems, and remove the seeds. Save and dry the seeds separately if you want that extra heat.*

Makes 6 servings | Make the Aleppo Pepper Powder | Place the dried peppers in a Vitamix and blitz until the mixture has a powdery consistency. Add the remaining ingredients and blitz for 5 more seconds or until well combined. Store in an airtight container at room temperature for up to 3 months.

Make the Potato Chips | Wash the potatoes and slice them using a mandoline set to ⅛ inch thickness. In a heavy-bottomed, high-sided pot, heat the oil to 275°F. Working in batches of a dozen or so, carefully place the sliced potatoes in the oil, making sure not to overcrowd the pot. Stir the potatoes often at the start, then flip them all over halfway through frying. When the moisture bubbles subside, use a slotted spoon to carefully remove the chips and place them directly onto a kitchen cloth or paper towel to absorb any excess oil. Transfer the chips into a bowl when they are still a little warm and toss them with about 2 tbsp Aleppo Pepper Powder. Store in an airtight container lined with a kitchen towel or paper towel at room temperature for up to 5 days.

CONTINUES

CARAMELIZED GARLIC, GERMAN BUTTER POTATO + PINE NUT SOUP /

¼ cup olive oil
8 cloves garlic
2 onions, roughly chopped
8 German butter potatoes, skins on + scrubbed clean, quartered
2 tsp salt
1 tsp white pepper
¼ tsp ground nutmeg
½ cup raw pine nuts

Note | *Remember when blending hot ingredients to always leave a small air vent at the top of the container to let the pressure and steam release while blending. We recommend removing the plastic cap in the center of the Vitamix lid and covering it loosely with a kitchen towel.*

Makes 6 servings | In a large saucepot on low heat, add the olive oil and garlic cloves, allowing them to slowly caramelize to a light brown color, and release that sweet and mellow roasted garlic smell. Add the onions and sweat until they are soft and translucent. Add all the remaining ingredients and 6 cups water, bring the soup up to a simmer, and cook for approximately 40 minutes or until the liquid has reduced by a quarter.

Working in small batches, blend the soup in a Vitamix until it is silky-smooth. Once blended, check for seasoning and adjust as needed.

PLATING /

1 recipe Caramelized Garlic, German Butter Potato + Pine Nut Soup (left)
1 recipe Aleppo Pepper Powder Potato Chips (page 143)
¼ cup Smoked Sunflower Oil (page 51)
Fresh bittercress, for garnish
Pepper, to taste

Evenly distribute the soup between six bowls. Top each bowl with a small stack of Aleppo Pepper Powder Potato Chips, and drizzle a little Smoked Sunflower Oil on top. Garnish with fresh cress or microgreens and some fresh ground pepper, to taste.

RUTABAGA //

Caramelized Rutabaga, Quince Gastrique, Quince Coulis, Fermented
Porcini Puree, Pickled Onions, Pickled Sitka Spruce Buds, Vegetable Bottarga

Serves 6 | Winter vegetables, take a bow to the almighty rutabaga, the season's workhorse.
This quintessential crop packs a rich and mellow earthy flavor, with a texture between a turnip and
a parsnip. Its versatility lends itself to both sweet and savory dishes, keeping populations nourished
all over the world through those dismal cold months. Here we have a little fun spotlighting the rutabaga and quince in their peak moments, while using some preserved and fermented ingredients from
seasons past. With all the components, this dish is a flavor blaster, sure to excite your hibernating
winter taste buds.

FERMENTED PORCINI MUSHROOMS /

2.2 lb porcini mushrooms
20 g salt (2% of the weight of the porcini mushrooms)

Makes 2 cups | Clean the porcini mushrooms using
a brush or kitchen towel, removing all dirt and debris.
Cut them into 2-inch pieces and lay out flat on a baking
sheet lined with parchment paper. Freeze for 4 hours.
(Freezing the mushrooms breaks down their cellular
structure, allowing more of their liquid to be released
for the fermentation process.) Remove from the freezer
and toss with the salt.

**Either Ferment the Mushrooms in a Vacuum
Bag** | Place the salted frozen mushrooms in a single
layer in a vacuum bag, making sure to include all the
salt. Vacuum on high suction and seal the very top of
the bag in order to have room to puncture and reseal
through the fermentation process.

Or Ferment the Mushrooms in a Jar | Alterna-
tively, add the salted mushrooms to a sterilized 32 oz
mason jar with a lid. Fill a resealable plastic bag with
2% salted water and lay it on top of the mushrooms to
stop any air interfering with the fermentation process.
Cover the container with the lid but leave a small gap
to let gases out.

With either method, ferment the mushrooms at room
temperature (72°F) for approximately 5 to 7 days. Make
sure to check the mushrooms daily. For the vacuum
method, the bag may start to inflate with gas. You can
make a small cut at the top of the bag to release the
gas, and then reseal it. For the jar method, make sure
that the mushrooms are completely submerged in their
juices. You'll also want to taste the mushrooms after a
few days, checking the acidity of the liquid; it should
be tart but not too overpowering. The final product
you're ultimately looking for is a tangy umami flavor,
balancing salty and sour with a mushroom aroma.

Once you have the desired flavor, strain out the liquid
from the mushrooms through a fine-mesh strainer.
Reserve the liquid and the mushrooms separately in
two airtight containers. Store these in the fridge for up
to 2 days, or freeze them to preserve the flavors without
further fermentation.

CONTINUES

FERMENTED PORCINI PUREE /

2 Yukon Gold potatoes
½ cup Fermented Porcini Mushrooms (page 147)
1 tbsp reserved liquid from the Fermented
    Porcini Mushrooms (page 147)
½ tsp pepper
2 tbsp maple syrup

Makes 2 cups | Score the potato skins with a paring knife around the outside of the potatoes, cutting just through the skin. Add to a large pot with 8 cups salted water and bring to a boil. Once boiling, reduce the heat to a simmer and cook the potatoes until fork-tender. Strain out the potatoes and carefully peel off the skins. Let the potatoes cool slightly. Place the peeled potatoes and all the remaining ingredients in a Vitamix and blend until smooth. Transfer to an airtight container and store in the fridge for up to 5 days.

QUINCE COULIS /

2 large quinces
Juice of 1 lemon
½ cup sugar

Makes 2 cups | Peel the quinces and set the peels aside to be used for the Quince Gastrique (right). Remove and discard the cores and give the quinces a rough chop. Place the chopped quinces, lemon juice, sugar, and 1 cup water in a small saucepot and bring up to a simmer. Simmer for approximately 15 minutes, then transfer to a Vitamix and blend to a smooth consistency. Transfer to a container and allow to cool. Seal the container and store in the fridge for up to 7 days.

QUINCE GASTRIQUE /

½ cup birch syrup
Peels of 2 large quinces from Quince Coulis (left)
½ cup red wine vinegar
1 tsp salt
½ tsp pepper

Makes ½ cup | In a pan on medium-high heat, warm the birch syrup and quince peels; pay close attention to the birch syrup as it begins to caramelize and reduce, as it will burn rather quickly. Once the birch syrup has reduced by half, pull the pan off the heat and add the vinegar to stop the caramelization process; keep your hand out of the way, as this process will generate a lot of steam. Place the pan back onto the heat and season with salt and pepper. Continue to cook until the liquid has reduced by half. Remove from the heat and set aside. Store in an airtight container in the fridge for up to 1 week.

CARAMELIZED RUTABAGA /

2 tbsp olive oil
4 cups peeled and cut into 1-inch cubes rutabaga
1 tsp salt
1 tsp pepper
2 tbsp Quince Vinegar (page 46)
2 tbsp Quince Gastrique (above)

Makes 6 servings | In a large frying pan on high heat, heat the olive oil. Add the cubed rutabaga and sauté for 1 minute, until you see some caramelization. Season with salt and pepper, then add the Quince Vinegar and Quince Gastrique. Cook on medium-low heat until the rutabaga is cooked through, approximately 10 to 15 minutes, and nicely glazed with the gastrique. Check for seasoning. Serve immediately with any gastrique left in the pan.

PLATING /

1 ½ cups Quince Coulis (left)
1 recipe Caramelized Rutabaga (left)
1 ½ cups Fermented Porcini Puree (left)
1 ½ cups (approximately 30 petals) Pickled Onions
   (page 35)
½ cup Pickled Sitka Spruce Buds (page 35)
Fennel fronds, for garnish
¼ block Vegetable Bottarga (page 45), grated

Lay out six shallow bowls. Place ¼ cup Quince Coulis
in the center of each bowl. Distribute the Caramelized
Rutabaga evenly on top of the coulis and drizzle any
remaining gastrique around the rutabaga and onto
the bottom of each dish. Spoon dollops (about ¼ cup
per plate) of the Fermented Porcini Puree around the
rutabaga. Top the dish with Pickled Onions, a sprinkle
of Pickled Sitka Spruce Buds, and some fennel fronds.
Using a Microplane, grate the Vegetable Bottarga over
each plate, giving a generous coating of shavings.

SPRING //

// You know spring has officially arrived when our foragers come out of hibernation. The thaw of the land, and our souls, is accelerated when we put those first delicate blossoms and spring shoots on the plate. Some of the most unique flavors appear on our spring menu through the wildcrafted ingredients picked by forager Lance Staples and our team. Wild blossoms get processed into vinegars and syrups for us to enjoy throughout the year, as most have extremely short harvesting windows. Spruce tips and other wild buds awaken the palate through their naturally bright textures and flavors. With how short-lived and unpredictable it can sometimes be, spring keeps us on our toes, and we are always ready and eager to dance alongside it.

STINGING
NETTLE SOUP //

Serves 6 | This vibrant and velvety soup is nutrient-rich, creamy, and fresh. Stinging nettle is a wild leafy plant that is most prolific in spring and best enjoyed in the earlier part of the growing season. Nettles are high in iron and similar in flavor to spinach. You can make this soup all year round by replacing the nettles with more spinach.

4 cups stinging nettles (see Note)

4 cups spinach

1 cup sliced onions

4 cloves garlic, roughly chopped

Salt and pepper, to taste

½ cup dry white wine

1 lb Yukon Gold potatoes, diced in approximately
   1-inch pieces

2 tbsp maple syrup

¼ cup Almond Crème Fraîche (page 28), for serving

Note | *The tiny needle-like hairs that cover stinging nettles can cause skin irritation or rash. When handling raw nettles, always wear gloves or use tongs!*

Wash the stinging nettles, then blanch (see page 21) in a pot of boiling water for 30 seconds. Use a slotted spoon to remove the nettles from the pot and place them directly into an ice bath. Repeat the process with the spinach. Remove both from the ice bath, squeeze out as much water as possible, and set aside in a separate bowl.

Place the onions and garlic in a medium pot on medium heat and season with salt and pepper. Sauté for approximately 5 minutes, until soft. Before the onions begin to brown, add the white wine and continue to cook until the liquid in the pot is reduced by half. Add the diced potatoes and cover with 8 cups water. Simmer for 20 minutes or until the potatoes are cooked through and the liquid has again reduced by half.

Remove the pot from the heat and transfer the soup to a metal container, placed in an ice bath. Allow the soup to cool for 10 minutes. Working in batches, add half of the soup to a Vitamix with half of the blanched nettles and spinach. Blend to a smooth consistency, then pass through a fine-mesh strainer. Repeat this process with the other half of the ingredients. Whisk in the maple syrup and season with salt and pepper to taste.

To serve, heat the soup on low heat until warm. Do not boil during this stage, as you will overcook your greens and the soup will start to discolor and change in flavor. Garnish with a drizzle of our Almond Crème Fraîche and some fresh-cracked black pepper.

Nettle

FIDDLEHEAD
GOMAE //

Serves 6 | We flip tradition with this gomae recipe, made from wild-foraged fiddleheads! Fiddleheads are the young shoots of the wild ostrich fern, recognizable from their coiled-up circular shape. Green and foresty in flavor, they need little help to showcase their uniqueness and are often best served with just a little butter or oil and salt and pepper. But we're going full flavor here, tossing them in our house sesame dressing and adding even more depth with a little sake thrown in for good measure. Fiddleheads pack an awesome crunch, and their shape makes them well suited to hold sauce.

4 cups fiddleheads (see Note)
2 tsp salt
⅓ cup sesame seeds
1 tbsp sugar
1 tsp dry sake
1 tsp mirin
1 tbsp soy sauce

Note | *Foraging for fiddleheads requires experience and good plant knowledge, as there are copycats that are considered inedible. They should also never be consumed raw! Fiddleheads are a spring delicacy with a relatively short availability window, but time it right and you should be able to find fiddleheads at your local farmers' market. If fiddleheads are not available in your area, you can substitute cut asparagus.*

Clean the fiddleheads thoroughly under cold water, picking off any brown leaves or husks from the stems and coil. Trim off the very end where the harvest cut was made, and let them soak in cold water to remove any dirt and debris.

In a large pot, bring 12 cups water and the salt to a boil. Strain the fiddleheads out of their soaking water and add them to the boiling water. Blanch for 1 minute, then remove with a slotted spoon and transfer directly to an ice bath. Leave them in the ice bath for 1 minute, then strain.

Make the Gomae | Lightly squeeze out any excess water from each fiddlehead at the same time as uncoiling each one, leaving a long spiraled little fern. Set aside to be mixed in with the gomae.

Heat a small pan on low heat and add the sesame seeds. Toast until the seeds begin to pop and change to a light amber color. Separate ¼ cup sesame seeds for the gomae and set aside the rest of the toasted seeds to finish the dish.

Place the toasted ¼ cup sesame seeds and the sugar in a mortar and pestle and grind to a smooth, thick paste. Transfer to a large mixing bowl, then add the sake, mirin, and soy sauce and mix well. Add the uncoiled fiddleheads to the bowl and mix until evenly coated.

Serve in individual dishes or family style topped with the reserved toasted sesame seeds.

RED-FLOWERING CURRANT //

Puff Pastry Tart, Vanilla Caramelized Whey Ricotta,
Red-Flowering Currant Jelly

Serves 6 | We get excited when red-flowering currants blossom. These harbingers of spring have berries that don't taste all that special, but their racy pink flowers make for the perfect aromatic preserve—and awaken our senses after a long, wet winter. Add the fresh caramelized whey ricotta—light, fluffy, and delicate in flavor—paired with an airy puff pastry, and you have a not-too-sweet delightful dessert. Top this pastry with any seasonal jam to enjoy all year round.

PUFF PASTRY TART /

DOUGH
1 cup pastry flour + ¼ cup for dusting
1½ tsp sugar
¼ tsp salt
2 tbsp unsalted butter, room temperature
¾ tbsp fresh lemon juice

BEURRAGE
¾ cup unsalted butter, room temperature
¼ cup pastry flour

Note | *Remember to keep your surface dusted with a small amount of flour to prevent the dough from sticking. If you're pressed for time, you can put the dough in the freezer between rotations to speed up the process. You can prepare the pastry squares in advance and bake at a later time. Just freeze them, thaw, and follow the baking instructions below.*

Makes 6 (3 × 3-inch) pastries | Make the Dough | If using a stand mixer, fit it with the dough hook attachment, then add the flour, sugar, salt, butter, and lemon juice to the bowl. Set the mixer to low, then slowly pour in ⅓ cup cold water until the dough comes together and is pulling away from the sides. Remove from the mixing bowl, turn out onto a floured work surface, and knead by hand for 4 minutes.

Alternatively, if mixing by hand, place the 1 cup of pastry flour in a circular mound on a clean work surface. Using your hand, create a well in the center.

Add the sugar, salt, lemon juice, and ⅓ cup cold water to the well. Stir the ingredients in the center, gradually incorporating more of the flour from the outside, working until it's all combined. Break the butter into small pieces and begin to knead them into the flour mixture. It's important to keep kneading for 10 minutes to build gluten and structure in the dough.

When fully kneaded, shape the dough into a flat rectangle about 4 × 6 inches in size. Wrap with plastic wrap and rest in the fridge for 30 minutes.

Make the Beurrage | Using a stand mixer fitted with the paddle attachment, whip the butter for 30 seconds. Scrape down the sides of the bowl. Add the flour and continue mixing until all the ingredients are incorporated.

Shape the beurrage to about the same size as the dough (a flat rectangle about 4 × 6 inches). Wrap in plastic wrap and refrigerate for 30 minutes or until the butter firms up, making it easier to handle.

Make the Puff Pastry | Dust a clean work surface with flour and roll out the beurrage to a 8 × 6-inch rectangle. Place the chilled dough on top of the lower half of the beurrage and fold the other (top) half over the top of the dough. Gently pinch the sides to attach them together.

CONTINUES

a second baking sheet underneath your main baking sheet. This acts as a buffer for the bottom of the pastry from the heat of the oven and helps prevent it from burning. Bake for 15 minutes.

RED-FLOWERING CURRANT JELLY /

    3 cups red-flowering currant blossoms
    Juice of 1 lemon
    4 tbsp pectin powder
    4 cups sugar

Makes 3 (16 oz) jars | In a medium pot, bring the blossoms and 6 cups water to a boil. Reduce the heat and simmer on low for 15 minutes. Remove from the heat and strain the liquid into a bowl, discarding the blossoms. Allow to cool slightly, then add the lemon juice.

Pour the liquid back into the pot and add the pectin powder, making sure to whisk it in evenly. Bring back to a boil, stirring often, then stir in the sugar. Continue to boil for 2 more minutes, then remove from the heat. While the liquid is still warm and hasn't yet set, pour into three 16 oz sterilized mason jars and cover with their lids. Store in the fridge for up to 3 months.

VANILLA CARAMELIZED WHEY RICOTTA /

    8 cups whole milk
    2½ cups buttermilk
    1 cup heavy cream
    1 cup sugar
    1 tbsp fresh lemon juice
    1 vanilla pod, scraped, or 2 tsp vanilla extract
    1 tsp salt

Makes 1½ cups | In a large pot on low heat, warm up the whole milk, buttermilk, and cream for about 20 minutes, stirring often, until it reaches 190°F and the milk solids have separated from the whey. Remove from the heat and let stand for 10 minutes.

Gently roll out the combined dough and beurrage to a 6 × 9-inch rectangle, being careful not to let any butter break through the dough. Then fold the rectangle into thirds to create a rectangle about 6 × 3 inches in size. Cover with plastic wrap, and place back into the fridge for another 25 minutes. Repeat this rolling, folding, and chilling process five more times, rotating the dough 90 degrees at each turn, until you've reached a total of six folds, making sure to refrigerate for 25 minutes between each turn. This step is very important as it will keep the butter cold, making it easier to layer the pastry and preventing it from melting and falling flat. At the end of the sixth fold, wrap and refrigerate for a final 30 minutes.

When the dough is ready to use, preheat the oven to 410°F. Evenly roll the dough out to a 6 × 9-inch rectangle and cut into six 3-inch squares. Line a baking sheet with parchment paper and lay out the squares on top. Stack

Line a large strainer with cheesecloth and place a container underneath. Empty the contents of the pot into the strainer. Tie the tops of the cheesecloth together and let the whey slowly drain (for about 1 hour) through the cheesecloth into the container below. For this recipe we're aiming for a less creamy, denser ricotta-style texture, but still fluffy. Continue to strain out the whey until you reach the desired texture. Once there, transfer the ricotta from the cheesecloth to a large bowl. Cover and refrigerate.

Transfer 3 cups of the whey (discarding any remaining whey) to a small pot and simmer on medium heat until the liquid reduces by two-thirds. Add the sugar, lemon juice, and half of the vanilla and turn the heat down to low. Continue to cook, stirring often, until the liquid has reduced again by half. Transfer this whey caramel to a glass or metal container and place the container over an ice bath, allowing it to cool.

Remove the ricotta from the fridge and mix in the salt, cooled whey caramel, and remaining vanilla. Store in a sealed container in the fridge for up to 5 days.

PLATING /

    1 recipe Puff Pastry Tart (page 159)
    1 recipe Vanilla Caramelized Whey Ricotta (left)
    1 cup Red-Flowering Currant Jelly (left)
    Picked red-flowering currant blossoms and leaves,
      for garnish

Preheat the oven to 375°F. Lay the puff pastry squares onto a baking sheet lined with parchment paper. Generously spoon the ricotta on top of each pastry square. Bake for 5 minutes, until the ricotta is warmed through and soft on the outer edges. Remove from the oven and carefully transfer to a plate. Pour the Red-Flowering Currant Jelly over the ricotta and garnish each tart with red flowering currant blossoms and a few leaves.

RADISH //

Spring Radishes, Ashed Spring Onion Almond Sauce,
Shaved Rhubarb, Pickled Ramps, Rhubarb + Ramp Vinaigrette

Serves 6 | Full disclosure, our team was addicted to this dish when it was on the menu. At the end of shift, with tall glasses of rosé in hand, we'd delight in dragging a crisp radish through the thick and creamy almond sauce. At the risk of sounding trite, this is the best crudité plate you'll ever have.

Note | *For this dish, we use all the varieties of radishes available to us through our farmers each season. You should be able to find most of those listed below at your local farmers' market. If not, use whatever you can find. Try to leave an inch of stem on each one.*

RHUBARB + RAMP VINAIGRETTE /

½ cup diced rhubarb
½ cup ramp vinegar from Pickled Ramps
   (page 31, see Note)
½ tsp salt
¼ tsp pepper
6 tbsp grapeseed oil

Note | *The ramp vinegar called for here is from our jarred Pickled Ramps, which also get used in this dish. If you don't have it made, substitute with white balsamic vinegar.*

Makes 1½ cups | Place the diced rhubarb, ramp vinegar, salt, and pepper in a Vitamix. Blend until smooth. With the blender on medium, slowly add and emulsify the grapeseed oil. Store in a sealed container in the fridge for up to 1 week (the leftover marinade can be used for another batch of radishes or as a salad dressing).

ASHED SPRING ONION ALMOND SAUCE /

6 spring onions
2 tbsp finely diced shallots
1 tsp minced garlic
2 tbsp olive oil
1 tsp salt
½ tsp pepper
¼ cup sherry vinegar
2 tbsp maple syrup
¼ tsp charcoal powder
½ cup ground raw almonds

Makes 2½ cups | Using an open flame, char the spring onions until they are nice and dark. Allow to cool, then roughly chop them. Set aside.

In a large pan on medium heat, sweat the shallots and garlic in the olive oil until soft and translucent. Season with salt and pepper, then add the sherry vinegar, maple syrup, and 1¼ cups of water. Cook on medium heat for approximately 2 minutes. Turn off the heat and mix in the charcoal powder, ground almonds, and chopped spring onions.

Transfer in small batches to a Vitamix and blend until smooth and creamy. Store in an airtight container in the fridge for up to 5 days.

CONTINUES

PLATING /

6 French breakfast radishes
6 amethyst radishes
6 red radishes
6 ping pong radishes
1 recipe Rhubarb + Ramp Vinaigrette (page 163)
¾ cup shaved rhubarb
1 recipe Ashed Spring Onion Almond Sauce
   (page 163)
½ cup sliced Pickled Ramps (page 31)
1 cup watercress
Sea salt

Note | *This recipe can be plated individually, the way we do in the restaurant, or as a bowl of marinated radishes with the sauce on the side as a dip.*

Wash and dry the radishes thoroughly, then marinate in the Rhubarb + Ramp Vinaigrette for 5 minutes. In the last minute, add the shaved rhubarb. This will give the radishes and rhubarb a light pickle and soften them a touch, while still keeping a nice crunch.

Lay out six plates and add a large spoonful of Ashed Spring Onion Almond Sauce to each plate. Using a palette knife, lightly spread a portion of the sauce across the plate. Remove the radishes and rhubarb from the vinaigrette and distribute them evenly between the plates, wedging them into the sauce. Garnish with the Pickled Ramps and watercress, and season with sea salt.

VICTORY GARDENS //

During WWI and WWII, people were encouraged to grow their own food to "do their part" for the war effort and contribute to securing a stable, sustainable food supply. As a result, neighborhood farmers became more involved in their local communities as people turned to them for their advice and expertise. When Vancouver master gardener and gardening coach Sam Philips joined forces with her colleagues—Lisa Giroday and Sandra Lopuch—to start a gardening collective, they based it on the historic Victory Gardens model, updated for today's households and businesses.

Today the Victory Gardens team designs, builds, and maintains gardens, as well as offers coaching to people on how to keep their own gardens growing and thriving. With their help, anyone can grow delicious, fresh produce in their own backyard, garden plot, or balcony planter.

The Acorn started working with Victory Gardens in 2013 with the goal of sourcing the freshest possible organic herbs and other hard-to-find ingredients for use in the restaurant. They helped build a garden specific to the herbs, edible blossoms, and vegetables that we wanted to serve most often. The Acorn's garnishes, cocktail ingredients, and savory herbs are now all from this prolific garden, including calendula, anise hyssop, shiso, parsley, basil, lavender, rosemary, tarragon, thyme, mustard green flowers, and cucumber flowers. Our involvement with them has brought a closer connection for The Acorn team to the ingredients we serve.

INSPIRATIONS | Grandparents, community, neighbors, sharing, friendships, and fresh food.
THE ACORN-AT-HOME | If you can't find an ingredient, consider growing it.

HOP SHOOT
SALAD //

Sautéed Hop Shoots, Maple Blossom Vinaigrette,
Browned Hazelnut Butter, Toasted Hazelnuts, Pickled Hop Shoot Stems

Serves 6 | We combine two unique ingredients here to create this warm spring salad: hop shoots and maple blossoms. This dish was an immediate hit at the restaurant and is both bright and earthy—with the acid from the pickled hop shoots grounded by the richness of the hazelnut butter—compelling you to eat through the complexity of its flavors.

Note | *The Pickled Hop Shoot Stems (page 31) that are used in both the Sautéed Hop Shoots and for plating, require 3 days' pickling, so be sure to prepare them in advance.*

BROWNED HAZELNUT BUTTER /

2½ cups raw hazelnuts, skins on
2 tsp salt

Makes 1½ cups | Preheat the oven to 350°F. Spread the raw hazelnuts on a baking sheet and toast them until their skins start to darken and blister, approximately 10 to 15 minutes. Remove from the oven, and working in batches while they are still warm, use a kitchen towel to rub off all the skins, shaking the towel clean between batches. Set aside ½ cup hazelnuts.

Place the remaining hazelnuts, salt, and ¼ cup water in a Vitamix and blend on medium speed. Use the tamper to work the hazelnuts around, keeping them moving in the blender. If you do not have a tamper, turn off the machine periodically and scrape the sides of the blender with a spatula. Turn the blender to high and let it run for 3 to 5 minutes or until the mixture is silky-smooth; once it begins to blend freely, keep the machine running until the butter is creamy with no pieces of hazelnuts remaining. This butter will take some time to come together. This can also be made in a food processor, although you will need to allow it to blend longer in order to achieve a smooth texture. Store in an airtight container in the fridge for up to 2 weeks.

MAPLE BLOSSOM VINAIGRETTE /

¼ cup Big Leaf Maple Blossom Vinegar (page 46) or high-quality white balsamic vinegar
Juice of 1 lemon
2½ tbsp maple syrup
1 tbsp Dijon mustard
1½ cups grapeseed oil
1 tsp salt
½ tsp pepper

Makes 2 cups | Place the vinegar, lemon juice, maple syrup, and Dijon mustard in a Vitamix and blend on medium speed until combined. Slowly drizzle in the grapeseed oil and continue to blend until emulsified. Season with salt and pepper. Store in the fridge for up to 1 month and use it as a dressing for your favorite salads.

CONTINUES

SAUTÉED HOP SHOOTS /

40 hop shoots (reserved from
   Pickled Hop Shoot Stems (page 31)
1 tsp olive oil
1 tsp salt
¼ tsp pepper
¼ cup Maple Blossom Vinaigrette (page 168)

Makes 6 servings | Trim away any large leaves
from the hop shoots, cut or snap off the ends (if you
didn't already do this to make the Pickled Hop Shoot
Stems, page 31), and discard. Heat a large sauté pan on
high heat. Add the olive oil and hop shoots and sauté
for approximately 20 seconds, until the hop shoots
have wilted slightly. Season with salt and pepper. Add
the Maple Blossom Vinaigrette and stir the shoots to
completely coat them in vinaigrette. Remove from
the heat and serve immediately, as directed.

PLATING /

¾ cup Browned Hazelnut Butter (page 168)
1 recipe Sautéed Hop Shoots (left)
½ cup toasted hazelnuts reserved from Browned
   Hazelnut Butter (page 168), roughly chopped
6 tbsp Pickled Hop Shoot Stems (page 31),
   drained from pickling liquid
2 cups peppercress, for garnish

Lay out six plates. Evenly distribute the hazelnut butter
in the center of each. Curl the warm hop shoots over
the hazelnut butter, and drizzle with the remaining
vinaigrette from the pan (about 1 tbsp per plate).
Sprinkle with chopped toasted hazelnuts and Pickled
Hop Shoot Stems, and garnish with peppercress.

Big Leaf Maple
Blossom

ELDERFLOWER
PANNA COTTA //

Elderflower Panna Cotta, Knotweed Crisps, Salmonberry Sauce

Serves 6 | This floral take on a classic creamy panna cotta gets a wild kick with tangy Knotweed Crisps and salmonberries—making it an exceptional representation of what spring tastes like in British Columbia!

KNOTWEED PUREE /

1 cup finely chopped Japanese knotweed (see Note)
2 tbsp sugar
1 tsp salt
Juice of 1 lemon

Note | *Trim the knotweed's leaves and stems. If it's later in the season and your knotweed is a little woodier, peel the tougher outer layer back. Roughly chop, then let soak in cold water to clean it inside and out. Remove from the water and finely chop.*

Makes ¾ cup | Place all the ingredients in a large saucepot and bring them to a simmer. Continue to simmer until the liquid has reduced by two-thirds. Transfer to a Vitamix and blend on high until silky-smooth. Store in an airtight container in the fridge for up to 5 days.

KNOTWEED CRISPS /

1 egg white
1 recipe Knotweed Puree (above)

Makes 6 servings | In a large bowl, whisk the egg white until you've reached stiff peaks. Using a spatula, carefully fold the Knotweed Puree into the egg white, making sure to incorporate evenly without overmixing.

Spread the mixture evenly onto a dehydrator sheet, about ⅛ inch thick. Dehydrate on high (165°F) for 8 to 12 hours until crispy. Alternatively, bake on a baking sheet lined with parchment paper in your oven at 200°F for approximately 15 minutes, rotate, then bake for another 15 minutes until dry and crispy.

Once dry and crisp, break the sheet apart into large bite-sized pieces. Store in an airtight container in a cool, dry place for up to 7 days.

SALMONBERRY SAUCE /

3 cups salmonberries, washed thoroughly
¼ cup sugar
2 tbsp fresh lemon juice

Makes 1 cup | Place all the ingredients in a Vitamix and blend until smooth. Strain through a fine-mesh strainer. Store in an airtight container in the fridge for up to 5 days.

ELDERFLOWER SYRUP /

¼ cup sugar
¼ cup water
¼ cup fresh elderflower blossoms

Makes ½ cup | Place all the ingredients in a saucepot and bring to a simmer. Simmer for 30 seconds, then remove from the heat and let cool at room temperature for 5 minutes. Strain through a fine-mesh strainer, pressing the blossoms with the back of a ladle to remove as much liquid as possible. Store in an airtight container in the fridge for up to 1 month.

CONTINUES

ELDERFLOWER PANNA COTTA /

1 cup heavy cream
1 recipe Elderflower Syrup (page 172)
1 tsp agar-agar powder

Makes 6 servings | Clean and thoroughly dry a rectangular silicone pastry mold with six 4 oz cavities. Place it on a baking sheet, and place the baking sheet on a flat, level work surface.

In a medium pot on low heat, bring the cream and Elderflower Syrup to a simmer, then whisk in the agar-agar. Simmer for another 5 minutes, whisking constantly to ensure that the agar-agar is dissolved. Strain through a fine-mesh strainer (ideally into a container with a spout for easy pouring). Pour the mixture into each of the mold's six cavities, filling them to the top.

Let the tray of panna cotta sit, uncovered, at room temperature for 20 minutes, then refrigerate for 30 minutes to cool fully.

PLATING /

1 recipe Elderflower Panna Cotta (left)
1 recipe Salmonberry Sauce (page 172)
1 recipe Knotweed Crisps (page 172)
Fresh salmonberries, for garnish
Wood sorrel or red-veined sorrel leaves, for garnish

Lay out six plates. Unmold the panna cotta one by one by gently bending the silicone and delicately flipping the panna cotta into your hand—be careful, they are fragile! Carefully place one on each plate. Add a spoonful of Salmonberry Sauce to each plate. Sprinkle with a few Knotweed Crisps and garnish with fresh salmonberries and wood sorrel.

WILD GARLIC
FRIED POTATOES //

Serves 6 | We couldn't write a cookbook and NOT include our brunch potatoes recipe. As with everything in this cookbook, even the simplest recipes are going to taste 100% better when you're using organic and farm-direct ingredients. Trust us on this one.

COOKING
12 to 16 German butter potatoes
4 cloves garlic
3 tbsp olive oil
1 tbsp salt
1 tbsp pepper
6 sprigs thyme

FRYING
2 tbsp olive oil
2 tsp salt
1 tsp pepper
½ cup chopped wild garlic

Note | *A two-step process is the secret to this dish, and totally worth it. Slow-cooking and cooling the potatoes first gives them a soft, light, and flavorful center and a crispy outside when fried.*

Leaving the skin on, clean and dice the potatoes into 1-inch cubes. In a large saucepot on medium heat, sweat the garlic in the olive oil until the garlic is soft and translucent. Add the potatoes, season with salt and pepper, and cover with 8 cups water. Heat the potatoes up slowly until they have reached a simmer, then immediately turn the heat down to just under a simmer, as if you were poaching the potatoes. Slowly cook the potatoes for approximately 35 minutes, until they are cooked through but do not break apart. The key is to be patient and take this step slow as this will impart more garlic flavor, and the potatoes will be much juicier!

Remove from the heat, add the whole sprigs of thyme, and allow the potatoes to cool for 10 minutes in the liquid. Strain the potatoes and lay them out on a baking sheet to fully cool before sautéing.

In a large frying pan, heat the olive oil on medium-high heat and add the potatoes. Season with the salt and pepper and fry until crispy on all sides. Once crispy, add the chopped wild garlic and fry until the garlic begins to brown slightly.

Serve these potatoes alongside your favorite brunch dishes or on their own with our Herbed Hazelnut Dip (page 197) or Fermented Zucchini Puree (page 208).

ASPARAGUS, JUNIPER-CURED EGG YOLKS, WILD GARLIC //

Lemon Maple Asparagus, Juniper-Cured Egg Yolks,
Garlic Pickled Knotroot, Wild Garlic Oil, Wild Garlic Powder

Serves 6 | Nothing screams spring quite like asparagus. And we love the flavor affinity that asparagus and egg have with one another. Here, we take it one step further, curing egg yolk with locally foraged wild garlic and dried juniper berries, then garnishing the dish with pickled knotroot for extra crunch. Serve this as an appetizer or side dish, or pair it with our house-baked Focaccia Bread (page 226) for lunch.

JUNIPER-CURED EGG YOLKS /

HARD-CURED EGG YOLKS
4 tsp ground juniper berries
1 cup salt
1 cup sugar
2 egg yolks

SOFT-CURED EGG YOLKS
4 tsp ground juniper berries
¼ cup minced wild garlic
1 cup salt
1 cup sugar
6 egg yolks

Note | *This recipe calls for BOTH hard- and soft-cured egg yolks. It takes 4½ days to hard-cure the yolks, so you'll want to plan ahead for this dish. Soft-cured egg yolks will take 1½ hours. The hard yolks take on much more of a salty juniper taste with a chewy center, and are grated over the dish for a salty umami topping. The soft yolks have a subtler juniper flavor and a soft runny center, and break up around the asparagus, almost doubling as a sauce.*

Makes 2 hard-cured and 6 soft-cured yolks | **Make the Hard-Cured Egg Yolks** | In a bowl, mix together the juniper berries, salt, and sugar. Evenly distribute about half of the salt mixture along the bottom of an 8-inch square glass baking dish. Using your finger, create two yolk-sized depressions in the salt mixture. Gently place an egg yolk in each depression, and evenly sprinkle the remaining salt mixture over the yolks. Cover and refrigerate for 4 days.

When ready, carefully remove the yolks with a spoon. Gently rinse under cold water to remove any excess salt mixture.

Place the cured yolks on a dehydrator sheet and dehydrate on medium (145°F) for 12 hours. Alternatively, bake the yolks on a baking sheet lined with parchment paper in your oven at 250°F with the door cracked open for 2 hours. Store in an airtight container in the fridge for up to 2 weeks.

Make the Soft-Cured Egg Yolks | In a bowl, mix together the juniper berries, minced wild garlic, salt, and sugar. Follow the method above, making six yolk-sized depressions in the salt mixture this time. Refrigerate these yolks for only 1½ hours. When ready, carefully remove the yolks with a spoon. Gently rinse under cold water to remove any excess salt mixture.

CONTINUES

WILD GARLIC POWDER /

2 cups finely chopped wild garlic scraps
    from Wild Garlic Oil (page 50)
1 tsp salt
1 tsp sugar
1 tsp citric acid

Note | *This recipe uses the wild garlic trim and scraps from our Wild Garlic Oil recipe. The idea is to use all parts of the wild garlic so nothing goes to waste.*

Makes ½ cup | Spread the garlic scraps onto a dehydrator sheet and dehydrate on medium (145°F) for approximately 6 hours. Alternatively, bake on a baking sheet lined with parchment paper in your oven at 200°F (with the door cracked open) for for 1 to 2 hours until dry and crispy.

Place the dried garlic scraps, salt, sugar, and citric acid in a Vitamix or spice grinder and blend until you've reached a fine powder or dust. Store in an airtight container in a cool, dry place for up to 1 month.

LEMON MAPLE VINAIGRETTE /

½ cup fresh lemon juice
½ cup olive oil
2 tbsp maple syrup
¼ tsp pepper
Salt, to taste

Makes 1 cup | In a small bowl, mix all the ingredients thoroughly together until well incorporated. Store in an airtight container in the fridge for up to 1 month.

BLANCHED ASPARAGUS /

30 stalks asparagus
5 (8-inch) lengths food-safe twine

Note | *To extend the life of raw asparagus, trim the ends and tie them in bundles with twine (as instructed below).*

Add 1 inch of water to a tall container and stand the asparagus bundles up in the container. Cover with a damp towel and store in the fridge.

Makes 6 servings | Wash the asparagus and trim the ends, leaving the tender stalks. (The woody ends are great for making stocks and soups.) Bundle together five sets of six stalks, securing them with twine tied twice around.

Bring a large pot of salted water to a boil and prepare an ice bath. Drop the asparagus bundles into the boiling water one at a time and boil for 2 minutes. Using tongs, transfer to the ice bath and let cool for 2 minutes. Remove and pat down with a towel. Remove the twine using kitchen scissors. If preparing ahead of time, keep the blanched asparagus in the fridge and bring back to room temperature before serving.

PLATING /

1 recipe Blanched Asparagus (left),
    room temperature
1 recipe Lemon Maple Vinaigrette (left)
6 Soft-Cured Egg Yolks (page 179)
1 recipe Garlic Pickled Knotroot (page 32)
¼ cup Wild Garlic Oil (page 50)
Red amaranth, picked, for garnish
2 Hard-Cured Egg Yolks (page 179)
¼ cup Wild Garlic Powder (left)

Toss the Blanched Asparagus in the Lemon Maple Vinaigrette. Lay out six plates and divide the asparagus between them, laying the stalks out side by side. Carefully place a Soft-Cured Egg Yolk on top of each plate of asparagus. Distribute four pieces of Garlic Pickled Knotroot around each plate, drizzle everything liberally with the Wild Garlic Oil, and garnish with red amaranth. Using a Microplane, finely grate the Hard-Cured Egg Yolks over top. Lastly, using a fine sieve, dust Wild Garlic Powder over each plate.

MOREL VELOUTÉ //

Sautéed Morel Mushrooms, Wild Rice, White Mushroom Velouté,
Lovage Oil, Sitka Spruce Cone Relish

Serves 6 | We often attack our menu with an "you eat with your eyes" approach. Color and contrast play huge roles, and we're so fortunate to live in a region where there's an abundance of tasty and colorful veg growing in our backyard. This recipe really showcases the tender quality that Sitka spruce cones have in the early stages of growth; they have a wonderful citrus flavor that really brightens up the whole dish. With this recipe, the goal is to keep the velouté as white as possible so the contrast of the sautéed morels and Lovage Oil pop in the bowl. Don't be fooled by the apparent lightness of this dish. It's rich, creamy, and hearty!

Note | *If you can't find Sitka spruce cones in your area, you can substitute the Sitka Spruce Cone Relish with our Garlic Scape Relish (below).*

SITKA SPRUCE CONE RELISH /

½ cup young, green foraged Sitka spruce cones
1 tbsp olive oil
1 red onion, finely diced
¼ cup sugar
¼ cup apple cider vinegar
2 tsp salt
1 tsp pepper
1 tsp agar-agar

Makes 1 cup | Using a paring knife or your fingers, trim the seed scales off of the core of the cones. These are the purplish-green leafy scales that contain the seed. Discard the cores or feel free to keep them for another use, such as steeping them with a little bit of your favorite oil for a nice infused oil.

In a small saucepot, heat the olive oil on medium heat and sweat the red onions until soft and translucent. Add the spruce cone scales, sugar, apple cider vinegar, salt, pepper, and ¼ cup water and simmer for 10 minutes, until the liquid has reduced by two-thirds. Whisk in the agar-agar and simmer for another 5 minutes.

Remove from the heat and allow to cool slightly, then transfer to an airtight container to cool completely.

Once cool, the agar-agar will help to thicken the relish and give it more body. Store in an airtight container in the fridge for up to 1 month.

GARLIC SCAPE RELISH /

½ cup small-diced onions
¼ tsp caraway seeds
1 tbsp olive oil
1 cup sliced (in small discs) garlic scapes
1 tsp salt
½ tsp pepper
1 cup white vinegar
¼ cup sugar

Note | *This is an alternative to the Sitka Spruce Cone Relish recipe (left) if you do not have spruce cones available.*

Makes 1 cup | In a medium saucepot on medium-low heat, sweat the onions and caraway seeds in the olive oil until soft and translucent. Add the remaining ingredients and slowly cook down the liquid until it reduces in volume by three-quarters. Transfer to an airtight container and allow to cool, then seal with a lid; the relish should be thicker and sticky when cool. Store in the fridge for up to 2 weeks.

CONTINUES

WILD RICE /

1 cup finely diced onions
3 cloves garlic, minced
2 tbsp olive oil
1¼ cups Canadian wild rice or
    whatever wild rice is available to you
Salt and pepper, to taste

Makes 4 cups | In a medium saucepot on medium heat, sauté the onions and garlic in the olive oil. Add the rice and 3 cups water and stir. Cover with a lid, leaving just a crack open for steam to vent out. Reduce to low heat and cook for approximately 40 minutes, removing the lid and stirring occasionally, until the rice has cracked open and is tender but toothy. Season with salt and pepper.

WHITE MUSHROOM VELOUTÉ /

1 medium onion, diced
4 cloves garlic, sliced
2 tbsp olive oil
1 lb white mushrooms, thinly sliced
½ cup dry white wine
2 tsp salt
1 tsp white pepper

Makes 6 cups | In a medium saucepot on medium heat, sweat the onions and garlic in the olive oil until soft and translucent. Add the mushrooms and sauté until soft. Try not to brown any of the vegetables; the goal is to keep the sauce as creamy-white as possible. Add the white wine and cook for 2 minutes or until the liquid is reduced by half. Season with the salt and white pepper. Add 2 cups water and simmer for 20 minutes or until the liquid has again reduced by half. Working in batches, carefully blend everything in a Vitamix until smooth and velvety. Check the seasoning.

PLATING /

2 tbsp olive oil
24 morel mushrooms, ends trimmed
Salt and pepper, to taste
1 recipe White Mushroom Velouté (left)
1 recipe Wild Rice (left)
6 white mushrooms, trimmed and thinly sliced
¾ cup Sitka Spruce Cone Relish or Garlic Scape
    Relish (page 183)
½ cup Lovage Oil (page 50)
Lovage leaves, picked, for garnish

Heat a large saucepot on medium-high heat. Once it's nice and hot, add the olive oil and morel mushrooms, season with salt and pepper, and cook for approximately 30 seconds, stirring often. Remove from the heat and set aside.

Lay out six shallow bowls. Evenly pour in the White Mushroom Velouté. In the center of each bowl, gently add a ⅔-cup mounded island of Wild Rice. Add the sautéed morels, four per bowl, and top with the sliced white mushrooms and 2 tbsp of the relish. Drizzle the Lovage Oil generously over the velouté and garnish with picked lovage leaves.

MOREL MUSHROOMS
+ CAULIFLOWER PANISSE //

Sautéed Morel Mushrooms, Cauliflower Panisse, Morel–Salted Fried Cauliflower,
Lovage Almond Cream, Mushroom Red Wine Jus, Pickled Morel Mushrooms,
Candied Lichen

Serves 6 | Fluffy, savory chickpea flour cake; hearty and lively mushroom jus; candied wild lichen. This dish has it all. Chantal, one of our front-of-house managers and a farmers' market enthusiast, sums it up best: "This dish manages to be total comfort food, while also being unlike anything I have ever eaten before." Mic drop.

LOVAGE ALMOND CREAM /

½ cup ground raw almonds
1 probiotic capsule
¼ cup chopped lovage leaves
3 tbsp maple syrup
1 tsp salt

Makes 1½ cups | Place the ground almonds and 1 cup water in a Vitamix. Open the probiotic capsule and empty the contents into the Vitamix, discarding the casing. Blend until smooth. Pour the mixture into a sterilized 32 oz mason jar, cover with a towel and secure it with an elastic band around the neck. Place on the counter at room temperature for 48 hours, allowing it to ferment.

After 48 hours of fermentation, transfer the almond mixture back to the Vitamix. Add the lovage leaves, maple syrup, and salt. Blend until well incorporated and the texture is creamy and smooth. Store in an airtight container in the fridge for up to 5 days. The cream may produce bubbles over time as it continues to ferment slowly in the fridge.

CAULIFLOWER CREAM /

4 cloves garlic, sliced
3 cups finely chopped cauliflower trim (see Note)
1 tbsp salt
1 tsp white pepper

Note | *This is a great way to use up cauliflower trim. Don't be afraid to use the leaves and stems here. It's all good in this recipe!*

Makes 4 cups | Place all the ingredients and 3 cups water in a medium pot and bring to a simmer. Cook uncovered for 20 minutes or until the cauliflower is soft. Working in small batches, add the mixture to a Vitamix and blend until smooth. Set aside to use in the Cauliflower Panisse (page 188). Store in an airtight container in the fridge for up to 2 days.

CONTINUES

CAULIFLOWER PANISSE /

1 recipe Cauliflower Cream (page 187)
2 tbsp fresh lemon juice
1 tbsp salt
1 tsp white pepper
1¾ cups chickpea flour, sifted
8 cups canola oil

Makes 6 servings | In a large saucepot, bring the Cauliflower Cream, lemon juice, salt, and pepper to a simmer, then slowly whisk in the sifted chickpea flour. Continue to whisk for about 4 minutes until there are no lumps and everything is thoroughly blended. Cook on low heat for about 15 to 20 minutes, whisking often to help prevent the mixture from sticking to the bottom of the pot. The mixture will thicken up fast, and the batter will start to fall away from the sides of the pot as you stir.

Line a 2 × 6 × 10-inch cake pan with parchment paper. Transfer the batter to the prepared pan. Even out the surface with a spatula and gently cover the entire surface with another piece of parchment paper. (The goal is to seal the top of the panisse to prevent air from reaching it and drying it out.) Cover with a lid or plastic wrap and refrigerate to set for 12 hours, or overnight.

When ready, remove from the fridge and gently peel the parchment paper off the top. Flip the set panisse onto a cutting board and portion into six pieces, about 2 × 5 inches each. These can be stored in an airtight container in the fridge for up to 5 days before being cooked.

To cook, in a high-sided pot, heat the canola oil to 350°F, then submerge the panisse pieces in the oil. Fry until golden brown, approximately 3 minutes. Use a pair of tongs or a slotted spoon to carefully remove them from the oil and place directly onto a baking sheet lined with a kitchen cloth or paper towel to soak up any excess oil.

MUSHROOM RED WINE JUS /

1 onion, roughly chopped
10 cloves garlic, crushed
1 cup peeled and roughly chopped carrots
1 lb cremini mushrooms, cleaned and quartered
½ cup olive oil
1 tbsp salt
2 tbsp peppercorns
2 cups dry red wine or whatever is open
   on your counter
⅓ cup tomato paste
1 cup roughly chopped Yukon Gold potatoes,
   cleaned with skins on
10 sprigs thyme, leaves picked

Makes 4 cups | Preheat the oven to 400°F. Line a baking sheet with parchment paper. Toss the onions, garlic, carrots, and mushrooms with 2 tbsp olive oil and spread them out evenly on the prepared sheet. Roast for 30 minutes, tossing every 10 minutes. Once well caramelized, transfer the vegetables to a large saucepot on medium-high heat and sauté in the remaining olive oil to brown them even further. Season with the salt and add the peppercorns. Continue to sauté—you want it to be slightly sticky on the bottom of the pot—until you've built up a good caramelization.

Deglaze the pot with the red wine, scraping any sticky bits off the bottom of the pot. Cook on medium heat until the liquid has reduced by two-thirds. Add the tomato paste and cook on low heat, stirring often, until the color has changed to a deeper red-brown, about 5 to 7 minutes, being careful not to scorch the paste. Stir in 12 cups water and the potatoes and simmer for about 20 minutes, until the liquid has reduced by half.

Strain the liquid through a large-holed strainer, using the back of a ladle to press out as much sauce as possible, mashing the cooked vegetables to do so. Discard the vegetables left in the strainer and transfer the sauce back to the pot. Bring to a simmer, add the thyme, and continue to simmer until the sauce reduces by a third.

CONTINUES

Strain the sauce through a fine-mesh sieve. Use right away or, if preparing in advance, cool over an ice bath, then transfer to an airtight container and store in the fridge for up to 5 days. Alternatively, you can freeze the sauce and, when ready to use it, thaw and blend it once more to achieve a smooth consistency.

CANDIED LICHEN /

1 cup sugar
2 cups reindeer lichen
Salt, to taste

Note | *There really is no substitute for reindeer lichen so if you don't have access to it, just omit this component of the recipe.*

Makes 6 servings | Preheat the oven to 250°F. Place a wire rack on top of a baking sheet and set beside your stove. In a small stockpot, bring 4 cups water and the sugar to a simmer. Working in batches, add ½ cup lichen to the pot, submerge in the sugar mixture, and simmer for 1 minute. This will help remove any excess acids contained in the lichen. Using a slotted spoon or tongs, remove from the pot and place on the wire rack to drain. Season with salt, and once it's cool enough to touch, fluff the lichen back up with your fingers. Repeat this process until all the lichen is done. Transfer the lichen to a baking sheet lined with parchment paper, and bake for 10 minutes or until completely dry.

Candied lichen is best eaten right away, but it can be stored in an airtight container lined with paper towel, kept in a cool and dry spot, for up to 1 month.

MOREL SALT /

¼ cup crushed dried morel mushrooms
¼ cup kosher salt

Makes ½ cup | Add the dried morel mushrooms to a food processor or Vitamix and blend to a powder consistency.

Combine the powder and the salt and mix until thoroughly combined. Transfer to an airtight container and store at room temperature for up to 1 year.

MOREL-SALTED FRIED CAULIFLOWER /

4 cups canola oil
18 (1-inch) pieces cauliflower
Morel Salt (left), to taste

Makes 18 pieces | In a heavy-bottomed, high-sided 6-quart pot, heat the oil to 350°F. Gently place half the cauliflower in the oil and deep-fry until golden brown, about 45 seconds to 1 minute. Using a spider or slotted spoon, remove the pieces from the oil and place in a bowl lined with paper towel to soak up any extra oil. Toss immediately with some morel salt. Repeat with the second batch of cauliflower. Serve immediately.

PLATING /

2 tbsp olive oil
24 morel mushrooms, ends trimmed
Salt and pepper, to taste
1 recipe Mushroom Red Wine Jus (page 188)
¾ cup Lovage Almond Cream (page 187)
1 recipe Cauliflower Panisse (page 188)
1 recipe Morel-Salted Fried Cauliflower (above)
1 recipe Candied Lichen (left)
1 cup Pickled Morel Mushrooms (page 32)

Heat a large saucepot on high heat until it is nice and hot. Add the oil and morel mushrooms and season with salt and pepper. Sauté for just 30 seconds, stirring often. Add the Mushroom Red Wine Jus and bring to a simmer, then remove from the heat and season to taste.

Add about 2 tbsp Lovage Almond Cream to each of six plates, then one Cauliflower Panisse.

Divide the Morel-Salted Fried Cauliflower and sautéed morels between the plates, and drizzle the jus from the pan on and around the panisse. Garnish with the Candied Lichen and Pickled Morel Mushrooms.

SUMMER//

// Summer is when we see the most visitors from around the world— fortunately, it's also the most abundant season in British Columbia for fresh ingredients, so it's a time when our menu really gets to sing. With farmers' markets in full swing and our own farmers hand-delivering the fruits of their labor, summer is the season with the most fully formed constellation of creators, growers, foragers, brewers, winemakers, and distillers from our own backyard. There is no other time of year that we can demonstrate, in one sitting, the vast variety of passions coming from such a disparate group of unique and talented individuals. And nothing brings us more joy than sharing their spirit through our expression of vegetables, with guests who have traveled a great distance to sit down and eat at our tables.

FRIED GARLIC SCAPES //

Fried Garlic Scapes with Sea Salt, Herbed Hazelnut Dip

Serves 6 | These curly bites are deliciously mild with a sweet hint of garlic, making them a perfect, simple early-summer snack. We've paired these fried scapes with our Herbed Hazelnut Dip, which is good with literally anything. Seriously addictive.

Note | *Garlic scapes are easily one of our favorite early summer veg. They are the shoots that grow from the bulbs of the garlic plant, and are harvested before they flower. Their pungent garlicy flavor mellows out when cooked, making them a versatile veg to serve as a side dish, or as a unique replacement for garlic in any summer recipes.*

HERBED HAZELNUT DIP /

1 cup raw hazelnuts, skins off
2 cloves garlic
¼ cup diced shallots
1 tsp salt
¼ cup apple cider vinegar
2 tsp flaked nutritional yeast
½ cup basil, chopped
¼ cup dill, chopped
¼ cup chives, chopped

Makes 2 cups | Place the hazelnuts and 3 cups water in a bowl or 32 oz mason jar and cover. Soak in the fridge overnight for approximately 8 to 10 hours. When ready, strain and rinse the hazelnuts, discarding the soaking liquid.

Add the soaked hazelnuts, garlic, shallots, salt, apple cider vinegar, ¾ cup water, nutritional yeast, and three-quarters of the herbs (basil, dill, and chives) into a Vitamix. Blend until smooth. Add the remaining herbs and blend again until the herbs are incorporated but still visible. Store in an airtight container in the fridge for up to 1 week.

FRIED GARLIC SCAPES WITH SEA SALT /

20 garlic scapes
12 cups canola oil
1 tsp sea salt
1 recipe Herbed Hazelnut Dip (left)

Makes 6 servings | Trim the woody ends off the garlic scapes. In a heavy-bottomed, high-sided pot, heat the oil to 350°F. Check the temperature by using a clip-on pot thermometer or candy thermometer. Gently place half the scapes in the oil and deep-fry until they are golden brown, about 45 seconds to 1 minute. Using a spider or slotted spoon, remove the scapes from the oil and place in a bowl lined with paper towel to soak up any extra oil. Sprinkle with the sea salt. Repeat with the second batch of scapes. Serve immediately with Herbed Hazelnut Dip.

GARDEN PEA AGNOLOTTI //

Garden Pea, Nasturtium + Walnut-Stuffed Agnolotti,
Pickled Garlic Scape Bulbs, Garden Pea Broth

Serves 6 | This rectangular handmade pasta is always a crowd pleaser and relatively easy to make. As with any stuffed pasta, it's all about the filling. We get so enamored with the vibrancy of summer produce that we love to show it off! Sweet garden (or English) peas, peppery nasturtium leaves, and toasted walnuts pop not only in color, but in flavor too.

Note | *This recipe calls for 4 cups garden (or English) peas in total. You can shell the peas up to 2 days in advance and store the raw peas in an airtight container in the fridge, leaving you with the shells you will need to make the broth. While the standard pasta recipe calls for egg and milk, we have also given you a vegan version for the dough that is hard to refute. This recipe calls for the use of a pasta maker. Any household manual pasta roller will do. That's what we use in the restaurant!*

GARDEN PEA BROTH /

1 onion, halved
3 stalks celery, roughly chopped
3 cloves garlic, slivered
½ tsp seeded and minced bird's eye chili
2 tsp salt
1 tsp peppercorns
2 tbsp sugar
3 cups garden or English pea shells
(peas reserved for recipes to follow)

Makes 5 cups | Place all the ingredients, except the pea shells, in a stockpot, add 12 cups water, bring to a simmer, and cook for 30 minutes, until the liquid reduces by half. Add the pea shells and simmer for 5 more minutes to give the broth a brighter flavor. Remove from the heat and strain the liquid through a fine-mesh strainer. Store in an airtight container in the fridge for up to 3 days.

GARDEN PEA, NASTURTIUM + WALNUT PUREE /

1 tbsp salt, for blanching
2 cups shelled garden or English peas
(shells reserved for the Garden Pea Broth, left)
2 tbsp olive oil
1 onion, diced small
2 tbsp thinly sliced garlic
1 tsp ground cardamom
2 tsp salt
2 tsp sugar
1 cup toasted walnut pieces
2 cups tightly packed nasturtium leaves,
washed and dried

Note | *We love the peppery, bittersweet nasturtium plant. Originally we grew it in our garden for its edible blossoms, but ended up also using the leaves in purees and sauces to give dishes a boost of vibrant green. Since we eat with our eyes first, color is everything. You can substitute arugula for nasturtium if you're having trouble finding it.*

CONTINUES

Makes 4 cups | In a medium saucepot, bring 2 cups water and the salt to a boil. Blanch the peas for 30 seconds. Strain the peas and place the strainer directly into an ice bath to chill. Place the empty pot back on the stove, add the olive oil, and sweat the onions and garlic on medium heat for 2 minutes, until they are soft and translucent. Add the cardamom, salt, sugar, and walnuts and cook for another 2 minutes. Add 2 cups water and simmer for approximately 15 to 20 minutes, or until the liquid has reduced by two-thirds.

Cool the liquid by pouring it into a metal bowl or container set in an ice bath. Once cool, transfer the liquid to a Vitamix along with 1 cup of the blanched peas and the nasturtium leaves. Puree until the mixture is silky-smooth. Store in an airtight container in the fridge for up to 2 days. Set aside the remaining blanched peas for serving.

Nasturtium

AGNOLOTTI /

PASTA DOUGH
3½ cups all-purpose flour + extra for dusting
12 large egg yolks
2 large eggs
1 tbsp olive oil
1 tsp salt

VEGAN PASTA DOUGH
3 cups all-purpose flour + extra for dusting
4 tbsp olive oil
1 tsp salt

3 cups Garden Pea, Nasturtium + Walnut Puree (page 198)
Semolina flour, for dusting
2 tbsp salt

Note | *You can prepare the dough and let it rest for up to 24 hours before rolling it out. Or, if you are making these ahead of time, you can freeze the uncooked agnolotti on the sheet pan. Once frozen, transfer them to a sealed container or freezer bag and store in the freezer until you're ready to use them. From frozen, cook in salted boiling water for 2 to 3 minutes.*

Makes 6 servings | Either Make the Dough in a Mixer | Place all the ingredients and 2 tbsp water in the bowl of a stand mixer fitted with the dough hook attachment. Mix on medium speed until all the ingredients come together. Once incorporated, continue mixing for another 5 minutes, then remove the dough from the bowl and knead by hand for 2 to 3 minutes.

Or Make the Dough by Hand | For the non-vegan pasta dough, place the flour on a clean work surface, shaping it into a mound. Create a well in the center of the mound with your finger, making sure to leave a little flour at the bottom of the well. The well should be approximately 5 inches in diameter with high-sided walls. In the center of the well, add the egg yolks, whole egg, olive oil, 2 tbsp water, and the salt. Using your fingers, break the egg yolks and stir in a circular motion, slowly incorporating flour from the sides as you go.

For making the vegan dough by hand, follow the previous directions to create the flour well. In the center of the well, add the olive oil, 1 cup water, and salt. Using your fingers, stir in a circular motion, slowly incorporating flour from the sides as you go.

For both doughs, take your time at this stage. If the flour is incorporated too quickly, the dough will come out with lumps. Once you've brought all the flour into the center, use your hands to bring together all the pieces of dough and form them into a tight ball. With the palm of your hand, press the dough down and away from you, then reshape the dough into a ball. Repeat this for 5 minutes.

Knead and Rest the Dough | Clean off your work surface with a bench scraper, then dust with fresh flour and knead the dough for 15 minutes. Kneading for this length of time helps to build up the gluten in the dough, giving it a better chew. When ready, the dough should be springing back to the touch and have a nice shine. Wrap tightly with plastic wrap and allow it to rest in the fridge for 1 hour.

Make the Pasta | Set up a clean work surface and dust it with flour. Unwrap the pasta and cut it into three equal pieces. Press out each piece into a flat, rectangular shape and run it through your pasta maker starting on the thickest setting and working your way to the thinnest setting (approximately ⅛ inch thick). As the finished sheet of pasta comes off the pasta roller, lay it out on a floured work surface and cut it into rectangular sheets, each approximately 12 inches long and 3 inches wide. You can dust each sheet with flour and stack them to save space.

Pull one sheet of pasta off the top of the stack. Fill a large piping bag with the Garden Pea, Nasturtium + Walnut Puree. Fit the end of the bag with a wide tip, approximately ½ inch in diameter. Pipe a straight line of filling lengthwise onto the pasta sheet, leaving enough pasta along the edge to cover the filling.

Fold the pasta over the filling. Press firmly along the fold to seal. Use a wheeled pasta cutter or a sharp knife to cut lengthwise along the edge of the filled pasta tube to trim the pasta, making sure to keep the sealed tube intact. Using the tips of your fingers, pinch the tube of pasta into equally sized sections approximately 1 inch long, creating a seal between the pockets of filling. Use the wheeled pasta cutter to cut along the pinched and sealed edges and separate your agnolotti. Place the agnolotti on a baking sheet dusted with semolina flour. Repeat this process until all the dough is used up.

To Cook | Fill a large pot with water and add the salt. Bring to a boil, then gently drop in the agnolotti and cook for approximately 1 to 2 minutes, depending on your preferred level of doneness (we always prefer al dente). Use a slotted spoon to remove the agnolotti from the water and onto a plate or baking sheet lined with parchment paper.

PLATING /

1 recipe cooked Agnolotti (left)
1 cup blanched peas (reserved from Garden Pea, Nasturtium + Walnut Puree, page 198)
1 recipe Pickled Garlic Scape Bulbs (page 32)
½ cup Garden Pea, Nasturtium + Walnut Puree (page 198)
20 to 30 nasturtium leaves, washed and dried
Edible blossoms, for garnish
1 recipe Garden Pea Broth (page 198), warmed in a pot

Lay out six deep-rimmed plates or large flat-bottomed bowls. Place six to seven pieces of cooked agnolotti on the bottom of each and sprinkle with blanched peas and Pickled Garlic Scape Bulbs (if you're using whole pickled garlic cloves, slice them lengthwise before serving). Pipe or spoon in drops of the Garden Pea, Nasturtium + Walnut Puree around the pasta. Garnish with nasturtium leaves and edible blossoms. Pour some warmed Garden Pea Broth around the bowl, just enough to cover the bottom edge of the pasta.

MUSHROOM //

Kelp Salt Roasted King Oyster Mushrooms, Confit Leeks,
Charred Onion Kelp Sauce, Seared Leek Rings, Sea Asparagus

Serves 6 | In this playful dish, we prepare and serve the king oyster mushrooms as you would a scallop, and they're surprisingly similar in texture and flavor. To further draw on elements of the sea, we incorporate kelp salt in the roasting and a Charred Onion Kelp Sauce.

Note | *At the restaurant, we use Haida Gwaii kelp, sustainably and respectfully picked by a licensed professional. You can find dried whole-leaf kelp or kombu at your local specialty store.*

CHARRED ONION KELP SAUCE /

3 (4 × 5-inch) sheets dried kelp
1 onion, halved and peeled
6 cloves garlic, crushed
2 tbsp olive oil
1 tbsp sherry vinegar
1 tbsp maple syrup
1½ tsp salt
1 tsp pepper

Makes 2 cups | Preheat the oven to 350°F. Spread the kelp sheets evenly on a baking sheet lined with parchment paper and toast in the oven for 5 minutes, or until they turn light brown. Remove from the oven and allow to cool. Once cool, crumble and set aside.

Char the onion halves over an open flame until both halves are coated in a deep, blackened char (you can use a barbecue or your gas stove burner flame on high). Let the onions cool, then chop into ¾-inch-thick pieces.

In a pan over medium heat, sauté the onions with the garlic in the olive oil. Once you've reached a deep caramelization, approximately 10 minutes, deglaze the pan with the sherry vinegar. Add the crumbled kelp, 1 cup water, maple syrup, salt, and pepper. Cook until the liquid has reduced by half, approximately 20 minutes. Transfer into a Vitamix and blend to a smooth consistency. Store in an airtight container in the fridge for up to 1 week.

CONFIT LEEKS /

3 tbsp olive oil
3 cups sliced leeks (¼-inch-thick slices, see Note)
Salt and pepper, to taste
1 cup chopped sea coriander

Note | *Trim off the dark green tops of your leeks and save them to use in a stock. Clean the outside of each leek and cut lengthwise from the bottom to top, slicing only halfway through. Butterfly the leek open. Chop into ¼-inch pieces and run them under cold water to remove any dirt that could have been trapped inside the leek. Dry with paper towel.*

Makes 1½ cups | In a pot on high heat, heat the olive oil, add the leeks, and season with salt and pepper. Sweat until the leeks begin to soften, then turn the heat down to low. Continue to cook for another 10 minutes, until soft.

Cut the pale white/light green base of the sea coriander (the first 2 to 3 inches) into 1-inch pieces. Make sure to discard the green tops, as they are inedible in large amounts. Add to the leeks and cook for 5 more minutes. Remove from the heat and store in an airtight container in the fridge for up to 5 days.

CONTINUES

KELP SALT /

4 (4 × 5-inch) sheets dried kelp
2 tbsp salt
1 tsp sugar
Zest of 1 lemon

Makes ½ cup | Preheat the oven to 350°F. Spread the kelp evenly on a baking sheet lined with parchment paper. Toast in the oven for 5 minutes, until light brown. Remove from the oven and allow to cool. Transfer the toasted kelp to the Vitamix and blend on high until it reaches the consistency of a fine powder. In a bowl, combine the kelp powder with the salt, sugar, and lemon zest and mix until blended. Store in an airtight container at room temperature for up to 1 month.

KELP SALT ROASTED KING OYSTER MUSHROOMS /

12 king oyster mushrooms
3 tbsp olive oil
2 tsp Kelp Salt (above)

Makes 6 servings | Preheat the oven to 375°F. Thoroughly clean the mushrooms with a brush or kitchen towel. Slice each mushroom into ¾ inch thick medallions or coins (3 to 4 pieces per mushroom depending on their size). Score one side of each mushroom piece with a cross-hatch pattern

Add the mushrooms to a large bowl and toss with the olive oil and Kelp Salt. In a large frying pan, sear the scored side of the mushrooms until they've reached a nice dark caramelization, approximately 2 minutes. Transfer to a baking sheet lined with parchment paper, scored side down. Roast in the oven for 15 to 20 minutes, until soft. Serve immediately.

SEARED LEEK RINGS /

6 (½-inch) rings leek (using the white, tender base only)
1 tsp olive oil
Salt and pepper, to taste

Makes 6 servings | Heat the oil in a medium pan on medium-high heat and sear the leek rings on one side until they are caramelized and slightly charred, approximately 1 minute. Remove from the heat and season with salt and pepper. Once cool enough to touch, pop out the individual rings.

PLATING /

1 cup Charred Onion Kelp Sauce (page 203)
1 recipe Confit Leeks (page 203)
1 recipe Kelp Salt Roasted King Oyster Mushrooms (left)
Olive oil, to taste
Salt and pepper, to taste
1 recipe Seared Leek Rings (above)
1 cup sea asparagus

Lay out six plates. Add 2 tbsp Charred Onion Kelp Sauce over two spots on each plate. Spoon 2 tbsp Confit Leeks beside the Kelp Sauce. Place approximately 4 pieces of Kelp Salt Roasted King Oyster Mushrooms on each plate, scored side up. Drizzle lightly with olive oil and season with salt and a little black pepper. Add the Seared Leek Rings to each plate and finish with some fresh sea asparagus.

KING OYSTER MUSHROOMS

WALLA WALLA ONION
+ NOOTKA ROSE CONSOMMÉ //

Serves 6 | These giant sweet onions are milder and less pungent than your typical white or yellow variety, and this clean and beautiful broth truly showcases them front and center. Combining onions and roses might be weird to think about, but the rich and deep flavor of the onions is lifted by the light and floral summery notes of the dried Nootka rose petals, creating a sweet and earthy consommé. This is a wonderful broth to serve on its own or as a base stock for your favorite dumpling or noodle soups.

DRIED NOOTKA ROSE PETALS /

½ cup fresh Nootka rose petals

Makes ¼ cup | If you're lucky enough to have fresh, in-season rose petals, a great way to preserve them for use throughout the year is simply to dry them. To do so, spread them out on a dehydrator sheet and dehydrate on medium (145°F) for 8 hours. Or you can place the petals in a paper bag with the top of the bag open slightly (this allows for air circulation and for humidity to escape) and leave them in the bag at room temperature for approximately 1 week, or until completely dry, making sure to shake the bag a few times throughout. Once dry, store in a dry container at room temperature for up to 1 year.

WALLA WALLA ONION
+ NOOTKA ROSE CONSOMMÉ /

1 tbsp olive oil
2 Walla Walla onions, skins on, cut in large slices (see Note)
5 cloves garlic, crushed
¼ cup sherry vinegar
2 tbsp maple syrup
1 tbsp salt
1 tbsp peppercorns
2 bay leaves
1 recipe Dried Nootka Rose Petals (above)
6 sprigs thyme

Note | *Keeping the skins on the onions helps to preserve a richer, deeper color in the broth. The benefit to the clarification process we use in this recipe is that you don't lose any flavor. Instead, you're left with a rich and tasty clear broth without needing to use egg to clarify.*

Makes 6 servings | Heat a medium stockpot on medium heat and add the olive oil, onions, and garlic. Sauté, stirring continuously, until the onions begin to caramelize. Adjust the heat as needed so as not to burn the onions. Continue until the onions reach a deep, dark caramelization. Deglaze the pot with the sherry vinegar and cook the liquid down until the onions are almost dry. Add the maple syrup and salt. Then pour in 16 cups water and add the peppercorns, bay leaves, and Dried Nootka Rose Petals. Simmer for 25 minutes. Add the thyme and simmer for 5 minutes more (adding the thyme at the end like this preserves its freshness). Remove from the heat and strain the liquid through a fine-mesh strainer.

Clarify the Broth | Transfer the broth into ice cube trays or small containers and place in the freezer. Line a large strainer with a coffee filter and place it over a large pot. Once frozen, remove the broth from the freezer and place into the lined strainer. Allow the frozen broth to slowly thaw and drip through the filter. Give this process time, and try not to disturb the frozen cubes (see Note). Once everything is fully thawed, you'll have a delicious clarified broth that you can reheat and enjoy! Store the clarified broth in a sealed container in the fridge for up to 5 days.

FRIED ZUCCHINI BLOSSOMS //

Fermented Zucchini Puree, Fried Zucchini Blossoms, Apricot Chili Sauce

Serves 6 | Zucchini stuffed inside a zucchini! This meta vegan snack needs a few days to prepare, but the reward is worth it: Creamy zingy filling inside a lightly battered and fried blossom is the closest thing to heaven we can find here on earth.

FERMENTED ZUCCHINI PUREE /

4 large zucchini
10 cloves garlic, smashed
3 tbsp roughly chopped dill, including stems
3 tbsp roughly chopped basil, including stems
4 tsp salt

Makes 4 cups | Wash the zucchini and slice into 1-inch coins. In a large bowl, mix the zucchini with the garlic, dill, and basil. Transfer the mixture to a sterilized 64 oz mason jar. Stir the salt into 4 cups water to dissolve, then pour over the zucchini mixture. Fill a resealable plastic bag with 2% salted water and place it over the surface of the water inside the jar. This bag will spread to the inside edges of the jar and help keep the vegetables submerged. Cover the top of the jar with a towel or piece of cheesecloth and fasten it with a rubber band or string.

Allow the zucchini mixture to ferment at room temperature (72°F) for 2 to 3 days, checking every day to ensure the vegetables are fully submerged under the salt water. When ready, strain out the liquid using a spoon or spatula to press out as much liquid as possible, and add the vegetables to a Vitamix. Blend until smooth. Store in an airtight container in the fridge for up to 1 week.

APRICOT CHILI SAUCE /

½ cup small-diced onions
4 cloves garlic, crushed
1 tbsp olive oil
2 cups pitted and roughly chopped apricots
1 tsp seeded and finely chopped cayenne pepper
2 tbsp sugar
1½ tsp salt

Makes 1½ cups | In a large pan on medium heat, sweat the onions and garlic in the olive oil until soft and translucent. Add the apricots, cayenne pepper, sugar, and salt and cook down the mixture, allowing the liquid to release from the apricots. Continue on low heat until the liquid has almost completely evaporated. Remove from the heat and place the mixture in a Vitamix. Blend until smooth. Store in an airtight container in the fridge for up to 5 days.

CONTINUES

FRIED ZUCCHINI BLOSSOMS /

1 cup Fermented Zucchini Puree (page 208)
12 zucchini blossoms (see Note)
½ cup all-purpose flour
1 tsp baking powder
½ cup soda water
8 cups canola oil
Sea salt, to taste
1 recipe Apricot Chili Sauce (page 208)

Note | *Zucchini blossoms are highly perishable, so it's best to enjoy them the same day you harvest or purchase them. Thoroughly clean the zucchini blossoms with a dry pastry brush to remove any debris on the outside, and check the insides to make sure there are no hidden critters. You can make this recipe with the blossoms exclusively, or pair the blossoms with baby zucchini for a little more substance to the dish.*

Makes 6 servings | Fill a pastry bag fitted with a ½-inch piping tip with the Fermented Zucchini Puree. Carefully fill the center of each blossom with approximately 1½ tsp puree, just enough so you are still able to twist the blossom tips together to close.

In a medium bowl, whisk together the flour, baking powder, and soda water to create your batter. Line a baking sheet with a kitchen towel or paper towel.

In a heavy-bottomed, high-sided pot over high heat, bring the canola oil up to 350°F. Using tongs, dip the filled blossoms into the batter, letting go of them and then picking each back up at one end to let any excess batter drip off. Gently place into the hot oil and fry for just 1 minute, until golden brown, rotating halfway through. Transfer to the prepared baking sheet to soak up any excess oil. Season with sea salt and serve immediately with the Apricot Chili Sauce for dipping.

LEGUME //

Assorted Beans + Peas Dressed with Serrano Pepper Cherry Vinaigrette, Pickled Tomatoes, Smoked Tomato + Pepper Broth, Marinated Cherries

Serves 6 | This is a wonderfully fresh summer side dish or appetizer. It's a great way to showcase all the tender legumes from your garden. There's a little kick in the vinaigrette to keep things interesting, and the broth can be served hot or cold, as we do in the restaurant. Feel free to garnish this dish with any fresh-picked garden herbs.

MARINATED CHERRIES /

1 small shallot, diced
2 tsp olive oil
2 tbsp sherry
¼ cup sherry vinegar
½ tsp salt
4 cups cherries, pitted and halved

Makes 1½ cups | In a small pot on medium heat, sweat the shallots in the olive oil until translucent. Deglaze the pan with the sherry and cook until the liquid has reduced by half. Add the sherry vinegar and continue to cook until the liquid has reduced by three-quarters. Season with salt and remove from the heat. Cool in the fridge for 10 minutes before marinating the cherries.

Toss the halved cherries in the marinade. Cover and refrigerate for at least 30 minutes to allow the liquid to cool completely and the cherries to soak in the juices. Store in an airtight container in the fridge for up to 7 days.

SERRANO PEPPER CHERRY VINAIGRETTE /

¾ cup cherries, pitted and halved
2 tsp sugar
¼ tsp salt
4 serrano peppers, destemmed and seeds removed
¼ cup fresh lemon juice
½ cup grapeseed oil

Makes 2 cups | In a small saucepot on medium-low heat, combine the cherries, sugar, and salt. Cook, stirring often to prevent the cherries from sticking to the pot, until almost all the liquid is cooked out.

Char the serrano peppers over an open flame until cooked and slightly charred (you can use a barbecue or your gas stove burner flame on high). Transfer to a Vitamix and add the cooked cherries, lemon juice, and grapeseed oil. Blend on high speed for 1 minute. Store in the fridge for up to 1 week.

SMOKED TOMATO + PEPPER BROTH /

1 onion
4 cloves garlic
½ bulb fennel
8 serrano peppers
Applewood chips, for smoking
1 tbsp olive oil
2 tbsp tomato paste
2 cups dried tomatoes (see Note)
¾ cup roughly chopped celery
2 tsp salt
1 tsp pepper

CONTINUES

Note | *For dried tomatoes, we use sliced tomatoes that are dried directly on site at the farm. The closest and easiest thing to substitute would be store-bought sundried tomatoes packed without oil. With this recipe, we smoke the vegetables to add a depth of flavor, and you will see different methods for using a conventional or stovetop smoker, or smoking gun. With a conventional or stovetop smoker you smoke the vegetables first and then make the broth; with a smoking gun you make the broth and then smoke. If you do not have means to smoke vegetables, feel free to omit these steps and prepare the sauce without smoking.*

Makes 6 cups | **If Using a Conventional or Stovetop Smoker** | Cut the onion, garlic, fennel, and serrano peppers in half, then smoke them with applewood chips for 30 minutes.

Make the Broth | Roughly chop the (smoked or unsmoked) vegetables. In a large pot on medium-high heat, place the olive oil and chopped vegetables and sauté until you've achieved a nice golden caramelization. Add the tomato paste and cook for approximately 5 minutes, stirring often to prevent the tomato paste sticking to the bottom of the pot (if it starts to stick, add a small splash of water to release it from the pot). Add the dried tomatoes and celery and season with salt and pepper.

If Using a Smoking Gun | Remove the pot from the stove and let the sides of the pot cool slightly, then cover tightly with plastic wrap. Poke a small hole in the plastic wrap, just big enough to fit the smoking gun nozzle, and smoke the vegetables with the applewood chips. Once the smoke has dissipated, repeat this process once more, then remove the plastic wrap.

Continue with the Broth | With the pot back on the stove, add 8 cups water and bring the liquid up to a low simmer. Simmer for 30 minutes, then season with salt and pepper to taste. Strain the broth into a bowl through a large-holed sieve or strainer, using a ladle or spatula to press as much of the juice out of the vegetables as possible. Strain the broth again, this time through a fine-mesh strainer to remove any small impurities. This broth will keep in the fridge for up to 4 days, or the freezer for up to 1 month, and can be enjoyed on its own, or as the base for your favorite vegetable soup.

DRESSED BEANS + PEAS /

12 sugar snap peas
12 snow peas
6 dragon tongue beans
12 green beans
2 cups fava beans, skins removed
1 cup Pickled Tomatoes (page 35)
¼ cup Serrano Pepper Cherry Vinaigrette (page 213)

Makes 6 servings | Wash the legumes under cold water, removing the tough strings along the sides of the snap peas and snow peas along the way. Cut them into 1-inch bite-sized pieces. (Cutting on a bias creates more room for the sauces to get inside—which is a good thing!)

Remove the Pickled Tomatoes from the pickling liquid and add to a large bowl. (You can reserve the pickling liquid to use a second time.) Add the legumes and Serrano Pepper Cherry Vinaigrette, and mix until everything is well coated.

PLATING /

1 recipe Dressed Beans + Peas (above)
1 cup Marinated Cherries (page 213)
Fresh garden herbs, chopped, for garnish
2 cups Smoked Tomato + Pepper Broth (page 213)

Lay out six bowls. Place ½ cup Dressed Beans + Peas in the center of each bowl, and place a small handful of Marinated Cherries around them. Garnish with the fresh garden herbs of your choice (basil works very well with this dish). Finish with ⅓ cup Smoked Tomato + Pepper Broth, poured into each bowl around the vegetables.

CUCUMBER //

Poona Kheera Cucumber Salad, Pickled Serrano Peppers, Serrano Pepper
+ Plum Relish, Charred Serrano Pepper Vinaigrette, Cucumber Powder, Purslane

Serves 6 | What is better than a fresh summer cucumber salad? We love this heirloom variety, with its crisp, sweet, and hardy qualities. It gets an extra kick from the heat of the serrano peppers laced throughout the dish. Wash it down with your favorite summer beer.

CUCUMBER POWDER /

1 long English cucumber
1 tbsp sugar
1 tsp salt
½ tsp citric acid

Makes ¼ cup | Keeping the skin on, slice the cucumber into thin strips and lay them on a dehydrator sheet. Dehydrate on medium (145°F) overnight for 12 hours or until the cucumbers are completely dry. Alternatively, you can dry them on a baking sheet lined with parchment paper in your oven at 165°F (with the door cracked open) for approximately 4 hours.

Transfer the dried cucumbers and the sugar, salt, and citric acid to a spice grinder (or the dry container of your Vitamix) and blend to a fine powder. Store in an airtight container at room temperature for up to 1 month.

SERRANO PEPPER + PLUM RELISH /

4 Santa Rosa plums, pitted
2 serrano peppers, seeded
½ tsp salt
¼ tsp pepper
1 tbsp plum vinegar or white balsamic vinegar

Makes 1 cup | Finely and uniformly dice the plums and serrano peppers. Mix together with the salt, pepper, and vinegar to evenly coat. Store in an airtight container in the fridge for up to 1 week.

CHARRED SERRANO PEPPER VINAIGRETTE /

3 serrano peppers
1 shallot, peeled
¼ cup fresh lemon juice
2 tbsp maple syrup
1 tbsp Dijon mustard
1 tsp salt
½ tsp pepper
1 cup grapeseed oil

Makes 1 cup | Use an open flame to char the serrano peppers and shallot whole until they have a nice charred crust all over, then allow to cool. Remove the stem and seeds from the peppers, then roughly chop the peppers and the shallot. Transfer the peppers and shallot to a Vitamix and add the lemon juice, maple syrup, Dijon mustard, salt, and pepper to the blender. Blend on high until smooth. Turn the blender to medium speed and slowly drizzle in the grapeseed oil until it is completely emulsified.

Note | *Serrano peppers are similar in heat to jalapeños. If you're spice-averse, it is best to taste each pepper before cooking (since some are hotter than others) and adjust the amount of peppers according to your taste.*

CONTINUES

PLATING /

2 Poona Kheera cucumbers, peels on,
   washed and thinly sliced
¼ cup Charred Serrano Pepper Vinaigrette
   (page 217)
1 recipe Serrano Pepper + Plum Relish (page 217)
½ cup Pickled Serrano Peppers (page 35)
2 cups purslane, washed and dried
2 tbsp Cucumber Powder (page 217)

Add the sliced cucumbers to a large bowl and toss
with the vinaigrette. Lay out six plates and distribute
the dressed cucumbers evenly along the bottom of
each. Add the Serrano Pepper + Plum Relish and
the Pickled Serrano Peppers around the cucumber
slices, and top with the purslane. Using a small fine-
mesh strainer, dust the top of each plate with the
Cucumber Powder.

SUMMER
FRUIT SALAD //

Heirloom Tomatoes, Yellow Watermelon, Lemon Cucumbers,
Peaches, Pears, Sun Jewel Melon, Cherries, Melon Seed Vinegar,
Sorrel Yogurt, Toasted Hazelnuts

Serves 6 | Sometimes we just want to showcase the unparalleled flavor of our farm-fresh summer fruits and vegetables. Even after all these years, it's hard to control our excitement at the season's first arrival of heirloom tomatoes! Or the flavor explosion of a perfectly ripe peach. We appreciate the tender sweet flavor of lemon cucumbers and grow them in our own garden.

MELON SEED VINEGAR /

¾ cup melon seeds and guts reserved from the
    Sun Jewel melon (used in the Plating, page 222)
1 cup white wine vinegar
1 tsp salt
1 tsp pepper
3 tbsp sugar

Note | *This recipe is all about using the scraps that would otherwise end up in your compost bin. You can make it ahead of time, using the scraps from your favorite melon if you don't have access to the sun jewel variety!*

Makes 1 cup | Add all the ingredients to a small saucepot on medium heat and bring to a simmer. Simmer for 5 minutes, strain through a fine-mesh strainer, then set aside to cool. Store in a sealed airtight container in the fridge for up to 1 month.

TOASTED HAZELNUTS /

1 cup raw hazelnuts
1 tsp salt
2 tsp sugar

Makes 1 cup | Preheat the oven to 400°F. Spread the hazelnuts out onto a baking sheet and roast for 10 minutes or until they're light brown and have a

nutty aroma. Remove from the oven and allow to cool, then roughly chop into smaller pieces. Toss in a bowl with the salt and sugar. Store in an airtight container at room temperature for up to 3 weeks.

SORREL YOGURT /

1 cup sorrel (see Note)
2 tbsp maple syrup
½ tsp salt
1¼ cup 5% plain Greek yogurt

Note | *We grow red-veined sorrel in our garden, as we love the dramatic color of the veins through the leaves. The fresh, lemony flavor it imparts adds that touch of acid to a dish in a unique and colorful way. You can use any garden or French-variety sorrel for this sweet, tangy, and creamy recipe.*

Makes 1¼ cups | Place the sorrel and maple syrup in a Vitamix and blend until smooth. Transfer to a bowl and add the salt and Greek yogurt, stirring until all the ingredients are well incorporated. Store in an airtight container in the fridge for up to 5 days.

CONTINUES

PLATING /

3 medium heirloom tomatoes

2 peaches

2 lemon cucumbers

12 cherries, pitted

1 pear

2 cups thinly sliced yellow watermelon (rinds discarded)

1 skin-on Sun Jewel melon, cut in ½-inch slices
  (seeds and guts reserved for Melon Seed Vinegar,
  page 221)

¼ cup Melon Seed Vinegar (page 221)

1 recipe Sorrel Yogurt (page 221)

1 recipe Toasted Hazelnuts (page 221)

Fresh mint or lemon balm leaves, for garnish

Pepper

Note | *At The Acorn, we compress the watermelon using
a vacuum sealer to increase the density and translucency
of the fruit. Essentially, this is a process that squeezes out
the air pockets throughout the watermelon, intensifying its
flavors along the way. You likely won't have a vacuum sealer
at home, so the real key to this dish is that you use perfectly
ripe ingredients.*

Prepare the Fruit | Cut the tomatoes into thin
wedges, approximately ½ inch thick. Remove the pits
from the peaches and cut into wedges.

Keeping the skins on, cut the lemon cucumbers into
thin slices. Cut the cherries in half. Halve the pear,
core it, then slice into long thin wedges.

Assemble the Salad | In a bowl, gently toss the
prepared fruit with the Melon Seed Vinegar. Lay out
six plates. Place three 1 tbsp dollops of the Sorrel
Yogurt on each plate, and lay the fruits over and
around the yogurt, evenly dividing them between all
the plates. Sprinkle the Toasted Hazelnuts over top
and garnish with fresh mint or lemon balm leaves.
Finish with cracked black pepper.

PANZANELLA SALAD //

Heirloom Tomatoes, Arugula, Lemon Basil Vinaigrette,
Toasted Focaccia Bread, Smoked Paprika + Sunflower Seed Crumb, Basil Puree

Serves 6 | Our take on this classic Italian salad involves fresh-baked Focaccia Bread, peak-season Klippers Organics heirloom tomatoes, Smoked Paprika + Sunflower Seed Crumb, and creamy Basil Puree. It's yet another example of our love affair with summer.

Note | *This dish is all about letting your ingredients sing, and you'll likely find the best tomatoes at your local farmers' market. Don't worry about being too precious about the plating. Having torn and rustic edges will help the Focaccia Bread soak up all the flavors.*

LEMON BASIL VINAIGRETTE /

2 cups tightly packed basil leaves
¼ cup fresh lemon juice
1 tsp Dijon mustard
¼ cup grapeseed oil
¼ cup olive oil
1 tsp salt
½ tsp pepper

Makes 1 cup | Place all the ingredients in a Vitamix and blend until emulsified. Store in an airtight container in the fridge for up to 5 days; the color will eventually fade to a darker green, but the flavor will remain.

SMOKED PAPRIKA + SUNFLOWER SEED CRUMB /

¾ cup sunflower seeds
1 tsp smoked paprika
¼ tsp salt
¼ tsp sugar
⅛ tsp red pepper flakes

Makes ½ cup | Preheat the oven to 350°F. Place the sunflower seeds on a baking sheet lined with parchment paper. Toast in the oven for 10 minutes.

Remove from the oven and allow to cool. Transfer to a food processor and add all the other ingredients. Pulse until the mixture is roughly chopped into a crumb consistency. Store in an airtight container in the cupboard for up to 3 weeks.

BASIL PUREE /

1 cup tightly packed basil stems and leaves
1 tsp Dijon mustard
1 tbsp fresh lemon juice
½ tsp salt
¼ cup olive oil

Makes ¾ cup | Place the basil, Dijon mustard, lemon juice, and salt in a Vitamix. Blend until smooth. Turn the Vitamix to medium speed and, with the blender still running, slowly drizzle in the olive oil until it is completely emulsified. Store in an airtight container in the fridge for up to 4 days.

CONTINUES

FOCACCIA BREAD /

1 medium russet potato, peeled
6 tbsp olive oil,
½ cup washed and thinly sliced leeks
1½ tsp active dry yeast
3½ cups all-purpose flour
1¼ tsp salt
2 tbsp roughly chopped rosemary
1 tsp sea salt

Makes 1 (10 × 15-inch) loaf | Cut the potato into
quarters and place in a small pot. Cover with 6 cups
water. Bring to a simmer and cook for approximately
20 minutes, or until tender. Strain the water from
the potatoes, making sure to reserve 1 cup of potato
water for the dough. Allow the potatoes to cool, then
coarsely mash with a fork.

Meanwhile, place 2 tbsp of the olive oil in a small
saucepot on medium heat and sweat the leeks for
5 minutes. Remove from the heat and allow to cool.

Transfer the 1 cup reserved warm potato water to a
bowl and sprinkle the yeast over top. Set aside for
5 minutes or until the liquid begins to bubble.

In a stand mixer fitted with the paddle attachment,
place the yeast water, flour, salt, leeks, and crushed
potatoes. Mix on medium-low speed for approximately
5 minutes, until the dough all comes together. Remove
the bowl from the mixer and cover the top with plastic
wrap. Set in a warm area of your kitchen to rise for
1 hour.

Brush the inside of a 10 × 15-inch baking pan with
2 tbsp olive oil. Turn the dough out onto the prepared
pan and shape it to the edges of the pan using your
fingers. Brush lightly with a little more olive oil and
cover with plastic wrap. Place the pan back into a
warm area of your kitchen for 1 more hour to rise.

Preheat the oven to 425°F. Once the dough has doubled
in size, carefully remove the plastic wrap. Using your
fingers, make small indents on top of the dough and
then brush the dough with the remaining olive oil.
Sprinkle the chopped rosemary and sea salt over top.

Bake on the middle rack of the oven for 15 minutes,
turn the pan 180 degrees, and bake for another
8 minutes. Remove from the oven and set on a wire
rack to completely cool. Store in an airtight container
at room temperature for up to 2 days.

PLATING /

3 large heirloom tomatoes, cut in small wedges
3 cups heirloom cherry tomatoes
6 cups arugula
¼ cup olive oil
¾ loaf Focaccia Bread (left)
1 recipe Lemon Basil Vinaigrette (page 225)
1 recipe Basil Puree (page 225)
3 cups basil leaves
1 recipe Smoked Paprika + Sunflower Seed Crumb
  (page 225)

In a large bowl, toss together the tomatoes and arugula
and set aside.

Place the olive oil in a large pan on medium-high heat.
Tear the focaccia into 1-inch bite-sized pieces and
add to the hot pan, tossing to make sure all sides of
the bread are lightly coated with the oil. Continue to
toast and toss until the bread pieces are golden brown
and crispy (keep them moving around, as they will
burn easily).

Add the warm toasted bread to the bowl with the
arugula and tomatoes and evenly dress with the Lemon
Basil Vinaigrette, tossing to coat.

Lay out six plates. Distribute the salad among the plates
and, using a spoon, add dollops of the Basil Puree
in and around the salad. Top the salad with the basil
leaves and finish with a generous sprinkling of the
Smoked Paprika + Sunflower Seed Crumb.

TOMATO TART //

Almond + Hazelnut Tart Shells, Herbed Hazelnut Dip,
Marinated Tomatoes, Garden Herbs

Serves 6 | These little tarts are deceivingly filling. The dehydrated Almond + Hazelnut Tart Shells maintain a soft and nutty density that flakes under your fork. Our Herbed Hazelnut Dip makes another appearance as the tart filling, with peak-season cherry tomatoes hitting you with that acid and sugar to keep you wanting more.

ALMOND + HAZELNUT TART SHELLS /

¾ cup raw hazelnuts
¾ cup ground raw almonds
3 tbsp potato starch
2 tbsp tapioca starch
1 tsp salt
½ tsp black pepper
2 sprigs thyme, leaves picked
1 tsp agave or maple syrup
Olive oil, for tart molds

Note | *You need six round, removable-bottom tart molds for this recipe, each approximately 3½ to 4 inches in diameter and ½ to ¾ inch tall. If you would prefer to bake the tart shells rather than dehydrate them, you can do that in a 350°F oven for 20 minutes; baking them will turn up the crunch!*

Makes 6 shells | Place all the dry ingredients and the thyme in a food processor and blitz until it reaches as fine a consistency as you can get. With the machine still running, add ¼ cup water and the agave syrup and continue to blend until everything is well mixed, stopping to scrape down the sides of the container halfway through. Transfer the mixture to a large bowl and finish mixing by hand, making sure there are no dry spots and that everything is fully incorporated.

Lightly brush the inside of your tart molds with olive oil. Divide the dough into six and press into the molds. Place the molds directly onto the dehydrator tray and dehydrate on high (160°F) for 6 hours. After 6 hours, separate the shells from the molds and return them to the dehydrator for 6 more hours. Store in a airtight container lined with paper towel at room temperature for up to 7 days.

MARINATED TOMATOES /

1 cup olive oil
4 cloves garlic, sliced
2 sprigs dill
2 sprigs basil
1 tsp salt
½ tsp pepper
1 tbsp sugar
½ tsp red pepper flakes
2 cups halved baby gem tomatoes

Makes 2 cups | Place all the ingredients, except the tomatoes, in a saucepot on low heat and cook for 10 minutes. Remove from the heat and let cool for 15 minutes, then pass through a strainer, reserving both the liquid and solids. Place the tomatoes in an airtight container and pour the liquid over top (make sure it is completely cooled first). Allow to marinate for at least 3 hours in the fridge before serving; the longer the better. Store in an airtight container in the fridge for up to 3 days.

CONTINUES

PLATING /

6 Almond + Hazelnut Tart Shells (page 229)
1½ cups Herbed Hazelnut Dip (page 197)
1 recipe Marinated Tomatoes (page 229)
2 cups basil leaves
Edible blossoms and herbs, for garnish

Lay out six plates and place one tart shell on each.
Fill each tart shell with ¼ cup Herbed Hazelnut Dip.
Strain the tomatoes from the olive oil (reserving the oil)
and top each tart with approximately ⅓ cup tomatoes.
Drizzle the olive oil marinade over the tart and plate.
Garnish with basil leaves and edible blossoms
and herbs.

KLIPPERS ORGANICS //

When Annamarie and Kevin Klippenstein started their organic farm in 2001—in the Similkameen Valley in British Columbia's interior—it was ahead of the curve. With patience and care, they showed farmers' market customers how good fresh food grown without pesticides or genetic modification can taste. They also introduced many to heirloom-variety tomatoes. Behind the scenes, they were perfecting a healthy farm ecosystem that encourages beneficial bugs and healthy crops. Now their farm is thriving, with 40 acres of land, a table-on-the-farm restaurant, and loyal customers.

Klippers Organics grows food that's ready to eat. It's not picked early for a longer shelf life at the grocery store. Instead, it has a chance to ripen. In those extra days in the sun, fruits and vegetables undergo a sugaring process that boosts nutrients and adds flavor. Then the farm sells the freshest produce directly to customers at farmers' markets and to select restaurants, including The Acorn.

Annamarie and Kevin met The Acorn team at a fundraiser for Growing Chefs, a charity that helps teach children how to connect with food from seed to stalk. The Acorn was immediately hooked on Klippers Organics produce because of its excellent quality. Annamarie says this ongoing relationship is built on strong mutual respect: she's honored by how the restaurant presents the farm's food, and The Acorn team deeply appreciates Klippers Organics' passion and the care they take with what they grow and how they grow it.

INSPIRATIONS | Flavors, taste, heirloom varieties, the ripening process, high nutrient values, and healthy ecosystems.
THE ACORN-AT-HOME | Talk to farmers at your local farmers' market to learn about how they grow food and what their specialty varieties are.

ROASTED CARROTS //

Roasted Carrots, Preserved Plum Mostarda,
Shropshire Blue Cheese, Sweet Cicely

Serves 6 | With this ingredient-driven side dish, we're using a unique blue cheese that gets its yellow color naturally from ground annatto seed. It's a delicate blue that has just enough funk to it, and it pairs beautifully with these preserved plums and roasted early season carrots. We've been fortunate to eat these little baby farm carrots straight from the soil at Klippers Organics; they're perfectly crunchy, and delightful.

PRESERVED PLUM MOSTARDA /

- 2 tbsp yellow mustard seeds, soaked overnight (see Note)
- 1 large onion, cut in small dice
- 4 cloves garlic, thinly sliced
- 3 tbsp olive oil
- 1½ tsp salt
- 1 tsp pepper
- 1 tbsp sugar
- ¼ cup fresh lemon juice
- 1 tbsp dry mustard
- 2 cups large diced Preserved Plums (page 40), liquid strained
- 2 tsp finely chopped thyme leaves

Note | *Soak the yellow mustard seeds in 2 cups water for 12 to 24 hours. When ready, strain out the liquid.*

Makes 2½ cups | In a medium saucepot on medium heat, sweat the onions and garlic in the olive oil until they are soft and translucent. Season with the salt and pepper and add the sugar and lemon juice. Cook until the liquid has reduced by half. Add the dry mustard and Preserved Plums and continue to cook until the liquid has again reduced by half. Add the thyme and the soaked mustard seeds for the last 2 minutes, then remove from the heat. Store in an airtight container in the fridge until ready to use, up to 1 week.

ROASTED CARROTS /

- 12 early-season or young carrots, each about 8 inches long
- 3 tbsp olive oil
- 8 sprigs thyme, leaves picked
- Salt and pepper, to taste

Makes 6 servings | Preheat the oven to 400°F. Wash and scrub any dirt off the carrots; you do not have to peel or trim them. In a large bowl or pan, mix the carrots with the olive oil and thyme. Season with salt and pepper. Lay the carrots and thyme out on a baking sheet lined with parchment paper. Roast for 15 to 20 minutes or until the carrots are cooked through but still retain some crunch. Cooking time will vary depending on the size of your carrots. Serve immediately.

PLATING /

- 1 recipe Roasted Carrots (above)
- ¼ cup crumbled Shropshire blue cheese
- ½ cup Preserved Plum Mostarda (left)
- Sweet cicely or other garden herbs, for garnish

Lay out the roasted carrots on a serving plate. Add the cheese over top, and drizzle with the Preserved Plum Mostarda. Garnish with sweet cicely or garden herbs of your choice.

CHARRED PEACH //

Charred Peaches, Chickpea "Meringue," Red Currants,
Red-Veined Sorrel, Candied Pineappleweed Pistachios, Pineappleweed Granita

Serves 6 | Here in British Columbia, the Okanagan is famous for its peaches. We get ours from Klippers Organics, as they will never early-pick a peach. They wait for them to ripen to the point that they're about to fall off the tree, heavy with their own juices. It's almost a shame to do anything other than just eat them fresh! We do plenty of that too along the way, but this cheeky play on peaches and cream—using Chickpea Meringue and Candied Pineappleweed Pistachios—coalesces the flavors of summer beautifully.

For a deeper and more meaningful pineappleweed experience, top this dessert with Pineappleweed Granita. This is one of our favorite granitas ever at The Acorn. It's super delicious and messes with your head a little—being that it's a plant with an uncanny resemblance to pineapple. Such a cool and novel way for us to bring a local, tropical flavor to the table.

CANDIED PINEAPPLEWEED PISTACHIOS /

2 cups packed fresh pineappleweed
2 tbsp sugar
½ tsp salt
1 cup toasted pistachios

Note | *We know you're going to like this: make a double batch so you have candied pistachios to snack on!*

Makes 1 cup | Wash and dry the pineappleweed, then spread out on a dehydrator sheet. Dehydrate on medium (145°F) for 11 hours. Alternatively, dry on a baking sheet lined with parchment paper in your oven at 165°F (with the door cracked open) for 3 hours. With either method, make sure the pineappleweed is completely dry to the touch; if not, you can extend the drying time. Once ready, grind the pineappleweed in a spice grinder or Vitamix until it becomes a fine dust.

Preheat the oven to 325°F. In a medium mixing bowl, mix together the sugar, salt, and pistachios with 1½ tbsp dried ground pineappleweed. Spread the mixture onto a baking sheet lined with parchment paper and bake

for 20 to 25 minutes or until the sugars have completely melted and begin to caramelize. Remove from the oven and allow to cool completely. Store in an airtight container at room temperature for up to 6 months.

PINEAPPLEWEED GRANITA /

2 cups packed pineappleweed,
    washed and spin-dried
¾ cup + 1 tbsp fresh lemon juice
¼ cup sugar

Makes 4 cups | Place all the ingredients plus 3 cups water in a Vitamix and blend until the pineappleweed is smooth and the sugar has dissolved. Pour directly into a 4 x 4 x 2-inch deep cake pan and place in your freezer. Every hour, stir the mixture with a fork to create frozen but fluffy ice shavings. Repeat until evenly frozen and flaky all over. Cover with a lid to prevent frost buildup while waiting to serve. To serve, use a fork to scrape the granita into a bowl, then carefully spoon onto the dish.

CONTINUES

CHARRED PEACHES /

3 ripe peaches

Note | *At the restaurant, we char the peaches using a butane torch instead of the cast-iron skillet. We recommend using one if you have it. You can also use it in the plating to torch the Chickpea Meringue just a touch to add more of a burnt marshmallow flavor.*

Makes 6 servings | Cut the peaches in half and dry the cut side with a towel to remove any excess moisture. Heat a cast-iron skillet on high. Once hot, sear the peaches cut side down for 30 seconds each, until they develop a nice charred or blackened crust; be careful not to overcook. Carefully remove from the pan. Cut each peach half into thirds.

PLATING /

1 recipe Charred Peaches (above)
2 cups Chickpea Meringue (page 27)
¾ cup Candied Pineappleweed Pistachios (page 237)
18 leaves red-veined sorrel
½ cup red currants
Pineappleweed Granita (page 237), for garnish
   (optional)

Lay out six plates. Place three segments of peach on each plate. Add the Chickpea Meringue to a piping bag and pipe the meringue around the peaches, then sprinkle each plate with the Candied Pineappleweed Pistachios. Garnish with sorrel leaves, fresh red currants, and the Pineappleweed Granita, if using.

CORN TART //

Sautéed Corn, Pâte Brisée Tart Shells, Camembert Cream,
Red Onion Relish, Arugula, Espelette Pepper Powder

Serves 6 | Peak-season corn tastes as incredible raw as it does cooked, and you just can't go wrong with corn sautéed in butter with salt. We served wheels of raw corn picked right off the stalk at a Klippers Organics farm dinner to celebrate the vegetable in its purest form! This dish delivers on all levels, with a flaky tart shell, sweet and tangy red onion relish, and creamy Camembert. The perfect way to elevate lunch!

ESPELETTE PEPPER POWDER /

10 Espelette peppers
1 tsp salt
2 tsp sugar

Makes ½ cup | Wash the peppers and cut off the stems. Cut each pepper in half and scoop out the seeds with a spoon. Wash your hands after handling. Lay the peppers out on a dehydrator sheet and dehydrate on medium (145°F) overnight for 12 hours or until completely dry.

Alternatively, you can dry them on a baking sheet lined with parchment paper in your oven at 165°F (with the door cracked open) for approximately 4 to 5 hours. Place all the ingredients in a spice grinder or Vitamix and blend until it becomes a fine powder. Transfer to an airtight container and store at room temperature for up to 6 months.

RED ONION RELISH /

1 large red onion, cut in small dice
1 tsp minced garlic
1 tbsp olive oil
2 tsp Espelette Pepper Powder (above)
1 tsp salt
¼ cup white wine vinegar
2 tbsp sugar

Makes 1 cup | In a pan on medium heat, sweat the onions and garlic in the olive oil. Cook, stirring often, for approximately 4 minutes, until the onions are soft and translucent. Add the Espelette Pepper Powder, salt, vinegar, and sugar and cook until the liquid has reduced by half. Remove from the heat and transfer to a bowl, then place in the fridge to cool before serving. Store in an airtight container in the fridge for up to 7 days.

CAMEMBERT CREAM /

1 9 oz/250 g wheel Camembert cheese
1 tsp salt
¼ cup heavy cream

Makes 1½ cups | Combine the ingredients in a pot and heat on low until the cheese has softened. Remove from the heat. Using a hand blender, blend until smooth and creamy. Store in an airtight container in the fridge for up to 6 days.

CONTINUES

TART SHELLS /

2½ cups all-purpose flour + extra for rolling
½ tsp salt
20 sprigs thyme, leaves picked and chopped
1 cup cubed cold unsalted butter

Note | *This tart shell is done in a classic Pâte Brisée style—flaky, buttery, and rich. If you find your dough is starting to stick when rolling it out, use a bench scraper to gently loosen it from your work surface. Feel free to add a little more flour before continuing to roll it out.*

Makes 6 shells | Sift the flour into a large mixing bowl, then add the salt and chopped thyme. Using a pastry cutter or bench scraper, cut the cold butter into the flour until it becomes coarse and crumbly. Slowly pour in ½ cup ice-cold water and mix the dough until it comes together and you can form a ball. Wrap the dough in plastic wrap and refrigerate for 2 hours.

Remove the chilled dough from the fridge. Lightly dust a clean work surface with flour and roll out the dough into an ⅛-inch-thick rectangle. Using a 5-inch tart ring, cut out six tart shells. Transfer the shells to a baking sheet lined with parchment paper and refrigerate for 30 minutes.

Preheat the oven to 350°F. Remove the baking sheet from the fridge. Using a fork, dock the tart shells all the way around the edges and into the center. Bake in the oven for 20 minutes. Remove from the oven and set aside to cool at room temperature. These are best enjoyed fresh, but can be stored in a paper towel–lined airtight container at room temperature for up to 3 days.

SAUTÉED CORN /

6 cobs corn, shucked
3 tbsp unsalted butter
Salt and pepper, to taste
½ cup Red Onion Relish (page 241)

Makes 6 servings | Using a serrated knife, cut the corn kernels off the cobs. In a pan on medium heat, sauté the corn kernels in the butter for 4 minutes. Season with salt and pepper to taste. Transfer a quarter of the corn to a Vitamix and blend until smooth. Mix the blended corn back in with the rest of the corn, along with the Red Onion Relish. Mix until well combined. Serve soft, gooey, and warm. Store in an airtight container in the fridge for up to 5 days.

PLATING /

3 cups arugula (or substitute with any salad green)
6 Tart Shells (left)
1 recipe Camembert Cream (page 241)
1 recipe Sautéed Corn (above)
Watercress, for garnish
⅛ cup Espelette Pepper Powder (page 241)

Lay out six plates. Add ½ cup arugula to the bottom of each plate, then place a tart shell on top. Add 2 tbsp Camembert Cream to each tart shell and evenly spread it over the surface of the shell; top with the sautéed corn and garnish with watercress. Dollop any remaining cream on each plate beside the tart. Sprinkle with Espelette Pepper Powder.

CORN GRITS //

Hominy Corn Grits, Sautéed Chanterelles, Charred Corn + Padrón Peppers,
Smoked Onion Corn Sauce, Pickled Corn, Lamb's Quarters

Serves 6 | Another great way to celebrate corn is in fritter form. Crunchy and pillowy, sweet and savory, these fried grits are a satisfying chew. Our team at The Acorn has a Rorschach-inspired game when making the grits to see what country or continent the ripped bites resemble. Is it Africa? Italy? You be the judge . . .

PICKLED CORN /

1 to 2 cobs corn, shucked
½ cup Pickling Liquid (page 31)

Makes 6 servings | Using a serrated knife, cut the kernels off the cobs until you have filled 1 cup. Set aside in a bowl or 32 oz mason jar. In a pot over medium-high heat, bring the Pickling Liquid up to a simmer, then immediately pour it over the corn. Allow the corn to steep in the pickling liquid uncovered for at least 1 to 2 hours at room temperature before serving. This can be store in an airtight container in the fridge for up to 1 month.

SMOKED ONION CORN SAUCE /

1 Walla Walla or sweet yellow onion
4 to 5 cobs corn, shucked
3 cloves garlic, sliced
2 tbsp olive oil
2 tbsp fresh lemon juice
6 sprigs thyme
1 tsp salt
½ tsp ground black pepper

Note | *We smoke the corn in this recipe, but you can omit that step if you want.*

Makes 2 cups | Remove the skin from the onion and cut in half. Using tongs, blister the corn and onion over an open flame. Using a serrated knife, cut the kernels from the cobs (reserving the cobs) until you fill 2 cups. Break the cobs in half and place in a medium pot with 4 cups water. Simmer for 20 minutes, until the liquid is reduced by half. Strain out the cobs and reserve the stock.

Meanwhile, roughly chop the charred onion halves and place in a large frying pan with the corn kernels, garlic, and olive oil. Sauté on medium heat for approximately 4 minutes. Add the lemon juice and chopped thyme and season with salt and pepper. Transfer to a metal baking sheet and cover tightly with plastic wrap. Smoke the vegetables using either of our smoking methods on page 22. Once the smoke has dissipated, repeat the smoking process. Return the mixture to the frying pan and sauté again for 5 minutes, then add to the pot containing the corn stock.

Bring the stock to a simmer and cook until the liquid has reduced by half. Transfer to a Vitamix and puree until smooth. Store in an airtight container in the fridge for up to 5 days.

CONTINUES

CHARRED CORN
+ PADRÓN PEPPERS /

12 padrón peppers
3 cobs corn, shucked
3 tbsp olive oil
Salt and pepper, to taste
2 tsp fresh lemon juice

Note | *Ready to play pepper roulette? Padrón peppers are fun and flavorful, with a mildly smoky profile. Similar in size and color to a shishito, they grow locally in British Columbia. While 90% of them are mildly spicy, approximately 1 in 10 will hit you with that jalapeño heat!*

Makes 6 servings | Wash and dry the padrón peppers, then char them whole—either over an open flame or using a grill for 30 seconds each side. Next char the corn for 1 minute per side. Rub the corn with 2 tbsp olive oil and season with salt and pepper. Using a serrated knife, cut the seasoned kernels off the cobs. Transfer to a large bowl with the charred padrón peppers and toss with the remaining olive oil and the lemon juice and season with more salt and pepper. Set aside to be sautéed for serving.

HOMINY CORN GRITS /

8 padrón peppers
2 cobs corn, shucked
1 onion, cut in small dice
5 cloves garlic, minced
2 tbsp olive oil
1 tbsp salt
1 tsp pepper
2 tsp flaked nutritional yeast
1 cup cornmeal
¾ cup hominy grits
8 cups canola oil

Makes 6 servings | Wash the peppers and remove the stems and seeds, then chop them into a small dice. Using a serrated knife, cut the kernels off the corn cobs (reserving the cobs). In a large saucepot on medium heat, sweat the peppers, corn kernels, onions, and garlic in the olive oil until slightly caramelized. Add 6 cups water and the salt, pepper, nutritional yeast, and reserved corn cobs. Simmer for 10 minutes, then remove the cobs and discard.

Turn the heat down to low and whisk in the cornmeal and hominy grits—whisking thoroughly to make sure there are no lumps. Cover and cook on the lowest heat, stirring every 5 minutes, for 1 hour. Check the seasoning and adjust if necessary.

Line the bottom of a square or rectangular baking sheet (with sides at least 2 inches tall) with parchment paper. Pour the grits into the pan and allow to cool slightly before placing, uncovered, in the fridge to cool completely for 1 hour. You can store in an airtight container in the fridge for up to 5 days.

Line a baking sheet with a kitchen towel or paper towel. Heat the canola oil in a heavy-bottomed, high-sided pot to 350°F. Break the grits, by hand, into small 2-inch pieces. In batches of eight, fry the grits in the oil for 2 minutes at a time, then remove with a spider or slotted spoon and place on the prepared baking sheet to soak up any excess oil. Keep warm in the oven until ready to serve.

SAUTÉED CHANTERELLES /

- 24 medium golden chanterelle mushrooms
- 2 tbsp olive oil
- 2 tsp minced garlic
- Salt and pepper, to taste
- 1 tbsp sherry vinegar

Note | *You'll want to make these chanterelles last so you can serve them hot from the pan. If you made your Smoked Onion Corn Sauce ahead of time, reheat it in a saucepot so it's ready to serve once the chanterelles are done.*

Makes 6 servings | Trim the ends of the chanterelles and clean them using a brush, removing all dirt or debris. Heat a large frying pan on high heat until it's nice and hot. Add the olive oil and chanterelles and sauté for 30 seconds. Season with salt and pepper, and cook for another 2 minutes, moving the mushrooms around for even cooking, until nearly all of the liquid from the mushrooms has reduced. The cooking time will vary as the moisture content will always differ from mushroom to mushroom; golden chanterelles are resilient to heat, so be patient. Add the garlic and cook for 1 more minute, then deglaze the pan with the sherry vinegar and remove from heat right away. Serve immediately.

PLATING /

- 1 recipe Hominy Corn Grits (left)
- 1 recipe Charred Corn + Padrón Peppers (left)
- 1 recipe Sautéed Chanterelles (above)
- 1 recipe Smoked Onion Corn Sauce (page 245)
- 1 recipe Pickled Corn (page 245)
- 3 cups picked young lamb's quarters leaves, washed

Lay out six plates and distribute the grits evenly between them. If reheating is needed, quickly sauté the Charred Corn + Padrón Peppers then add them to the plates. Distribute the Sautéed Chanterelles around the plates and generously spread the Smoked Onion Corn Sauce on top and around the ingredients. Sprinkle the Pickled Corn around the dish, and garnish with lamb's quarters.

COCKTAILS//

// Welcome to The Acorn bar! In this chapter we're showcasing some of our signature cocktails and nonalcoholic beverages. With a great amount of inspiration coming from our kitchen team, we've found similar, creative ways to approach our bar program. Our emphasis is on craft, local, and seasonal. Here in Vancouver we're lucky enough to have the support of our local farmers and suppliers, our very own fresh herb and blossom garden down the block, an incredible list of local breweries, some fantastic wine from all around the province, and an ever-growing list of kick-ass distillers. Even with the clouds and rain, it seems we can get everything under the sun. If it can be found locally,

RITES OF SPRING //

Spring is one of the most exciting times for us at The Acorn. The dark, damp winter months give way to a wave of available ingredients, most of them able to be enjoyed fresh and raw. The simple sugar snap pea is the star of this drink, which announces our departure from the stores of our root cellars and hints at the excitement of what the summer will bring. What began as a play on the classic French 75, this effervescent aperitif delivers bold and refreshing vegetal notes, tempered by the warmth of black pepper and fresh ginger.

GINGER + BLACK PEPPERCORN BITTERS /

3 tbsp peppercorns
3 inches peeled fresh ginger, grated
¼ tsp dried wormwood
3 cups Everclear or another high-proof neutral spirit

Makes 3 cups | Combine all the ingredients in a sterilized mason jar and cover. Allow to infuse at room temperature for at least 2 weeks, swirling or shaking the contents daily. Strain the contents first through a fine-mesh strainer and then through a coffee filter and into a mason jar or airtight container. Seal, and store at room temperature; bitters will keep indefinitely.

SNAP PEA + GINGER SYRUP /

3 cups sugar
2 cups sugar snap peas, ends trimmed
  and strings pulled
1 tsp citric acid
1 to 2 inches peeled fresh ginger

Note | *Fresh produce syrups keep for approximately 2 weeks. If you have some left over, we suggest mixing in soda for a refreshing Italian-style drink, adding to your favorite teas, or using as the sweetener in dressings or over breakfast parfaits. The possibilities are endless.*

Makes 6½ cups | In a heat-resistant bowl or container, combine 4 cups freshly boiled water and the sugar, and stir until it dissolves into a simple syrup. Set aside to cool.

Add the sugar snap peas, citric acid, ginger, and cooled simple syrup to a Vitamix and blend until smooth. Allow to rest for 15 minutes. Strain through a fine-mesh strainer into a nonreactive container and cool completely before using. Store in a sealed container in the fridge for up to 2 weeks.

RITES OF SPRING COCKTAIL /

1 oz London dry gin (we use Long Table Distillery)
¼ oz dry vermouth (we use Rathjen Cellars
  and Ampersand Distillery Imperative)
1 oz Snap Pea + Ginger Syrup (left)
½ oz fresh lemon juice
1 dash Ginger + Black Peppercorn Bitters (left)
Dry sparkling wine
Edible springtime flower, for garnish

Note | *Scale up the liquor and other ingredients in this recipe to serve it as a bright and seasonal punch bowl.*

Makes 1 cocktail | Chill a champagne flute. In a steel shaker, combine the gin, vermouth, Snap Pea + Ginger Syrup, lemon juice, and bitters. Fill with ice and shake, then double-strain into the chilled flute. Top with dry sparkling wine until the flute is three-quarters full. Garnish with a fresh, edible springtime flower.

FLOR DE VERANO //

The summer flower featured here is the intoxicatingly perfumed elderflower. Its distinct flavor has become incredibly popular within the world of cocktails, and its availability within the Pacific Northwest—if even just for a brief period of blooming—made it a no-brainer when we were considering an ingredient for our seasonal drink menu. We always make a large batch of Elderflower Syrup to have on hand and stretch the season for as long as we can. For this cocktail, we made the syrup into a granita, or shaved ice, which melts in the cocktail as you enjoy it, transforming the flavor profile from smoke and spice to sweet and floral. We chose the warming notes of cinnamon, sweet vermouth, and smoky mezcal to contrast the normally light and floral characteristics of elderflower.

ELDERFLOWER SYRUP /

2 cups sugar
2 cups fresh elderflower blossoms, stems removed
    (or 1 cup dried)

Note | *You can use dried elderflower blossoms as an alternative to fresh, just reduce the measurement to 1 cup.*

Makes 3¾ cups | Combine the sugar with 2 cups of water in a medium pot and bring to a gentle boil, stirring until the sugar is dissolved, then remove from the heat. Pack the elderflower blossoms in a sterilized 16 oz mason jar and pour the hot sugar water over top. Allow the jar to cool uncovered at room temperature. Cover and steep the blossoms overnight, up to 12 hours, swirling or shaking the jar several times throughout (dried blossoms need only 6 hours). The flavour should be sweet and floral. Strain the blossoms from the liquid using a fine-mesh sieve. Store the syrup in an airtight container in the fridge for up to 1 month.

ELDERFLOWER GRANITA /

1 recipe Elderflower Syrup (left, or
    find at a specialty food or liquor store)
Zest and juice of 2 limes
½ cup sugar

Makes 1 cup | Combine all ingredients in a pot, stirring constantly over low heat until the sugar is dissolved. Remove from the heat and pour directly into a 4 x 4 x 2-inch-deep cake pan and place in the freezer. Every hour, stir the mixture with a fork to create frozen but fluffy ice shavings; repeat until evenly frozen and flaky all over. Use right away or store, covered, in the freezer for up to 1 month.

CINNAMON SYRUP /

3 whole cinnamon sticks
2 cups sugar
2 cups water

Makes 3¾ cups | Combine all ingredients in a pot and bring to a gentle boil. Lower the heat and simmer for 10 minutes. Remove from the heat and allow to cool. Discard the cinnamon sticks and store the syrup in an airtight container in the fridge for up to 1 month.

CONTINUES

FLOR DE VERANO COCKTAIL /

1½ oz blanco tequila
½ oz mezcal
¼ oz sweet vermouth (we use Marrow Vermouth)
1 oz fresh lime juice
½ oz Cinnamon Syrup (page 255)
1 dash star anise bitters (we use Ms. Betters
  Pineapple Star)
2 to 3 tbsp Elderflower Granita (page 255)
Lime zest, for garnish

Makes 1 cocktail | Chill a stemless wine glass. In
a steel shaker, combine all the ingredients except the
Elderflower Granita and lime zest. Fill with ice and
shake, then double-strain into the chilled glass. Add
just enough fresh ice to break the surface of the liquid.
Using a fork, shave off 2 to 3 tbsp frozen granita and
place gently on top of the ice in the glass. Garnish
with freshly grated lime zest.

OMA-SAKE //

Inspired by omakase, a Japanese term that means "chef's menu", we created Oma-Sake—a play on words—as our sake-based cocktail that rotates using our seasonal inspirations. It has an overall lower alcohol % to keep everyone cheerful without pushing boundaries. This drink for us is always light, refreshing, and subtle in flavor to let the delicate sake notes shine bright. At the time of writing, we're up to our ninth version of the cocktail. We build our Oma-Sake in a stemless wine glass. Anything elegant and around that size will do, but the tapered nose helps draw aromas to the nose of the imbiber.

Note | *Artisan Sake Maker makes such great sake that we could never imagine substituting this. If you're in British Columbia, consider yourself lucky and go get yourself a bottle. It's best fresh, so we recommend going straight to Granville Island and getting it directly from the team there. If you can't get it, find another sake that's light, fresh, and dry with notes of melon and pear.*

SESAME-GINGER BITTERS /

3 quarter-sized slices fresh ginger
⅓ cup black sesame seeds
¼ tsp dried wormwood
3 cups Everclear, or another high-proof neutral spirit

Makes 3 cups | Combine all the ingredients in a large sterilized jar. Seal the jar and allow to rest at room temperature for 1 week, agitating daily. Strain through a coffee filter into a large sealable bottle, or airtight container. Store at room temperature; bitters will keep indefinitely.

SHISO-INFUSED VERMOUTH /

12 to 15 shiso leaves
3 cups dry vermouth (we use Rathjen Cellars and Ampersand Distillery Imperative)

Makes 3 cups | Tear the shiso leaves into a large sealable container or jar. Add the vermouth, cover, and allow to rest for 1 day, agitating several times. Strain through a fine-mesh strainer. Store in an airtight container (ideally the original vermouth bottle with lid) in the fridge for up to 3 months.

SANTA ROSA PLUM SYRUP /

2.2 lb ripe Santa Rosa plums
1 cup sugar

Makes 2 (32 oz) mason jars | Pit and slice the plums, then place them in a large pot and mash lightly. Add the sugar and 4 cups water. Bring up to a simmer and cook for 10 minutes, stirring occasionally. Remove from the heat and allow to cool. Strain, squeezing as much liquid from the plums as you can, using a slotted spoon to press against a large colander first, then strain again through a fine-mesh strainer. Store in a sealed container in the fridge for up to 2 weeks.

OMA-SAKE COCKTAIL /

1½ oz Osake Junmai Nama Sake
½ oz Shiso-Infused Vermouth (left)
¾ oz Santa Rosa Plum Syrup (above)
1 dash salted water
1 dash Sesame-Ginger Bitters (left)
Club soda or carbonated water
Mint leaf, for garnish

Makes 1 cocktail | In a stemless wine glass, combine the sake, vermouth, syrup, saline, and bitters. Fill with ice to the top of the glass, add the club soda until all the ice is covered, and give it a gentle stir. Garnish in the center with a mint leaf.

MASA SHIROKI, ARTISAN SAKE MAKER//

Masa Shiroki started importing premium Japanese sake to Canada in 2000 because he wanted to do something culturally meaningful to reflect his Japanese roots. Seven years later, he decided to take the next step and start making his own sake in Vancouver with locally grown rice, the northernmost crop of rice found in the world. Today, with a popular tasting counter on Vancouver's Granville Island—a destination for visitors from around the world—and a number of awards along the way, he provides many with a first sake-drinking experience. It's as enjoyable as visiting a winery, talking to a sommelier, and sipping fine wine.

Masa makes premium sake from the fermentation of rice, water, and yeast. Those familiar with sake imported from Japan or California will notice that the local rice in his made-in-Vancouver sake, which Masa sells under the Osake label, results in a uniquely savory flavor profile. Masa spent years studying wine, developing his recipes, and cultivating local rice to create an appealing, fresh, and delicate taste.

Masa initially started selling sake to The Acorn for cocktails—most recently we've been using the classic Junmai Nama in a signature cocktail called Oma-Sake (page 259)—but soon suggested it also be made available to enjoy by the glass. He says the acidity in the sake, together with its pear, melon, apple, and savory umami impressions, creates a remarkable synergy when paired with the rich flavors of The Acorn's dishes.

INSPIRATIONS | Japanese sake-making traditions, local ingredients, rice, synergistic food pairings, and fruity, savory, and umami flavors.

THE ACORN-AT-HOME | Pair sake with the vegan and vegetarian dishes you cook. The flavors will be as complementary as wine.

SUMMER ISLES //

This recipe is a punch in style, which means we combine a spirit with water, spice, sugar, and citrus. Way back in the late 17th century, punches were served at massive estate parties with freshly grated nutmeg, showing guests how exotic and hospitable the host was. We went all out fresh and seasonal with this lovely summer sipper. This can be easily dialed up to fill a punch bowl, but we prefer making it to order, fresh as can be.

Note | *You can find some very lovely nutmeg graters at your local kitchen supply store, or the finest grater in your drawer will get the job done.*

HYSSOP SYRUP /

2 cups fresh-picked hyssop leaves
2 cups sugar
½ tsp citric acid

Note | *Our hyssop comes from The Acorn's garden. We pick enough hyssop to loosely fill 2 cups.*

Makes 3¾ cups | In a pot of boiling water, blanch the hyssop leaves for 1 minute, then quickly transfer to an ice bath for 30 seconds. Bring 2 cups water to a boil and remove from the heat. Carefully transfer to a Vitamix and add the blanched hyssop leaves and the sugar. Blend until smooth, then let stand for 15 minutes. Strain into a clean sealable container, stir in the citric acid, and seal. Store in the fridge for up to 3 weeks.

RASPBERRY-WINE REDUCTION /

2 cups raspberries
3 cups dry red wine
1 cup brown sugar
¼ cup fresh lemon juice
½ tbsp vanilla extract

Note | *Raspberries were in season when we created this little number, but the drink is also great with blackberries or pretty much any other berry you can fancy or find.*

Makes 4 cups | In a large pot, combine the berries, red wine, sugar, and lemon juice and bring to a gentle boil. Cook for 10 minutes, stirring occasionally. Remove from the heat, allow to cool, then strain through a fine-mesh sieve, discarding the solids. Add the vanilla extract to the liquid and stir. Seal and store in an airtight container or 32 oz mason jar in the fridge for up to 2 weeks.

SUMMER ISLES COCKTAIL /

1 oz aged rum (we use Diplomatico Mantuano)
1 oz aged rum (we use Havana Club 3-year)
1 dash absinthe (we use Okanagan Spirits Taboo Genuine)
1 oz fresh lemon juice
1 tbsp Hyssop Syrup (left)
Club soda or carbonated water
1 tbsp Raspberry-Wine Reduction (left)
1 fresh raspberry
Freshly grated nutmeg

Note | *Taboo Genuine Absinthe is made in the heart of the Okanagan with backyard anise, fennel, and wormwood. You can use your favorite absinthe in its place. Diplomatico Mantuano is smooth, rich, and fruity, but you could try any aged and blended rum. Havana Club's 3-year rum is fresh and slightly fruity, but you could find another young column still rum.*

Makes 1 cocktail | In a steel shaker, combine both rums, the absinthe, lemon juice, and Hyssop Syrup. Fill with ice and shake, then double-strain into a Collins or tall, narrow glass. Add approximately 3 oz of club soda until the glass is about two-thirds full. Fill with ice, leaving just a finger of room. Float the Raspberry-Wine Reduction on top. Garnish with a fresh raspberry and grated nutmeg.

WHAT'S UP DOC? //

Summer moves into fall, and as our heat-loving crops diminish, others are just coming into their own. The humble carrot, having had its sugars concentrated by the first frosts of the year, is at its best. The goal with this cocktail was to elevate this unexpected martini ingredient to its highest potential—balancing its natural sweetness with the acidity of a pickled garnish and the added complexity of dill, caraway, and fennel. We use agar-agar here to clarify the carrot juice, minimizing separation in the glass and maintaining the classic elegance of the martini. The subtle balance of sweetness, acidity, and savory notes make this an excellent cocktail for beginning the meal and opening the palate.

DILL BITTERS /

1 bunch fresh dill
2 tbsp dried dill
½ tsp dried wormwood
3 cups Everclear, or another high-proof neutral spirit

Makes 3 cups | Combine all ingredients in a sterilized 32 oz mason jar, cover and let rest at room temperature for 2 weeks, swirling or shaking the contents daily. Strain through a fine-mesh sieve and then again through a coffee filter to remove all solids. Store at room temperature; bitters will keep indefinitely.

FENNEL OIL /

1 bulb fennel with fronds
1½ tbsp fennel seeds
2 cups grapeseed oil

Makes 2 cups | Chop the fennel bulb into small pieces and place in a small pot. Add the fennel seeds and grapeseed oil and heat over medium heat until everything is warm; do not boil. Transfer to a non-reactive container and allow to rest at room temperature for 24 to 48 hours. Strain through a fine-mesh sieve and then strain again through a coffee filter to remove all solids. Store in a sealable nonreactive container or 16 oz mason jar in the fridge for up to 3 months.

CLARIFIED CARROT SHRUB /

1 tbsp fresh lemon juice
4½ lb carrots, peeled
2 pinches agar-agar
4 tbsp white balsamic vinegar

Makes 4 cups | Place the lemon juice in a non-reactive container. Juice the carrots, and add the juice to the lemon-prepared container to prevent oxidation. Measure 1 cup carrot juice into a small pot, setting aside the remaining carrot juice. Whisk the agar-agar into the carrot juice in the pot, while bringing it to a boil. Boil for 2 to 3 minutes, then remove from the heat.

Pour the heated carrot juice into a large bowl and add the fresh carrot juice slowly, stirring continuously to combine. Pour into a freezer-safe container and freeze. Once frozen, remove from the freezer and thaw the frozen block through a jelly bag hanging over a bowl. As it melts, only clarified juice will filter through the bag into the bowl. Patience is your friend here, as rushing this step will result in juice that isn't fully clarified.

Once fully strained, discard the pulp and add the vinegar to the bowl. Stir gently to combine. Transfer to a mason jar or airtight container and store in the fridge for up to 1 month.

CONTINUES

PICKLED CARROT RIBBONS /

2 heirloom carrots
1 cup Pickling Liquid (page 31), cold
2 fronds fresh dill

Makes 2 cups | Wash and peel the carrots, then shave into uniform ribbons, lengthwise. Cover with water.

Drain the carrots, pat dry, and pack into a sterilized 16 oz mason jar. Pour in the cold Pickling Liquid and add the fresh dill fronds. Rest at room temperature for 12 hours before serving. Store in the fridge for up to 2 weeks.

WHAT'S UP DOC? COCKTAIL /

1½ oz vodka (we use Liberty Distillery Truth)
½ oz akvavit (we use Sheringham Distillery)
½ oz dry vermouth (we use Rathjen Cellars
   and Ampersand Distillery Imperative)
1 oz Clarified Carrot Shrub (page 265)
1 dash Dill Bitters (page 265)
3 to 4 drops Fennel Oil (page 265)
1 Pickled Carrot Ribbon, skewered (above)

Makes 1 cocktail | Chill a Nick and Nora glass (or a stemmed martini glass). Combine the vodka, akvavit, vermouth, carrot shrub, and bitters in a mixing glass. Stir with ice until you reach your desired dilution, then strain into your chilled glass. Garnish with three to four drops of the Fennel Oil and a skewer of Pickled Carrot Ribbon.

POMME D'OR //

The days begin to grow shorter, with hints of cooler fall weather on the horizon, and our local farmers bring us quinces and apples to play with. In this cocktail we stand up to the natural richness of sugar-poached quince with the bold flavors of dark rum and dry sherry and the pungent spice and raisin notes of Bitter Truth's Jerry Thomas' Own Decanter bitters. All of these complex flavors are elevated by a splash of effervescent apple cider from Vancouver Island.

QUINCE SYRUP /

2 quinces
2 cups sugar
½ cinnamon stick
2 cloves
1 whole star anise

Makes 3 cups | Clean the quinces and cut into chunks, removing the tough cores. Place in a large pot and add the remaining ingredients plus 2 cups water. Bring to a boil, then lower the heat and allow to simmer for 30 minutes, stirring occasionally. Strain through a fine-mesh strainer into a nonreactive airtight container. Seal and store in the fridge for up to 2 weeks.

POMME D'OR COCKTAIL /

1 oz dark rum (we use Diplomatico Mantuano)
½ oz Amontillado sherry (we use Lustau)
1 dash Bitter Truth Jerry Thomas' Own Decanter bitters (or Angostura bitters as a readily available alternative)
¾ oz Quince Syrup (left)
½ oz fresh lemon juice
1½ oz tart and dry cider (we use Sea Cider Pippins)
Apple slices, for garnish
Freshly grated nutmeg, for garnish

Makes 1 cocktail | In a cocktail shaker, combine all the ingredients except the cider. Fill with ice and shake briefly. Add the cider, then fine-strain into a Collins glass. Garnish with fresh slices of apple and grated nutmeg.

ODD SOCIETY SPIRITS //

Distillation is part science and part alchemy, and the founders of Odd Society—Gordon Glanz and Miriam Karp—harness both, along with an added measure of ingenuity. To bring an old-world distillation technique to Vancouver, Gordon studied in Edinburgh, Scotland, at Heriot-Watt University, earning a Master of Science degree in distilling and brewing. The distillery still participates in high-level whisky research in university labs, but Odd Society's best efforts and innovations are made for pure enjoyment.

Odd Society was founded in 2013, and started with vodka and gin made from locally grown grains. They now offer a lineup of whisky, vermouth, and liqueurs, plus some amazing limited releases. Their team are makers of refined rebellions in the form of unique, small-batch spirits, and each bottle tells a story. Odd Society's version of traditional sloe gin is made with local foraged salal berries to create a beautiful, dark, and rich local flavor. Their vermouth is based on a classic recipe but with arbutus and wild cherry bark for an intense complexity and heightened bitterness. Those with refined palates may even notice the subtle differences in Odd Society's spirits from British Columbia–grown grains and Vancouver water.

The Acorn's renowned cocktails rely on spirits from Odd Society, including a bespoke cask of Canadian rye whisky made specifically for the restaurant and aged 3 years. Collaborations like these keep our spirit fires stoked!

INSPIRATIONS | Refined rebellion, storytelling, distillation traditions, innovations, local flavors, whisky research.

THE ACORN-AT-HOME | Every good bartender can spin a good yarn. Start with spirits that tell their own story and you'll have lots to talk about.

AUTUMN ICED TEA //

We keep a list of nonalcoholic drinks on the menu and rotate them as often as our signature cocktails. It's important to us to offer nonalcoholic drinks so that everyone can feel like they're celebrating, or even just find a wonderful flavor to sip on. We think our non-alcoholic beverages deserve the same love and attention as our alcoholic ones. Some of us love tea. Some don't. But we think we could make a tea lover out of anyone with this drink. This cocktail is naturally sweet with no added sugar or sweetener. Shaken well with fresh juice, it has a fine frothy foam on top, so it looks great too.

Note | *We get our apples from Klippers Organics farm in the Okanagan. A while back, Klippers started juicing and bottling their apples at the farm and we're hooked on this juice. For a winter variation, simply add some cinnamon, allspice, and cloves. In the spring, try using chamomile tea instead and a stick of lemongrass. In summer, try fresh mint tea, and maybe switch to lime juice.*

CHILLED ROOIBOS TEA /

2 rooibos tea bags, or about 1 tbsp loose tea

Makes 4 cups | Bring 4 cups water to a boil and steep the tea for approximately 15 minutes. We're looking for intensity of flavor here. Strain and allow to cool. Transfer to a sealable container. Store in the fridge for up to 2 weeks.

AUTUMN ICED TEA NONALCOHOLIC COCKTAIL /

4 tbsp Chilled Rooibos Tea (left)
4 tbsp organic pressed apple juice
1 tbsp fresh lemon juice
Club soda or carbonated water
1 lemon wedge

Makes 1 cocktail | Combine the tea, apple juice, and lemon juice in a shaker, add ice, and shake hard. Pour the contents into a rocks glass. Top with a splash of soda and garnish with a lemon wedge. It's too easy!

CELLAR DOOR //

When the cold of winter is here, and comfort is key. With our cellars stocked full of apples, hazelnuts, and parsnips, we turn to the blended complexity of whisky and brandy for warmth. This drink features a play on traditional orgeat syrup, using toasted local hazelnuts in the place of almonds, and a Parsnip Foam made from Aquafaba (page 27) that mimics the added textural element of egg white, while at the same time adding complementary flavors. Freshly grated nutmeg tops off our winter homage to the Whisky Sour.

TOASTED HAZELNUT ORGEAT /

2 cups raw hazelnuts
3 cups sugar
1 oz brandy (we use Torres 10-year Solera)
¼ tsp orange flower water

Makes 8 cups | Preheat the oven to 350°F. Toast the hazelnuts on a baking sheet for 10 to 15 minutes, until golden. In a bowl, combine the sugar and 3 cups boiled water, and stir until the sugar is dissolved to create a simple syrup. Transfer the toasted hazelnuts and simple syrup to a Vitamix and blend until smooth. Strain through a fine-mesh strainer into a nonreactive container. (The nut solids could be reserved and baked into a nut brittle.) Add the brandy and orange flower water, stir to incorporate, and let sit, covered, at room temperature for 3 hours. Store in an airtight container in the fridge for up to 1 month.

PARSNIP FOAM /

1 tbsp fresh lemon juice
2 medium parsnips
Liquid from 3 (14 oz) cans chickpeas, or
    approximately 1½ cups Aquafaba (page 27)
1 cup apple juice
2 tbsp maple syrup

Makes 2½ cups | Place the lemon juice in a nonreactive container. Clean and juice the parsnips, and add the juice to the lemon-prepared container to prevent oxidation. Add the chickpea liquid or Aquafaba, apple juice, and maple syrup and stir until evenly blended. Fill a whipping cream canister with the liquid mixture and charge with one nitrogen gas cartridge. Keep the canister and any remaining liquid refrigerated for up to 1 week. If you don't have a canister, hand whip the ingredients together in a bowl to create soft peaks and use immediately.

CELLAR DOOR COCKTAIL /

1 oz Canadian whisky
½ oz brandy (we use Torres 10-year Solera)
1 oz fresh pressed apple juice
½ tbsp fresh lemon juice
¾ oz Toasted Hazelnut Orgeat (left)
Parsnip Foam (left)
Freshly grated nutmeg, for garnish

Makes 1 cocktail | Chill a large coupe glass. Combine the whisky, brandy, apple juice, lemon juice, and Toasted Hazelnut Orgeat in a shaker. Fill with ice and shake until chilled. Strain once, and then again into the chilled coupe. Carefully pipe or spoon enough of the Parsnip Foam over the cocktail for it to be uniformly covered. Garnish with freshly grated nutmeg.

WHISKY BUSINESS //

Well, there's a lot of history and inspiration behind this one. Where to start... In the mid-1800s, the Manhattan cocktail was born. If you cross a bridge into Brooklyn, you'll find a variation with that borough's name. Within Brooklyn you'll find even more adaptations, such as the Red Hook or Bensonhurst. We took inspiration from the Bensonhurst cocktail and used its formative style to work with Odd Society's No. 6 single-malt Canadian whisky. It was in high demand, so we were lucky to get some! We wanted a cocktail to showcase this local spirit while complementing its flavor. The result was spirit-forward with vegetal notes and a fresh aroma.

1 ½ oz single-malt Canadian whisky
(we use Odd Society)
⅓ oz extra-dry vermouth (we use Noilly Prat)
⅓ oz Cynar bitter liqueur
1 dash Bittermens Orchard Street Celery Shrub
1 oz akvavit (we use Sheringham Distillery),
in a small atomizer or spray bottle
1 lemon twist, for garnish

Note | *The Bensonhurst cocktail was a great inspiration, but each ingredient listed above really came together perfectly for this one: Odd Society's Canadian single-malt whisky (at the time of writing it was batch No. 6) showed hints of baking spice, apple, pear, cereal grain notes, and a little coconut. A Speyside Scotch could get the job done in its place, and we've even tried American straight rye, but it just isn't the same. Noilly Prat is the house that initially shipped dry vermouth across the Atlantic, and we find it works well in a variety of classics and classic-inspired cocktails. Cynar is an artichoke-forward, bitter liqueur with a surprisingly low alcohol %. Bittermens Orchard Street Celery Shrub just fit the bill perfectly. And Sheringham's akvavit continues to be our favorite local version of the Scandinavian-style spirit; it's so incredibly smooth.*

Makes 1 cocktail | Chill your favorite whisky glass. In a mixing glass, combine the whisky, vermouth, Cynar, and shrub. Fill with ice and stir gently for about 25 seconds. Place a large ice cube in the chilled whisky glass and mist with 3 sprays of akvavit. Strain the chilled cocktail over top. Garnish with a lemon twist.

ACKNOWLEDGMENTS //

SHIRA /

Thank you, Gabriel Cabrera for your magnificent eye. This book is as much yours as it is ours.

Special thanks to Robert McCullough and Lindsay Paterson for the opportunity and your endless patience, and to Emma Dolan for making these pages sing.

Much love to Julia Stiles, Nich Box, Liam Bryant, and Suzanne Andrews for your invaluable contributions. To Sophie MacKenzie for your involvement throughout. And to Janaki Larsen for the magnificent ceramic works used in the book.

To Carl Ostberg, for realizing our surrealist dreams. And to Scott August, our go-to for all things large format!

A special shout out to chefs Devon Latte and Lucas Johnston, who continue to sail this ship through unchartered waters.

A heartfelt thanks to Bill and Lynn Lewis for believing in me. To Phil Blustein, Katya Pine, Marty Rothman, and Jared and Laura Blustein (and baby Ever) for your unconditional love.

To Andreas Seppelt for the confidence to leap. Coco Culbertson for continually opening the door. Scott Cohen and Stephan Gagnon for your generosity. And to Michelle Godbout and Jim Cameron for your endless sage advice.

Love and thanks to Lizzy Karp and Pat Kelly—neighbors extraordinaire—for all the brainstorming sessions and bass checks.

Extra thanks to Miles Yeung, Louise Burns, and Lyndsay Sung for dining in style.

To Michelle Sproule, I'm forever grateful for your constant feedback and ability to always connect the dots.

Thank you, Amanda Cohen, David Zilber, Matty Matheson, and Andrew Morrison for penning your thoughts. I'm deeply honored.

Most importantly, to my partner in life, work, and love, Scott Lewis. Thank you for being my rock, for keeping me anchored but never letting me hit the ground, and for the limitless patience and love you bring to our family.

The Acorn restaurant and book would not exist today without the love and support from our community: family, friends, farmers, foragers, and especially our team, past, present, and future.

And of course, to every single guest who has ever graced us with your presence. I'm humbled and grateful for your trust.

BRIAN /

Thank you to all of my mentors throughout the years who have shown me so much courage, patience, and technique to help guide the future in food. A special mention to Heinz Nowatschin, may you rest in peace.

Thank you to my amazing partner, Christine, who has never doubted me, who has always been patient, and who has always understood the time and dedication it takes to push hard in this industry.

Thank you to my mom and dad, Deborah and Norm, who raised me to work hard, be honest, and love all those around you. To my brother and sister, Sarah and James, who have always been my biggest supporters and the heart that drives me. I owe you all so many holiday meals I have missed over the years.

A massive thanks to all of the amazing farmers and foragers who drive us to create the best out of what they work so hard to grow and find.

To Devon, who continuously pushes the boundaries of thinking outside of the box. To the many cooks, dishwashers, and servers who have made The Acorn what it is, and what it always will be.

And a huge thank you to Shira Blustein and Scott Lewis for your amazing support and trust over the years. The two of you work so damn hard to make sure The Acorn feels like a second home.

INDEX

garlic, black: Black Garlic Mayo, 69–70

garlic, Red Russian: Red Russian Garlic Confit, 120

garlic, wild
  Wild Garlic Fried Potatoes, 176
  Wild Garlic Oil, 50
  Wild Garlic Powder, 180
  as wildcrafted ingredient, 19

garlic scapes
  Fried Garlic Scapes with Sea Salt, 197
  Garlic Scape Relish, 183
  Pickled Garlic Scape Bulbs, 32, 35

Gastrique, Quince, 148

gin: Rites of Spring Cocktail, 252

ginger
  Black Garlic Mayo, 69–70
  Ginger & Black Peppercorn Bitters, 252
  Pickled Ginger, 37
  Sesame-Ginger Bitters, 259
  Snap Pea & Ginger Syrup, 252
  Vegan Kimchi, 79–80

Giroday, Lisa, 167

Glanz, Gordon, 271

Gluten-Free Flour Blend, 90

Gnocchi, 137–141

Gouda, goat: Salsify Cavatelli Pasta, 77

Grand Fir Buds, Pickled, 35

granitas
  Elderflower, 255
  Pineappleweed, 237

Gravy, Mushroom, 93

green beans: Dressed Beans & Peas, 214

grits
  Corn, 245–247
  Hominy Corn, 246

Guatemalan Blue Pumpkin Tuilles, 114

H

hazelnuts
  Almond & Hazelnut Tart Shells, 229
  Browned Hazelnut Butter, 168
  Hazelnut Cream, 132
  Herbed Hazelnut Dip, 197
  Hop Shoot Salad, 168–171

Toasted Hazelnut Orgeat, 275
Toasted Hazelnuts, 221

Hominy Corn Grits, 246

hop shoots
  Hop Shoot Salad, 168–171
  Pickled Hop Shoot Stems, 31–32
  Sautéed Hop Shoots, 171
  as wildcrafted ingredient, 15

House Gluten-Free Waffles, 94

Hyssop Syrup, 262

J

Japanese knotweed
  Knotweed Crisps, 172
  Knotweed Puree, 172
  as wildcrafted ingredient, 15

Jelly, Red-Flowering Currant, 160

juniper berries
  Juniper-Cured Egg Yolks, 179
  as wildcrafted ingredient, 15

jus
  Burdock Red Wine, 97–98
  Carrot, 123
  Mushroom Red Wine, 188–191

K

Kalettes, Sautéed, 110

Karp, Miriam, 271

kelp
  Apple Togarashi, 80
  Charred Onion Kelp Sauce, 203
  Crispy Kelp & Salsify Skins, 81
  Kelp Salt, 204
  Kelp Salt Roasted King Oyster Mushrooms, 204
  Seaweed & Beet Gastrique Glazed Chewy Beets, 132–133
  Shiitake XO Sauce, 69
  sustainably sourcing, 21

kimchi
  Kimchi Mayo, 80
  Vegan Kimchi, 79–80

King Oyster Mushrooms, Kelp Salt Roasted, 204

Klippenstein, Annamarie, 233

Klippenstein, Kevin, 233

Klippers Organics, 10, 113, 225, 233, 237, 241, 272

knotroots
  Garlic Pickled Knotroot, 32
  Pickled Knotroot, 32

knotweed, Japanese
  Knotweed Crisps, 172
  Knotweed Puree, 172
  as wildcrafted ingredient, 15

L

Lacto Caramelized Thumbelina Carrots, 124

Lacto Fermented Chanterelle Butter, 137

lamb's quarters
  Corn Grits, 245–247
  as wildcrafted ingredient, 15–16

larch
  Beet & Redwing Onion & Larch Tip Relish, 131–132
  as wildcrafted ingredient, 16

leeks
  Confit Leeks, 203
  Focaccia Bread, 226
  Seared Leek Rings, 204

Legume, 213–214

lemons
  Lemon Basil Vinaigrette, 225
  Lemon Maple Vinaigrette, 180

lemons, Meyer: Preserved Meyer Lemon, 41

lichen, reindeer
  Candied Lichen, 191
  as wildcrafted ingredient, 18

Licorice Fern Root Vinegar, 46

lime juice/zest
  Elderflower Granita, 255
  Flor de Verano Cocktail, 256

lovage
  Lovage Almond Cream, 187
  Lovage Oil, 50
  Parsley Root & Lovage Puree, 85

Lupoch, Sandra, 167

Luptak, Brian, 8–10

M

Maitake Mushrooms, Southern Fried, 90

Maple Blossom Vinaigrette, 168

maple syrup
  Bourbon Maple Syrup, 93
  Caramelized Black Salsify, 77
  Lemon Maple Vinaigrette, 180
  Maple Blossom Vinaigrette, 168

Now hop in the kitchen and give'r...

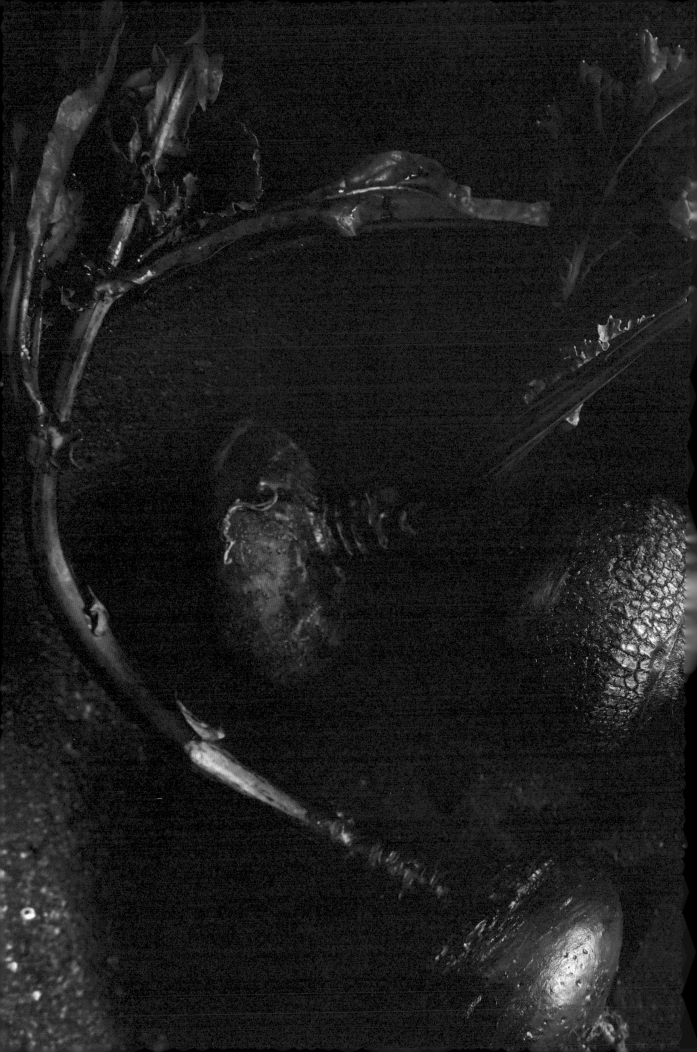